The Prodigal Tongue

BOOKS BY MARK ABLEY

SPOKEN HERE
Travels Among Threatened Languages

THE PRODIGAL TONGUE
Dispatches from the Future of English

The Prodigal Tongue

DISPATCHES
FROM THE
FUTURE OF ENGLISH

Mark Abley

HOUGHTON MIFFLIN COMPANY

BOSTON • NEW YORK   2008

For information about permission to reproduce selections from this book, write to Permissions, Houghton Mifflin Harcourt Company, 215 Park Avenue South, New York, New York 10003.

www.houghtonmifflinbooks.com

Library of Congress Cataloging-in-Publication Data
Abley, Mark.
The prodigal tongue : dispatches from the future
of English / Mark Abley.
p. cm.
Includes index.
ISBN 978-0-618-57122-2
1. English language—Variation. 2. English language—Influence
on foreign languages. 3. English language—Usage. 4. English
language—Globalization. I. Title.
PE1074.7.A35 2008 420'.9—dc22 2008007270

Printed in the United States of America

QUM 10 9 8 7 6 5 4 3 2 1

Lines from "Dear Tech Support" and "Dear Customer" by Shanta Acharya
are reprinted by kind permission of the author. Lines from *Collected Poems*
by Nissim Ezekiel are reproduced by permission of Oxford University
University Press India, New Delhi.

FOR MY DAUGHTERS,
KATE AND MEGAN

Loo! what sholde a man in thyse dayes now wryte, "egges" or "eyren"? Certaynly it is harde to playse every man bycause of dyversite and chaunge of langage.

— WILLIAM CAXTON, prologue to *Eneydos* (1490)

Each word was at first a stroke of genius . . . The etymologist finds the deadest word to have been once a brilliant picture. Language is fossil poetry.

— RALPH WALDO EMERSON, "The Poet"

Contents

1

Roarific

The Power of Language Change

W AS I IN ARCADIA OR ALHAMBRA? Was I speeding past
Temple City or City of Industry?
Somewhere amid the grind and spurt of traffic on a southern
California freeway, I slipped a Coldplay disc, *X&Y,* into my car's CD player.
The morning sun lit up the distant, snow-clotted San Gabriel Mountains, a
prospect as exhilarating as the opening song, "Square One." As the lead
singer, Chris Martin, evoked discovery, travel and the future, his tenor voice
seemed to soar high above the choking swarm of vehicles; half consciously
I swerved into the fast lane. But Martin's tone soon darkens. Several of the
cuts demonstrate loss, regret, uncertainty, and apprehension about what
the days after tomorrow hold in store for us. An SUV was maintaining an
aggressive stance inches behind my license plate, and I pulled back into one
of the middle lanes.

The CD reached its fifth track: a haunting, nine-note melody, repeated
softly, then with a surge of percussive volume. Martin sings about his fear
of the future, his need to speak out. When an early attempt at reassurance
fails, he probes deeper, asking if "you," his brother, feel incomplete or lost.
The song is called "Talk." To the underlying rhythm of a drummed heart-
beat, its lyrics summon up an anxiety specific to words and meaning:
the feeling that other people are addressing him in a language beyond his
grasp. It's as though language has lost its ability to connect us — as though
we've misplaced a key that would allow us, somehow, to understand what
words have come to mean. Birds kept flying somewhere above Walnut or
Diamond Bar, but all utterance now seemed strange, unfathomable. The
guitar riffs swooped and rose to match the breathtaking, lethal grandeur of
the California freeways, yet the song's lyrics were bleak.

Back home in Montreal, I found myself continually listening to *X&Y*. So were millions of other people in dozens of countries — this had been the world's top-selling album in 2005. One day I came across a futuristic, B-movielike video of "Talk"; it showed the perplexed band trying to communicate with a giant robot. A version of the video on the YouTube website had been watched more than 442,000 times in the previous ten months. Many hundreds of viewers had posted comments. Some of them were brief, uninhibited love letters. *ace this song iz wick id lol ace vid,* wrote a viewer from Britain. *coldplay is the BEST!!* added a thirteen-year-old Finn, using a Japanese screen name. *vid. is kind of err. but the song is roarific,* noted an American. A comment in English from China followed one in Basque from Spain and one in Spanish from Botswana.

If I were more of a joiner, I might have signed up for the official Coldplay.com online forum, which boasts tens of thousands of members. The forum makes national borders immaterial — Latvians and Macedonians, Indonesians and Peruvians, Israelis and Egyptians all belong. To them it doesn't matter that the band consists of three Englishmen and a Scot singing in a tongue that was once confined to part of an island off Europe's coast. Now, wherever on the planet these fans happen to live, music connects them. So does language. As long as they're willing to grope for words in the accelerating global language that Coldplay speaks, the forum gives all its members a chance to speak. Which is how the fifth song on *X&Y* ends. Martin admits that things don't make sense any longer. But as the melodies collapse around him, he invites us to talk.

All sorts of borders are collapsing now: social, economic, artistic, linguistic. They can't keep up with the speed of our listening, of our speaking, of our singing, of our traveling. Borders could hardly be less relevant on teen-happy websites like Facebook and MySpace. That morning, a Canadian in the exurbs of Los Angeles, I was listening to a British band while driving to meet a Mexican-American professor who began a memoir in Argentina full of sentences like this: "repente veo que ALL OF A SUDDEN, como right out of nowhere, estoy headed for the freeway on-ramp." Routes are merging. Languages are merging.

That professor celebrates a promiscuous, unruly mix of words. But many people contemplate such a mix with annoyance and fear, emotions they also feel about other kinds of language change, like the chatroom abbreviations in those YouTube comments. When you first peer at the weirdly spelled, lowercase fragments of speech, or listen to the staccato interplay of tongues in major cities like LA, you may be fearful that everyone else is talking in a language you don't speak. Is it mere unfamiliarity that inspires such unease, or is it something deeper?

Language enables us to feel at home in everyday life. But of late, language seems to have packed up its bags, slammed the door behind it, and taken to the open road. That's where we find ourselves: on the move. Every few days, if not every few hours, we become aware of a new word or phrase speeding past us. There's no going back, either — no retreat into the grammar and lexicon of the past. Our only home is this: the verbal space in which we're already traveling. The expressions in that space are often amazing — a generation or two ago, before our use of language went digital, no one would have believed some of what we routinely see, hear and type.

Yet from time to time, I too feel lost. In the future, wherever we are, what in the world will we say?

The way other people use language sometimes troubles us. But the reasons vary wildly. It may be the particular version of English spoken in Singapore, Sydney or San Diego. It may be the way teenagers talk — Joan Didion, describing the "blank-faced" girls and "feral" boys of southern California, criticized their "refusal or inability to process the simplest statement without rephrasing it. There was the fuzzy relationship to language, the tendency to seize on a drifting fragment of something once heard and repeat it, not quite get it right, worry it like a bone." It may be a pompously inflated polysyllabic phrase, a contortion of words in an ad, a noun that masquerades as a verb. It may be grammatical errors in a TV news bulletin, phrases abused on a radio talk show, spelling mistakes on a website. It may be the opaque language of bureaucracy — in March 2007, to take a random example, the Queensland Government Chief Information Office defined its task as "the development of methodologies and toolkits to strengthen the planning and project management capability of agencies." Say what? "The QGCIO also plays an integral part in building relationships and identifying opportunities for collaboration between agencies, cross-jurisdictionally, with the ICT Industry and with the tertiary sector." Even more than this kind of flaccid verbiage, my personal bugbear is the rhetoric of war, engineered to hide the truth: "collateral damage," "friendly fire," "transfer tubes," or "the excesses of human nature that humanity suffers" (such was Donald Rumsfeld's euphemism for the torture of Iraqi prisoners at Abu Ghraib). There are innumerable reasons why people get irritated about language.

Irritation can lead to anxiety. If words no longer bear their proper meaning, or are no longer pronounced the right way, or are now being combined with other words in some incorrect manner, what verbal defacements might scar the future?

Experts keep trying to reassure the public. Even in 1929, the British linguist Ernest Weekley felt it necessary to observe that "stability in language is synonymous with *rigor mortis.*" "People have been complaining about language change for centuries," says Katherine Barber, editor in chief of the *Canadian Oxford Dictionary.* "They're fascinated to learn that 'travel' started off as an instrument of torture — but they want the changes to stop now. I think people invest a lot in correct spelling and grammar because they worked very hard to learn it well in school — that's why there's a resistance. They say, 'It's terrible, they don't use the subjunctive anymore.' But the subjunctive has been disappearing for centuries." As the American scholar John McWhorter has pointed out, "There is no such thing as a society lapsing into using unclear or illogical speech — anything that strikes you as incorrect in some humble speech variety is bound to pop up in full bloom in several of the languages considered the world's noblest." Nobility, the linguists reiterate, is in the ear of the beholder. Many native speakers beg to differ.

Amid the commotion, rest assured: I have no ideological ax to grind. I'm not interested in persuading you to refine your punctuation, double your vocabulary or perfect your grammar. I write simply as someone who loves and cares about language; I believe its manifold powers of expression help make us truly human. Today the evidence of linguistic change, like that of climate change, is all around us. But I suspect that with both words and weather, we don't always ask the right questions. "Is language declining?" may not be the smartest inquiry to make. It might be more rewarding to ask: "Why does language change provoke such anxiety? What kinds of change can we expect to see in the future? And how should we try to cope?"

More than two thousand years ago, the Roman poet Horace compared words to leaves in a forest: just as trees lose their withered leaves and welcome fresh ones, so too do words fall away to be replaced by the new. The process is continual, and older than any of our languages. Yet words seem unusually volatile now. "We are living at the beginning of a new linguistic era," the eminent linguist David Crystal wrote in 2004. "I do not believe that 'revolution' is too strong a word for what has been taking place." He based his assertion on three interrelated phenomena: the planetwide spread of English in the late twentieth century, the disappearance of hundreds of other languages, and the sudden dominance of the Internet as a means of communication. When these topics are looked at together, Crystal argued, "we encounter a vision of a linguistic future which is radically different from what has existed in the past."

The nature of that difference is the central theme of these pages. Having devoted a previous book, *Spoken Here,* to the last-ditch struggles of minority languages, I promise to say little about that subject here. The awareness of a terrible loss — on average, a language goes extinct somewhere in the world every two weeks — underlies some of what follows. But loss is not the only story to be told. This book sets out to explore and interpret a verbal revolution.

∽

On a bright October afternoon, I was standing in front of a class of sixteen- and seventeen-year-olds in a small town west of Montreal. Their English teacher had invited me to give a writing workshop in the high school library. The hour was nearing its end when abruptly I switched course. Instead of talking about metaphors and similes, sweet conclusions and dynamite beginnings, I asked each student to jot down a few words or phrases that older people would not understand, and then provide a brief definition for each term. I gave the class no advance warning. The risk was that this impromptu assignment would induce a yawn-filled silence, a retreat into heavy-lidded boredom. But instead the students — especially the girls, I noticed — set about the task with enthusiasm.

"You mean *any* words?" said a preppy-looking girl in blue. "Even the ones that aren't in the dictionary?"

"Especially the ones that aren't in a dictionary," I replied.

I waited a couple of minutes — time was short — and asked for the results. Arms filled the air. Hands waggled. I'm a reader, a parent, a viewer, a listener; I thought that all together, the students might come up with a dozen words I didn't know. So much for the vanity of age.

Cheddar, said the first, meaning "money, lavish earnings." (I'll give this and all the other definitions in the students' exact words.) *He got owned,* said another: "rejected, shut down, beat up." *On the go,* added a third: "it's like going out, but not official." I recognized some of the expressions, of course; even a senior citizen of fifty can comprehend *eye candy* and *loaded, poser* and *flame.* Did these innocent, cool teenagers really believe their generation had invented *high*? But as I stood there in the sun-dappled library, I realized that the majority of the students' words and phrases left me bemused. What on earth was *burninate*? Was *d-low* somehow related to "below," "delay," "J Lo" — or to none of those terms? (Not wanting to keep the meanings secret — to d-low them, that is — I'll suggest that you'd burninate something only if you had the fire-breathing powers of a dragon.) More generally, by what learned or instinctive command had these young people enacted their self-assured takeover of the language?

Before the bell freed them from the joy of learning, the students handed in the slips of paper on which they'd scribbled their definitions. I have them still: scraps torn from notepads and workbooks, a page from a disintegrating paperback, a yellow Post-it note with a smiley at the top. Overlaps were surprisingly rare; just one word — *noob,* meaning somebody new, ignorant or inexperienced — was defined three times.

Looking at the sixty-six words now, I'm struck by the diversity of their origins. A few emerge from the online world of instant messaging: *rofl,* for instance, which gathers the initial letters of "rolling on the floor laughing." Others are abbreviations: *sup,* for instance, originally "What's up?" and now a synonym for "Hi, how are you?" Almost anywhere you go, the power of hip-hop seems unavoidable: surely that's how *homie* (friend) and *foshizzle* (I agree) migrated from America's inner cities to a small, WASPish town in Quebec. Hip-hop and cyberspace together encouraged the spread of *phat,* which morphed from "sexy" in the 1960s to "cool, great, wonderful" by the '90s, and which is now widely regarded as an acronym for "pretty hot and tempting" — its original meaning, in short. Drug culture is just as influential; blame or credit it for *fatty* (an oversized joint), *gacked* (on speed) and *pinner* (a small joint). It's unfortunate *That's so gay* has come to mean "That's stupid, not worth my time." But what could be the origins and adolescent meanings of *lag* and *One* and *die in a fire*?

It was humbling to read an impromptu definition of *scene,* a word I thought I knew, that deployed a word I couldn't quite pin down — "style (knock-off of emo)." *Emo*? It was even more humbling for me, a writer, someone whose livelihood depends on the rich and exact use of words, to realize how far the English language had slithered away from my grasp, not for reasons of ethnicity or culture but simply because of time. "But at my back I always hear / Time's wingèd chariot hurrying near," wrote the poet Andrew Marvell in the seventeenth century. It's not a chariot any longer; it's a Dreamliner.

Don't get me wrong. I'm not saying that all these expressions are destined to enter the permanent storehouse of English vocabulary. Many of them will be as fleeting as youth itself. Young men and women have always used slang as a weapon to cut their lives free from the nets cast by their elders — didn't I aspire, unsuccessfully, to be a groovy freak? Older people have no reason to try and memorize the throwaway lexicon of the young. But the cascade of teenage slang I faced that afternoon can stand as a symbol of the astonishing rate at which new words are pouring into English. Nobody can control this breakbeat language; nobody can even keep track of it.

The language is both inherently permissive and amazingly powerful. Yet while it soaks up terms from dozens of foreign cultures and nations, English also infiltrates and penetrates most of the world's other languages. Worry about the linguistic future is nothing unique to English-speakers. People around the world are struggling with verbal shock: angst about how we speak, how we read and write, the changing ways we communicate. Perhaps all this helps to explain why so many are convinced that language is deteriorating. It's as though — regardless of whether the supposed peak of eloquence was attained in the era of Shakespeare, Goethe or Proust — the language of the twenty-first century must inevitably mark a sad decline in accuracy, grace or both. Nervousness about falling standards makes us resort to grammar hotlines and seek the stern advice of language mavens. Google the phrase "proper grammar," and you'll find, as of November 2007, no fewer than 394,000 hits.

If technological innovations are usually cheered, linguistic innovations just as commonly come under attack. A few years ago Prince Charles attacked the "corrupting" effect of American English, saying, "People tend to invent all sorts of nouns and verbs and make words that shouldn't be. I think we have to be a bit careful; otherwise the whole thing can get rather a mess." His late compatriot Alistair Cooke bemoaned "the disastrous decline in the teaching of elementary grammar." But is language really in a state of free fall? Are speakers in the future condemned to be messier and less accurate than ourselves?

ᔕ

It's easy for me to say that words are evolving fast. But I need to prove the point. So let's perform a brief test. If you look back at the eleven paragraphs you've just read, describing my visit to a high school — and if you leave aside all the students' new expressions (*noob, foshizzle, sup* and so on) — you'll still find at least thirty words and usages that did not appear in the first edition of the *Oxford English Dictionary* (1884–1928), the most ambitious and scholarly effort yet made to assemble a complete record of the language. Some of these terms are obvious: Google, hip-hop and instant messaging were all born in the late twentieth century. So, slightly earlier, were Post-its and smileys. According to John Ayto's book *Twentieth Century Words*, "hotline" is believed to date back to 1955, "online" to 1950. More subtle, more thought-provoking, are recent coinages that evoke not technological inventions but concepts and ideas. The creators of the *OED* had no knowledge of "takeover," a word that appeared only in the mid-1940s, nor "permissive," a 1950s term, nor "inner city," a phrase from 1968. "Ethnicity" dates from 1953; one particular ethnicity, "wasp" (meaning white Anglo-Saxon Protestant), had been around for centuries, although the word remained absent from the language until 1962.

The list goes on. "Senior citizen" arrived in 1938, a year after "workshop" began to signify something more than just a room full of tools. "Angst," understandably, seems to have become an English word during the Second World War. Another wartime invention was "acronym." Both angst and acronyms have proliferated since. "Throwaway" was unavailable to the *OED*'s first editors; so was "cool," except as a term evoking temperature. Even "insecure," in its common usage, arose only in the 1930s.

Most surprising — given the ubiquity and apparent necessity of the term — the word "teenager" was not born until the early 1940s. "I never knew teen-agers could be so serious," declared a writer for *Popular Science Monthly* in 1941. The first verifiable use of "teenage" goes back another generation, to (of all places) Victoria, British Columbia, where a 1921 article in the *Daily Colonist* declared: "All 'teen age' girls of the city are cordially invited to attend the mass meeting to be held this evening." The *OED*'s staff had already finished work on the letter T by then, so anybody looking up "teenage" in the great dictionary is in for a shock: it's defined as a country term meaning brushwood for fences and hedges.

In 1921 few people outside the Victoria area would ever read the *Daily Colonist*. A copy took days to reach the East Coast, weeks to travel overseas. Today the *Times Colonist,* like almost every other newspaper, maintains a lively presence on the Internet. With some clicks of a mouse, anybody who has access to a computer can learn about the city, keep up with its goings-on, or send aggrieved letters to the editor. Thanks to technology, you don't have to live in Victoria to stay abreast of the Victoria news. Besides, the growth of immigration, cheap air travel and a global economy means that no English-speaking city in the world is ethnically homogeneous. I used to believe this wide dispersal of readers and speakers would encourage a uniformity of language — a smoothing out of differences. Even if a few slang expressions varied from place to place, surely the varieties of English were destined to become ever more similar.

Now I'm not so sure. Admittedly, many dialects and accents have faded over time — as long ago as 1962, in *Travels with Charley,* John Steinbeck lamented the decline of American regional speech. The little town of Lunenberg in southern Nova Scotia was settled by Swiss and German immigrants in the eighteenth century, and until recently dozens of German-based expressions could be heard in the area: "struddle," "mawger," "gookemole," "wackelass" and so on. Few of these terms, unfortunately, remain in daily use. Most of them have joined the silent, ever-growing army of lost words.

Yet robust dialects still flourish. Many people in Scotland, for instance, are convinced that their daily idiom, Scots, is so different from mainstream English that it should count as a separate tongue. In 2006 some portions of *Trawlermen,* a BBC-TV miniseries about fishermen off a coastal town in Scotland, had to be subtitled before being shown elsewhere in the United Kingdom. Matthew Fitt, a young writer appointed by the Scottish government to serve as National Schools Scots Language Development Officer, has written poems in which lines I can figure out ("be guid tae yirsel") are followed by lines I find totally incomprehensible ("sic a drochle / a peeliewally"). Fitt invents words on occasion — "cyberjanny" was his coinage for a virtual concierge who made an appearance in a Scots cyberpunk novel — but more often he simply puts into writing the everyday idiom of

Scottish people. Their accent can be so distinctive that many common words — "guid," for instance — look weird in standard English spelling, like a fullback in a tutu.

If you wander down the Royal Mile in Edinburgh, you'll pass a six-floor apartment building (a block of flats, I mean) on which a historic-looking plaque is kitted out with flags and emblems. But the plaque is far from old. The wording on it reads: AL THIS WARK WAS BEGUN BE DANCON ON 10 JANUARY 1989 AND ENDIT BE THEM ON 31 MARCH 1990. The use of Scots on the plaque makes a strong cultural and political statement. Part of its meaning is that, in the face of the rampantly global, Scottish people are determined to value and promote the local. Yet every vibrant dialect, not just Scots, generates new expressions; and these expressions can get in the way of a shared understanding. Think of all the acronyms that speak volumes to insiders and say nothing to everyone else.

TTC, for instance. If you're a sports fan, you probably associate those initials with The Tennis Channel. Unless you're a sports fan living in Toronto, in which case you'd first call to mind the Toronto Transit Commission. Anyone moving to the city finds TTC an essential trio of letters to figure out. In the American South, the letters also involve transportation: Trans-Texas Corridor. But in Paris, TTC is a hip-hop band; in Singapore, South Carolina, Essex and Oklahoma it refers to a college (four different colleges, that is); and in Wellington, New Zealand, it signifies the Tararua Tramping Club. ("Tramping" means hiking, if you're American, or rambling, if you're British.) The initials also belong to a European research project, Timing, Trigger and Control, whose website helpfully notes: "The TTC system was initially developed by RD12, an LHC Common Project financed by EP and SL Divisions and the four LHC experiment collaborations." TTC, in short, has dozens of disconnected meanings around the world.

For a stranger, mastering the language of a new place means getting to know its initials as well as its cultural and political references. And countries, like cities, have their own allusions, their own illusions. The playwright George Bernard Shaw once quipped that the USA and Britain are divided by a common language. It might be more accurate to say they're united by a different language. North Americans traveling in Britain would be well advised to realize that "randy" means what they know as "horny"; otherwise they could be as baffled as a Chicago girl I once met in a Glasgow youth hostel who couldn't fathom the reaction she caused by walking up to boys and saying, "Hi, I'm Randi."

Teenagers in London are less and less likely to speak in the traditional Cockney accent, but they're not switching over to the Queen's English, nor even to the Estuary English adopted by their parents and older siblings. Instead, many of them use a new transcultural idiom that goes by the name "Jafaikan." Besides the obvious Caribbean source, it draws on accents and words from Africa, South Asia and Australia. "Safe, man," wrote a *Guardian* journalist in a piece entitled "Learn Jafaikan in two minutes." "You lookin buff in dem low batties. Dey's sick, man. Me? I'm just jammin wid me bruds. Dis my yard, innit? Is nang, you get me?"

Migration is a fact of language. Now that the peoples of the world jam with their bruds on each other's doorstep, it may be necessary to understand the differences between, say, a hijab and a niqab, a khemar and a chador. In large cities, isolation from other cultures is impossible. The more we mix, the more we match. And just as our words keep flooding into other languages, some of their words inevitably seep into ours. English has already adopted terms from at least 350 other tongues, including Choctaw, Twi, Nootka and Araucanian.

Languages change when a minority people asserts itself as strongly as Jamaicans in Britain and Algerians in France have recently done. There's nothing new or alarming about this; Jewish immigrants to the United States a century ago had the chutzpah to make Yiddish a rich source of English expressions. Languages alter too when sheer proximity forces idioms to rub up against each other — to share a physical space is also to share a verbal space. In Montreal, English- and French-speakers routinely and genially wreak havoc on each other's languages. Soon after a collapsing overpass had killed several people, I heard a Quebec official say on English-language radio: "Circulation on Autoroute Dix-neuf will have a little perturbation."

In other words, traffic on Highway 19 will be chaotic.

ॐ

Technological change can add to our verbal unease. On a trip to New York in 2006 I happened to pass a notice board at the entrance to East Green, a quiet area of Central Park, that still told passersby: "Earphones are required for listening to radios and tapeplayers." The sign became outmoded as soon as the Discman and MiniDisc Walkman replaced the portable cassette player. In an era of iPods and MP3 players, the notice makes even less sense. The word "tapeplayers," once so shiny, bears the scuff marks of age. To keep up with technology, the notice board would require a fresh noun every few years.

Over the next few decades, advances in technology will bring us a megaload of gleaming words. But more important, the whole feel and, so to speak, headspace of the future will be unlike anything we can foretell. Words don't just give names to devices, they give flesh to ideas. Apart from the multitude of fresh vocabulary that speakers in 2100 will take for granted, and the subtly different threads of grammar that will knit their words together, it's likely they will pronounce the language in different ways than we do. The sounds and rhythms of English, French and many other languages have undergone substantial change within the past century.

To hear exactly how a language alters, we're lucky that the New Zealand Broadcasting Service sent mobile recording units around the country in 1946. The units had previously gathered soldiers' and nurses' wartime messages to their families at home. After the outbreak of peace, New Zealand decided to record the music being performed in outlying areas as well as the reminiscences of old-timers living there. "The recordings were made on fourteen-inch acetate disks," the linguist Margaret Maclagan explained to Australia's Radio National, "which were so soft that they didn't actually want to play them very often, so most of the people who were recorded never even heard themselves. They made the recordings in people's homes, or on farms or in the local town halls." Surprisingly, perhaps, the music proved less popular than the stories, and so the mobile units went back on the road for another two years, harvesting the voices of more than three hundred people.

Why is this of any interest now? Because New Zealand English is a young dialect. Other varieties of English, from North America and the Caribbean to India, South Africa and Australia, were already well established by the second half of the nineteenth century, when most of these speakers were born. They are, Maclagan explained, "the first generation of European people born in New Zealand. So they're the very first people who ended up speaking New Zealand English." This means, unusually, that almost the entire history of the dialect exists in recorded form.

Radio National played the voices of a brother and sister, a Mr. and Miss Bannatyne, who were small children in South Island in the 1890s. Their given names appear to be lost. Even in the late 1940s, Mr. Bannatyne spoke in what sounded very much like an English accent; he would have pronounced the word "fish" with a vowel sound recognizable to English-speakers elsewhere. But Miss Bannatyne pursed her mouth and swallowed her short *i*'s: *fsh*, she would have said. That's one of the most noticeable qualities of a New Zealand accent. She had it. He didn't.

What the New Zealand researchers found in those 1940s recordings holds true elsewhere. Women take on a new accent faster than men (this matters not only for its own sake, but also because mothers traditionally play the largest role in passing on language to children). People from a lower social class acquire a new accent more quickly than those from a higher class. And accents develop most quickly when people from many different places mix together. The more social flux and tumult there are in a community, the more likely its language is to alter. New Zealanders were fortunate to acquire their distinctive accent without rancor. In many countries today, mobility and social mixing have never been greater, and language can change with startling abruptness.

Even so, some kinds of change happen gracefully. Let's consider Somalia for a moment. It's hard to think of a nation more profoundly stricken by war, famine, displacement and ecological collapse. Somali culture, traditionally nomadic, was reliant on camel herding, and the decline of that practice has heightened the people's vulnerability to the ever more frequent droughts that plague the Horn of Africa. Over the centuries, the Somali language developed an astonishing range of words to embody a herding culture — *golqaniinyo*, for instance, meaning "a bite given on a camel's flank to render her docile during milking"; or *uusmiiro*, "to extract water from a camel's stomach to drink during a period of drought." What's striking is the confident way in which Somalis have taken their old camel-related words and applied them to new purposes.

Their use of language is dynamic. *Guree*, for example, once meant "to make room for a person to sit on a loaded camel." Now it refers to making space for someone in a full car or truck. More radically, *gulguuluc* used to mean "the low bellow of a sick or thirsty camel," but today the word applies to a poem recited in a low voice. *Haneed* once signified "the left side of a cow camel where one stands when milking." Its meaning has stretched to the point where the term now suggests good form or style. Yet the stretch-ing is a natural evolution, nothing forced or jagged. If English would only change as elegantly as the Somali words for camel culture, few people would have a serious objection.

Fat chance. In today's world many hundreds of millions of people speak English as a foreign language, with greater or lesser success. (One of them, translating an Israeli tourist brochure into English, recently turned a Hebrew phrase meaning "Jerusalem — there's no city like it" into "Jerusa-lem — there's no such city.") As their language lunges off into uncharted territory, native speakers often resent the bewildering, graceless changes they have witnessed since childhood. Can English still be ours if we don't know a *phat* from a *fatty*? If we respect traditional rules of spelling and grammar, will we soon be *owned*?

People with a different mother tongue are less likely to feel an intuitive bond to the particular version of English they learned. But they too can be upset by language change, especially if its effect is to make English seem even less straightforward, even harder to comprehend. Non-native speakers of the language far outnumber those for whom this is the tongue of earliest memory. And the future of English, some linguists now suggest, will de-pend heavily on those who did *not* speak it in their childhood.

‿つ

I will have much to say in this book about the exhilaration that language change provokes, the creativity it embodies. But it can also be deeply prob-lematic. It can leave older people voiceless in their own tongue. It can create havoc for lawyers, teachers, police officers and other professionals. It can divide a community. And what of the cultural loss it incites? The dramatic influx of new words into the language has left no room for thousands of old ones, which beat a quiet retreat into portly dictionaries and half-forgotten classics. Even the hardy survivor words carry meanings that swell or shrink over time.

The result, often, is confusion. We may think we know what a sentence or a paragraph means, but we can easily be deceived. When a language slams its foot down on the accelerator, the past shrinks and blurs in the rear-view mirror. Much of the difficulty we have in understanding the past is semantic — if its language consistently eludes us, so does its spirit, its psychology. The attempt to read any text from a bygone century can, in

Coldplay's words, make us "feel like they're talking in a language I don't speak." And as history becomes unintelligible, we lose touch with the roots of culture.

Consider a few lines from the Anglican *Book of Common Prayer*, still being used in many churches in the twenty-first century. Some of its wording goes back nearly half a millennium, to a time before William Shakespeare was born. I remember, as a boy, being puzzled by the invitation "Come unto me, all that travail and are heavy laden, and I will refresh you." Did I travail? Would I be refreshed? A few moments later, the priest declared Jesus to be "the propitiation for our sins." The what? That verse was prefaced by the command "Hear what comfortable words our Saviour Christ saith unto all that truly turn to him." There the language floored us — not just me, but also the vast majority of worshipers. For "comfortable" doesn't mean what we naturally assumed it did; it means, to quote the *Oxford English Dictionary,* "strengthening or supporting." That dictionary gives a dozen meanings for "comfortable"; nine of them were obsolete a century ago.

The Anglican prayer book employs the word in a geriatric sense that could only mislead contemporary readers. It's a good thing the book doesn't also — as far as I know — feature manure and commodes. To manure meant to manage or cultivate, which is why an Elizabethan author could say that England was "governed, administered and manured by three sorts of persons." And a commode, when it sauntered into the language, was a tall headdress worn by fashionable women. Hence an otherwise inexplicable couplet by the minor poet Edward Ward: "Stiff commodes in triumph stared / Above their foreheads half a yard."

More recent texts also run up against the shifting nature of language. As a university student, I learned a few favorite poems by heart. One of them was "Lapis Lazuli" by the Irish author William Butler Yeats. Its subject is the magnificent persistence of art in times of pain and horror. Written in the mid-1930s, as Europe lurched toward war, "Lapis Lazuli" is, I would still argue, one of the key poems of the last century. But, because of language change, it's a poem that has become hard to enjoy — even, for young people, to take seriously.

When the aging Yeats wrote, "Two Chinamen, behind them a third, / Are carved in lapis lazuli," he didn't know how offensive the term "Chinaman" would become (except in the game of cricket, where it continues to refer to a particular type of delivery from a left-armed spin bowler). When Yeats said, "Aeroplane and Zeppelin will come out, / Pitch like King Billy bomb-balls in," he couldn't predict that zeppelins would soon be a historical relic, even more antiquated than the expression "bomb-balls." When he used the phrases "hysterical women" and "all men have aimed at," he didn't know that feminists would dismiss such wording as sexist — his "men" refers to human beings, not just to adult males. And when the poet declared, "All things fall and are built again, / And those that build them again are gay," he wanted to evoke a brave insouciance in the face of grief. He certainly wasn't thinking about Judy Garland albums and rainbow bumper stickers.

As a euphemism or proud substitute for "homosexual," the word "gay" became widespread only in the 1960s. Its origins stretch back much further, perhaps to the Victorian era — although a 1942 *Thesaurus of American Slang* gives no hint of its current meaning, which spawned the derisive usage I encountered among high school students. Cole Porter could have had no clue about the adjective's future destiny when in 1932 he entitled a musical *Gay Divorce*. In "Lapis Lazuli," Yeats used "gay" four times, making it the poem's central word. But if you're a contemporary reader who has grown up equating gay with homosexual, you'll have a hard time forgetting the familiar meaning. The line "They know that Hamlet and Lear are gay" could well evoke an unwanted image of certain actors; and the poem's slow, resounding conclusion — "Their eyes, their ancient, glittering eyes, are gay" — verges on the ridiculous.

So far I've been speaking about the vocabulary of the past. But there's another difficulty: its syntax. The sentences we fashion today tend to be a lot shorter than they were in previous centuries, when authors were normally intimate with the rotund cadences of Latin and when they wrote out their texts by hand. Yeats grew up in the nineteenth century. His early readers had no telephones, no radios, no TV sets, no computers — the list of what they didn't have is almost endless. But they did have one thing most of us lack: time. They didn't need to hurry their reading. They didn't gobble sentences like mouthfuls of fast food.

And so they expected, even welcomed ornately sculpted phrases. They were at ease with sentences so complex that the syntax resembles architecture, and with a formal register of language that strikes most of us today as puffed up. To the great reformer William Wilberforce, a hundred-word sentence was merely routine. One of his finest pieces of writing — *An Appeal to the Religion, Justice, and Humanity of the Inhabitants of the British Empire, in Behalf of the Negro Slaves in the West Indies* — was published in London in 1823. A typical sentence begins like this: "For then, on the general ground merely of the incurable injustice and acknowledged evils of slavery, aggravated, doubtless, by the consideration that it was a slavery forcibly opposed on unoffending men for our advantage . . ."

He hasn't got to the main verb yet. He hasn't even got to the *subject.*

Wilberforce's lifelong struggle against slavery is the subject of Michael Apted's 2007 film *Amazing Grace.* The good characters in the movie say straightforward things like "To hell with caution!" and "Remember, God made men equal" and "If there's a bad taste in your mouth, spit it out." The evil characters speak pompously: "We have no evidence that the Africans themselves have any objection to the trade." We can't be sure, of course, exactly how Wilberforce talked; in conversation he's unlikely to have waited more than thirty words before reaching the subject of a sentence. It's clear, even so, that the film makes his enemies speak in an idiom reasonably true to the age — whereas Wilberforce, to appear heroic in our eyes, talks like us. We mistrust oratory. We like our heroes plainspoken.

Reading the past, we often stumble over the words we encounter. The words that are missing may be just as significant. Although Huck Finn is an adolescent boy, Mark Twain never conceived of him as a "teenager," for teenagers had not yet, so to speak, been invented. Oscar Wilde was undoubtedly a pederast, but how much sense does it make to call him gay? If we do so, we pluck him out of the nineteenth century and deposit him in ours. People in the past lived free of concepts from our own time, just as we walk around in blithe ignorance of ideas that will seem self-evident to our grandchildren. Those ideas will rely on words that have not yet been born.

છ

And then there's Shakespeare, the supreme cultural icon for writers and readers of English. Without knowing it, we repeat his words every day of our lives; they've become part of the fabric of our mental life. Brevity is the soul of wit, but if there's method in my madness, it might be too much of a good thing to lay it on with a trowel — there you have four Shakespearean phrases in half a sentence. He was an avid punster and word coiner too: the adjectives "vulnerable," "laughable," "barefaced" and "well-bred" all sprang to life in his plays. (So did "critic" as a noun and "puke" as a verb.) Knowledge of his work has often been considered essential to a humane education.

Yet in some eyes that notion betrays insufferable elitism. "It seems there are two kinds of people out there," the playwright and theater director Kim Selody told me: "those who were taught the plays in such a way that they knew what they were about, and those like me who somehow missed the story. Those that know the stories are in a club. I remember being in grade ten and studying *Macbeth*. We were asked to read the play on our own. The teacher jumped to the poetry and metaphors and allusions. I never really knew what the hell was going on. By the time I got to theater school and college, I was too embarrassed to admit that I really didn't know the stories and would just fake it." There are, Selody is convinced, countless fakers.

In the late 1980s, by then an established writer for young people, he took the plots of *The Tempest, Romeo and Juliet, Macbeth* and *Twelfth Night* and adapted them for children. A play called *Suddenly Shakespeare* was the result. "The main question I was responding to was 'What the heck is going on?' I purposely chose modern, simple language for the storytellers." But his choice of words gave rise to dissent: "Some of those in the club felt I was ruining the poetry of his work. This was a conscious choice on my part, because it was the poetry and allusions that had kept the story hidden from me."

Actors can work small miracles to get some of Shakespeare's meaning across, even when a word has fallen out of use — "the multitudinous seas incarnadine" becomes a bit less puzzling on the lips of a good Macbeth. But no performer conveys the exact rhymes that Shakespeare intended: in his day, "meet" and "mate," "see" and "say" were homonyms. And an actor's hardest challenge comes when very common words have altered in meaning. Addressing Ariel in act four of *The Tempest*, Prospero tells the sprite: "So, with good life / And observation strange, my meaner ministers / Their several kinds have done." None of those words are unusual. But do you have any clue what he's talking about? In that brief passage, "life," "strange," "meaner," "ministers," "several" and "kinds" all mean something different to Prospero than they do to you and me. To avoid such perplexity, many theater directors turn the Bard into slapstick, forcing their actors to ham up every speech with overblown gestures and endless bits of stage business.

Shakespeare's plays and poems have, in truth, become profoundly foreign to most speakers of his own language. The same fate has befallen the work of his contemporary Miguel de Cervantes (they died a few days apart in April 1616), perhaps the greatest writer in Spanish. "For most readers," the Hispanic scholar Orlando Alba told me, "it is very difficult (maybe impossible) to read and understand the original version of *El Quijote*. What students read in school is in fact a 'translation' to modern Spanish." The difficulties occur in both the vocabulary and the grammar. Cervantes has been left behind by the language he did so much to shape and by readers who remain in his debt. Similarly, audiences who watch Shakespeare's plays in a foreign language are liable to have a lot more fun than audiences who battle to decipher his English. The rapid pace of language change is making it harder and harder to produce his work in a way that an English-speaking crowd can comprehend.

Difficult, but maybe not impossible. "You don't need to do slapstick to make Shakespeare come alive," Leslee Silverman insists. "What you need to find is the emotional meaning behind the words. That hasn't changed." Silverman, who has achieved wonders as the artistic director of Manitoba Theatre for Young People, believes that "what the kids are hard-wired to feel is a response to the despair, to the compassion, to the big stories that are in language." When her company put on *Romeo and Juliet* in 2001, "we gave it the eye candy — a fashion walkway, with the kids on the one side being Montagues, the kids on the other side Capulets." Dressed in club gear, they danced to loud funk music. But apart from adding a little slang — the friar, realizing that Juliet had swallowed poison, blurted "Holy jumpin' Jesus!" — the production didn't mess around with the language.

Why not? asked a local critic. "If the stage was modern, the costumes were modern and the music was modern, then why wasn't the English? Perhaps the contemporary pizzazz was for the kids and the diction meant to appeal to the cultural desires of the parents. Either way, this was the only shortcoming." But for many, it was a shortcoming that effectively ruined the experience. "The children around me," the critic noted, "had a hard time understanding what was going on."

To Kim Selody, "language and its use is clearly the issue. Those parts of Shakespeare's writings that have fallen out of use today create a barrier to understanding the story." If we value the stories, we may have to detach them from Shakespeare's spectacular words. That's a painful task. But when

Selody is asked to justify his rewriting of the Bard, he reminds his critics that a child in a North American city now may well be somebody who "speaks English as a second language and whose cultural history is the *Ramayana* epic poem. I always like to ask those who are in the club, 'Do you know the story of the *Ramayana*?'"

༄

Most of this book will examine language change as it affects English, although these pages will also have a good deal to say about Japanese and French. Yet the dilemmas that beset English seldom afflict English alone. The world's most prominent languages are all in a state of flux. Let's take a quick look at another tongue caught between the weight of tradition and the demands of the new: Arabic.

Of the world's six thousand or so languages, Arabic and Hebrew appear to have the most invested in stability. Devout Muslims, like Orthodox Jews, believe their sacred texts are the immutable word of God. Christians, by contrast, read the Bible in translation, and their scriptures are subject to remorseless updating — in a twenty-first-century version from Australia, the Virgin Mary is described as a "pretty special sheila" who gives birth to "God's toddler." But in Islam, nobody can alter what God has said. Some Arabic texts from what we call the Middle Ages suggested that errors in language were also errors in morality — grounds, in fact, for damnation. So is Arabic immune to change? After all, the language of the Qur'an — *fusha*, to use its proper name — "is also the written language of classical Arabic literature, as well as the language of officialdom throughout Arab and Islamic history to this modern day."

The words are those of Issa Boullata, a distinguished Palestinian scholar of the Qur'an. Its text was written down — having been, in believers' eyes, revealed to the Prophet through the angel Gabriel — in what we call the seventh century. The *fusha* has provided a linguistic model ever since, one that is now heard daily on radio and television as well as in mosques and schools. Dubai even sponsors a lucrative competition, held each year during the sacred month of Ramadan, when boys and young men from around the world attempt to recite the 77,000 or so words of the Qur'an from memory, devoid of error or hesitation. Thanks to the *fusha*, Boullata explains, "if Arabs from different countries meet today, they will be able to speak in classical Arabic and have full understanding, especially in formal situations."

Yet time has transformed the language's very syntax. Most sentences in the classical tongue — the language of the Qur'an — follow a verb-subject-object order. But in daily life, the majority of Arabic-speakers now do what we do, and put the subject first. Not that they place much value on their everyday speech; most of them ascribe high value only to a form of the language that has been static for 1,300 years. They understand classical Arabic, they revere it, they love it — and they rarely hold a conversation in it. "If each person speaks in his or her own dialect," Boullata adds, "they will still understand each other, but sometimes with humorous misunder-standings." The confusion shows that in spite of the Qur'an's majestic pres-ence, Arabic has undergone dramatic change.

Stretching from the Atlantic Ocean to the Persian Gulf, it has a host of spoken dialects, some of which enjoy much higher prestige than others. The wealthy citizens of Beirut, for example, have tended to look down their noses at the accent of Palestinian refugees. Bedouins, villagers and city dwellers pronounce Arabic in different ways, often using different words to do so. So when pan-Arabic TV networks like al-Jazeera give voice to the colloquial language, they have to be careful not to confound their audience. Jokes and songs from one region of the Arabic-speaking world may be un-fathomable in another.

Arabic has always been willing to accept a modicum of foreign words. For every *al-jabr* it gave to Europe, a *faylasuf* would arrive in return (think "algebra," think "philosopher"). But since the early twentieth century, Boul-lata says, new inventions and scientific words "have been coming at such a fast speed that it was not easy always to find new Arabic terms, and people often resorted to adopting the foreign terms. So you have *telefon, telefizion, teleghram,* etc." Some of the borrowings led to innovations: to make a phone call in Arabic is *talfana.* Journalists were often the first to coin a word "because they needed to describe new inventions quickly to the read-ers; hence *sarukh* for rocket, for example. *Sarukh* was derived from the verb *sarakha,* to scream; therefore a rocket is the thing that screams as it is shot up in the air. And this word is still used successfully."

The journalists outpaced the linguists. Like Persian, French, Spanish and many other languages, Arabic has an academy to guide and regulate it; in fact it has several. "But," Boullata says, "what with scholarly discussions and debates, these academies are too slow in developing new terms in rela-tion to the speed needed to use them in daily communication. A joke is told that they invented a term for 'sandwich,' and it is the following: *al-shatir wal-mashtur wal-kamikh baynahuma* (the divider and the divided and the mixed pickles between them)."

Today, whether in Algiers or Cairo, Damascus or Baghdad, a wide gap separates the simplified grammar and diction used in the congested slums from the elevated style deployed by intellectuals. As a mother tongue, Arabic is growing at a faster rate than any other major language, and its speakers are on average younger. The implications are political as well as cultural. "The calls for holy war that adorn the walls in slums throughout the Middle East," Chris Hedges wrote in the *New York Times*, are written not in classical Arabic but in "a far simpler argot . . . Expressed in the cruder rhythms and pronunciations of street language, they become almost incomprehensible to educated Arabs, only widening a dangerous gulf between an elite that looks to the West and an enraged underclass." The jagged divisions within Arab society are mirrored by divisions in the language itself. Hedges proposed an analogy: "What if 80 or 90 percent of Americans spoke every day in the brutal and angry cadences of gangsta rap, while the members of a feudal upper class mused over their own demise in Elizabethan English?"

Even so, the combined influences of Islam, economic modernization and the mass media reduce the likelihood that the various dialects of Arabic will splinter into separate languages. The lasting power of the Qur'an should never be underestimated. It gives God a mother tongue, from which any change can appear an unworthy deviation. English has no such stabilizing text: it feeds on novelty. Changes are its meat and drink.

There remains, nonetheless, something a little uncanny about the process by which newborn expressions spread through society. Steven Pinker, who appears to know nearly everything about the inner workings of English, confesses in his 2007 book *The Stuff of Thought* that "the fortunes of new words are a mystery" and that "we still can't predict when a new word will take root." Pinker suggests that the most arresting neologisms are often ones that wither and die, for instead of merely naming something, they deliver an implicit editorial. "Soccer mom" has settled into American English, but the more recent "security mom" — a female voter worried about terrorism — may not last for long. Comment is free, and it goes out of date fast.

჻

To a writer, the prodigal scope and diversity of English are both a blessing and a curse. A blessing, because the language offers juicy specimens of almost any verbal trend you can imagine. But also a curse, because anything you say about English is liable to contradiction. In Melbourne, "garry" means to flirt; in Liverpool, it means an ecstasy tablet. What applies to a verb in Portland, Oregon, may not apply in Portland, Dorset, still less in Portland Cottage, Jamaica. The dispersal, flowering and transformation of English around the world raise a crucial question: will this remain a single language? Perhaps it will soon be an act of nostalgia to speak about English in the singular. For a time, the future may belong not to English but to Englishes.

Because of political, cultural and economic reasons, rather than strictly linguistic ones, today's English has a charismatic power. Ambitious people everywhere thirst to master the language. But as other idioms blur into it, especially in Asia and Africa, and as the many kinds of English spoken outside Britain and North America become louder and more confident, the language may be approaching an irrevocable split. Indian English, for example, is distinctive not just in its word-hoard, but also in aspects of its grammar and phonetics. French, Portuguese, Spanish, Italian and several other languages all branched out of Latin. It's conceivable that English will be the Latin of the new millennium.

Conceivable, but not inevitable. The combined influences of global business, media, politics, Hollywood and the Internet have an awesome linguistic power. They entail instant communication and instant comprehension, a requirement that may prove strong enough to pull English back from the brink of schism. The Roman Empire did not have CNN or Microsoft at its disposal. For the moment, a rough balance appears to exist between the forces working to pull English apart and those laboring to keep it united. The language's long-term future depends on which tendency — the centrifugal or the centripetal — proves stronger.

Its short-term future promises yet more growth. In 1997 the British Council released a major report by the linguist David Graddol entitled *The Future of English?* The question mark is significant, for Graddol's uncertainty matched his erudition. The growth of English, he argued, is unlikely to happen in a straightforward or predictable manner: "On the one hand, the use of English as a global lingua franca requires intelligibility and the setting and maintenance of standards. On the other hand, the increasing adoption of English as a second language, where it takes on local forms, is leading to fragmentation and diversity. No longer is it the case, if it ever was, that English unifies all who speak it." Beyond question, fragmentation and diversity have grown in the past few decades. Yet unless democratic governments are replaced by totalitarian ones, it's unclear who could possibly set and maintain the standards Graddol mentioned. I find it hard to imagine any organization with the breadth and authority to accomplish such a task. Still, for the first time in decades the heretical idea of regulating English is at least being discussed.

Graddol returned to the topic in a 2006 study, *English Next.* There he predicted that as early as 2010 or 2015, "nearly a third of the world population will all be trying to learn English at the same time." The demand for teachers and texts will be intense. "One Korean Internet provider," he notes, "is offering English courses for fetuses still in the womb." Never in human history has a single language been so widespread. "English is now," Graddol writes, "redefining national and individual identities worldwide; shifting political fault lines; creating new global patterns of wealth and social exclusion; and suggesting new notions of human rights and responsibilities of citizenship." That's an awful lot of power for any language to bear. But what exactly has this language become, and how might it change?

✍

In the remaining chapters I'll approach the linguistic future in a few sly, perhaps surprising ways. Texts that tell you precisely what to expect in the decades ahead are not just misleading, they're fraudulent — *nobody* knows what the future holds, in language or anything else. This book is not a crystal ball.

The future has always been cloudy; it always will be. It's best approached, I believe, by looking keenly and closely at what's happening now in the world, without prejudices or preconceptions. Such scrutiny will reveal a few common themes. Whether it be the growth of chatroom speech among teenagers or the rise of mixed idioms like Spanglish, we'll discover that people with little political or economic power can exert enormous influence on language. And whether it be the impact that English is having on Japanese or the effect that Asian languages are having on English, we'll find a tension between the informal and formal registers of language — between the top-down and the bottom-up forces that lead to verbal change. Although the language may not be going to hell in a handbasket — what *is* a handbasket, anyway? — some of its speakers appear ready to burninate a noob.

Talk 2u l8r.

2

Bouncebackability

How Words Are Created and Organized

DID "TEENAGE" REALLY GET its start in the somnolent capital of British Columbia? It seems unlikely. When exactly did "on the go" acquire the allure of a budding romance? Probably we'll never know. Words' origins are seldom easy to trace. Yet on occasion, new expressions — neologisms, to use the technical term — do emerge from a precise, well-defined source. I'll examine a few of those words and sources in this chapter, then go on to look at some ways in which people have tried to impose controls on language in the past, hoping to stop change in its tracks.

A few years ago a British biologist named Rob Wallace caught sight of a small monkey in the forests of northwestern Bolivia. With orange-brown fur on its cheeks, a golden crown and a white-tipped tail, it resembled an athletic teddy bear. Wallace, the coordinator of conservation programs in the region for the New York–based Wildlife Conservation Society, didn't recognize the animal. He and his colleagues watched the monkeys at several sites in Madidi National Park. They learned that the animals are monogamous fruit eaters, mating for life and enjoying it hugely. As the Wildlife Conservation Society delicately puts it, "These primates spend a lot of time bonding and are extremely tactile partners." By 2004 the scientists had made enough observations and taken enough pictures to know, beyond doubt, they had discovered a new mammal — a rare event in our age of burgeoning knowledge and succumbing wilderness. All the creature lacked was a name.

Wallace, as the discoverer, had the right to pick the monkey's name. Instead he and his colleagues set up an online auction in 2005 to sell off the naming rights. Money from the sale would go to a Bolivian nonprofit foundation dedicated to protecting the Madidi wilderness — no mean task in one of Latin America's poorest countries. Children placed bids; so did ce-

25

lebrities. But the winner was an Internet gambling company, Golden Palace, licensed in the Mohawk territory of Kahnawake. Having paid $650,000 for the privilege, the casino announced that the new species would be named the GoldenPalace.com monkey.

Until then, animals had not been named for private businesses. We talk about the black rhinoceros, not the "Guinness rhinoceros," and the pronghorn antelope, not the "Ferrari antelope." But corporate reticence is *so* twentieth century. The GoldenPalace.com monkey will always be identified with a website — even if the website closes down and the company goes belly-up, its brand will remain. The World Wide Web sprang to life in the early 1990s; within fifteen years the virtual realm had grown so powerful that one of its businesses could spend hundreds of thousands of dollars to label a creature in the wild. Companies have often found in animals a motif or inspiration for their products: think of Tiger beer and Jaguar cars, the Philadelphia Eagles and the Chicago Bulls. The online casino's offline monkey marks a reversal. A living species now carries the name of an entity that exists only on the Internet.

Other terms have humbler beginnings. "Womlu" sprang to life accidentally when a twenty-three-year-old freelance writer living in Los Angeles was typing a private message on an Internet forum devoted to the TV show *Buffy the Vampire Slayer*. Annika Barranti — "bettie" or "noirbettie" to other users of the forum — had befriended a user who went by the name of P@. She meant to say that something was "wonky," a British expression meaning messed up, out of sorts, askew. (As Giles and Spike, two of the show's key characters, came from England, Anglicisms dotted the script.) But, Annika explained to me, "my finger alignment on the keyboard was a bit wonky and I inadvertently typed 'womlu.' I thought P@ would find it amusing, so I left it as is, with a note of explanation at the bottom."

P@ was less forthcoming about himself — I can tell you only his sex (male) and nationality (American) — but he eventually e-mailed me to say that he too "found the mistake amusing, and we both opted to begin using 'womlu' as often as possible . . . Whenever something (generally computer-related) would not work, go on the fritz, or just be plain strange acting, we would deem it 'womlu.'" In August 2002, P@ posted a public message on the site complaining about the shortness of the upcoming *Buffy* season and offering a few suggestions to the show's creator, Joss Whedon. He wanted Buffy cloned; then he added: "*womlu*. Just throw the word on the show. A *womlu* demon would be fine."

It wasn't as crazy an idea as you might imagine. The writers of *Buffy the Vampire Slayer* were fearless at coining new words; an entire book, *Slayer Slang*, has been devoted to the topic. What other show would make its characters say "wiggins," "skulky," "mootville" or "Scareapalooza"? Willow, the show's lesbian witch, once complained: "She's like this cleavagey slutbomb walking around going, 'Ooh. Check me out, I'm wicked cool. I'm five by five.'" Womlu never made it on air. But other users of the *Buffy* forum picked up the word and ran with it: "You may have to copy the URL into a new window because Geocities is all womlu." "I was interested in the electrical components going womlu, and stopped listening when it came to oil and grease." "Doh! That was me. I'm on Heath's puter because mine is womlu." One user, attempting a parody of *The Lord of the Rings*, wrote, "Note to self: mention '*womlu*' — is important hobbit thing."

Buffy slipped away into the California sunset in 2003, apparently dooming the prospects for womlu — although it's conceivable, I realize, that this book will give it a new lease on life. After I interviewed her, Annika Barranti decided to take womlu down a commercial road. You can now buy its five letters, in black, lowercase form, on clothing and mugs. As she wrote on her blog in January 2007, "I am making [womlu] available in t-shirt and coffee mug form because I think it is awesome and I want to see it everywhere." A typing error has led to a moneymaking venture.

The short, strange history of womlu matters less than the serendipitous, even anarchic process of its creation. P@ and Annika asked nobody's permission before spreading womlu online; they had no qualms about turning a private term into a public one. New words like theirs enter the language freely: they have no barriers to surmount, either institutional or psychological.

The power of *Buffy* and other TV shows proves that even in a keyboard age, oral culture is alive and well. It's largely because of television that the speech and style of southern California's Valley Girls spread so fast. Many expressions join the language after being used in a movie or TV show — *The Simpsons* ("meh!") has been a particularly fertile source. Or think of "jumping the shark." The phrase originated in the early 1980s, when Fonzie, the main character of the sitcom *Happy Days*, donned water skis before implausibly vaulting over a shark. The stunt failed to boost the show's dismal ratings. Soon shark-jumping became a metaphor for any unsuccessful, high-profile effort to delay the inevitable. Other shows, including *Arrested Development*, *Dharma & Greg* and *South Park*, picked up the phrase and leapt with it. In 2002 "Jump the Shark" was the title of an episode in the final season of *The X-Files*. That show too spawned phrases that gained a wide currency in society at large, often being uttered by people who had no clue as to the terms' origin. "Trust No One" and "Deny Everything" each became the title of an alt-rock CD, one in Los Angeles, the other in London, while the makers of another TV show, *Charmed,* named an episode "The Truth Is Out There." I once came across yet another *X-Files* catchphrase, "Apology is policy," while plowing through a grim report on the failures of sewage treatment.

∽

The other day I was talking to my fourteen-year-old daughter.

"Can we go to a bookstore sometime so I can buy *Disco Bloodbath*?"

This was not a title I recognized, and instinctively I stalled for time.

"Why do you want to buy *Disco Bloodbath*?"

"Well, Anna has the book already, and she was reading us bits from it and it's really good. And I've seen part of the shockumentary on the Internet."

"The *what* on the Internet?" I said.

Megan is used to her father asking dumb questions. Sometimes she just gives me the look. This time she deigned to explain.

"Well, there's rockumentary, mockumentary, documentary and shocku-mentary, right?"

Right. For me there's one "real" word and three knockoffs — three that are a trifle suspect, verging on the illegitimate. But Megan is young. To her, all four terms are equally robust, equally legitimate and equally alive.

∽

Listening to teenagers is one way to discover how quickly the language is changing. Another is to read consumer magazines. Novelty is their stock-in-trade. One afternoon amid the clouds, I began to flip through Air Canada's in-flight magazine, *enRoute*. So much of what I found was new and strange that I put the issue in my hand luggage and carried it off the plane. I have it still. Its articles and ads exemplify some up-to-the-minute verbal fashions.

Those fashions include the blurring of traditional parts of speech. If you read an essay by a writer from an earlier century, like Samuel Johnson or Ralph Waldo Emerson, you may be put off by the orotund tone and the lengthy, intricately balanced clauses; but you should have no trouble telling an adjective from a noun or a verb. Now consider a single sentence from the contents page of *enRoute:* "With its hypersaturated colours and super-stylized people, manga- and anime-mad Tokyo brings a sci-fi megalopolis to life." "Manga" and "anime" are Japanese nouns, each of them deployed as the first half of a compound adjective; "sci-fi" is the abbreviation of two nouns, combined to form an adjective; "megalopolis" is a young noun that incorporates an adjectival prefix; and both "saturate" and "stylize" are verbs whose past participles have been whipped into service as adjectives and given the rhetorical icing of "hyper" and "super."

Compound adjectives offer an easy method for writers to cram lots of information into little space. The price is breathlessness. *En Route* contains a very short piece called "Gadgetwood" that packs a dizzying array of adjectival constructions into a mere five sentences. A partial list includes "wood grain clock" (modifying radio), "wooden tech" (toys), "nifty little SK65" (cellphone), "smooth burl" (wood), "Rotolog" (watch), "walnut wood" (inlays) and "deep-rooted clock radio" (memories — I kid you not). The effect, you'll notice, is to give nouns an ever greater prominence. They slot functionally into place like the linguistic counterparts of IKEA furniture. A few pages farther on, an article about luxury hotels includes a bevy of hyphenated adjectives, some of them familiar ("new-look," "gold-leaf"), others designed to sound new: "half-tester bed," "in-hotel restaurants," "over-sink video screens."

Many of the ads in *enRoute* forsake a common language, resorting instead to a specialized jargon incomprehensible to most readers. The jargon is liable to sink under the weight of acronyms. A full-page ad for Cadillac contains the following information: "Powered by an available 4.6L Northstar V8 VVT engine and AWD." On a later page, "The sleek and sexy ASUS W5A will create a scene wherever you go." Is that a threat or a promise? The small print of an ad for a telecommunications firm warns readers, "Quadband GSM/GPRS capable device required." But in terms of sheer impenetrability, no company outdoes Sony. Its full-page ad begins by addressing one of my deepest fears: "Don't Be a Casualty of Technology." You can avoid this mournful fate, alas, only if you purchase a "5.1ch DVD Dream System" with such "DAV-FX100W Features" as "Dts/Dolby Digital/Dolby Pro Logic II."

By definition, the ads of *enRoute* drip with brand names. But so do many of the articles. A column on global style describes how silhouettes are "turning up for a cameo on Dwell's Williamsburg-chic bedding and, in their cut-out positive form, lacily adorning Tord Boontje's lamps and Louis Vuitton sweaters." The writer of another article tells her readers to "enjoy Bastien Gonzalez pedicures at the Anne Sémonin spa." She describes a hotel in language that to me is almost utterly meaningless: "Combine Bang & Olufsen, Bose, Bulgari, designer Adam Tihany, retailer Harvey Nichols and acres of glass walls . . ." At least I can visualize the walls.

The verbal climax arrives in a piece by the magazine's "Scene columnist," Shinan Govani, pictured in dark glasses and light stubble. His subject is the opening of a Gucci boutique, an event that made the city of Vancouver just about chic enough for his taste. Previously, Govani says, the city has been "known more for Gore-Tex good sense than . . . for Gucci gorgeousness." Hyphenated compounds, like brand names, dot his prose: "It's the fashion house of cut-to-the-chase, loins-burning *sex*, where the men in the ads often look like on-call hustlers and the women's stilettos themselves are mini-pyramids to eroticism." Govani coins words with ironic verve: "'It's hot,' the Sweaty Betty declares, not at all content with the distinctly non-Vangroovy heat." "'It's all so yum,' coos a woman who's absolutely perfected the look of the West Coast fauxhemian." To my off-call, non-Vangroovy mind, all this bears no relation to real life; it's the language of hype, dead at the heart.

Forget that grumpy sermon. Govani's prose captures a few verbal trends. And trends are what a publication like *En Route* is all about. Whereas traditional journalism sets out to tell a story, one that will reveal a verifiable truth, "lifestyle journalism" seeks to embody the qualities it evokes and celebrates: mobility, glamour, hypermodernity and constant change. If you stick to old words, you can't be in the know. The narrative is subordinate to the style, style being essential to the message. In consumer magazines like *En Route*, neologisms serve an economic function.

Several months after picking up that issue, I met the magazine's editor, Ilana Weitzman, a slim, dark-haired young woman who talked both knowledgeably and eloquently about the language of her job. "We shamelessly create words," she told me over a vegetarian lunch in an Asian restaurant. "We created 'jetronaut' for our Future of Travel issue, and we invented 'hotelcultural tourism' for an article on Armenia. The magazine is very forward-looking, and part of that comes from toying with the language. But it's also native to English as it moves through different cultures — it's natural that it mutates."

En Route, the magazine of Canada's largest airline, is bilingual. It's based in Montreal, where two languages flourish. All of its editorial content, and many of its ads, appear in both English and French. Vivid translation is crucial. But the French versions of articles tend to be more linguistically conservative than the English — "a little touchy-feely" becomes *un peu de chaleur humain* (a little human warmth), and the enigmatic "place branding" turns into the straightforward *image territoriale*. Weitzman is well aware of this, and not happy about it: "On the French side there's an incredible resistance to neologisms. It's to the point where I tried to get the French team to use the word 'condo' — they wanted to use some antiquated term, because 'condo' hadn't yet found its way into the dictionary."

"Isn't 'condo' used in French ads all the time?" I asked.

"Oh sure. The difference between literature and ad copy is a huge divide. But the people who are the final arbiters — copyeditors and proofreaders — don't feel comfortable if they can't find a word in the dictionary." Weitzman recalled an article in English that had spoken of a "keyboard nipple" — hardly a common term, but not a neologism either. The French-language copyeditor was dubious. "I said to him, 'Just invent a word!' But he wouldn't. He wouldn't even import a word from France that we found online. Eventually we came up with the French for 'the button between two keys on a keyboard.'"

By the time a word like "metrosexual" is becoming familiar in society at large, *enRoute* is ready to leave it behind. The term reached most North American lips in 2003 (it had been coined in England in 1994) — but to Weitzman, "It's already old! You have to create a new word in order for it to have the same significance." Still young enough for her to consider it new was the label for a style of music, "grunk." It's unclear whether "grunk" started life as an amalgam of "grunge" and "punk" or of "grime" and "crunk" (itself a blend of "crazy" and "drunk"). No matter: writers and editors don't agonize about the word's lineage; they go ahead and use it. Coinages happen every day in French as well, but they take more time to leap onto the page.

Weitzman rose to leave. "It comes down to the trend-based things," she said. "When you write about trends, you have to do it in a trendy way."

❧

There was a time when eminent and trendy voices argued that English should be compelled to reject new words — that new words were, in fact, a sign of corruption. That time lay in the seventeenth and eighteenth centuries, and the main reason was the influence of France. The arguments made in that period clearly outline what would become, for the English language, a road not taken. The road we did take has made grunk and metrosexual, womlu and condo possible.

If Shakespeare was the greatest coiner of words in English, he had plenty of competition. Earlier poets and playwrights had shown a similar freedom, if not so much flair. Writers on the continent were also seizing their language by the scruff of its neck and shaking it up: Camões in Portugal, Rabelais and Ronsard in France. But French belonged only to a minority of people in the lands ruled by the king of France — and aside from the strength of regional languages like Provençal, Gascon, Breton and Basque, the French tongue was fluid, shape-shifting and highly variable. The government in Paris wanted to assert its power. Like so many regimes before and since, it found language a useful means of control. If that meant snuffing out the linguistic vitality and freedom enjoyed by Rabelais and Ronsard, so be it.

In 1635, under the aegis of the much-feared Cardinal Richelieu, the Académie Française was born. From the beginning, it had a mission to "cleanse the language of the filth it had acquired." The academy was limited to forty members, the "Immortals," whose first batch included not only writers but also a soldier, a physician, a sprinkling of priests and lawyers, and several politicians. With respect to language, the most deathless of the lot was an impoverished nobleman, translator and grammarian by the name of Claude Favre de Vaugelas. For it was Vaugelas who began to compile the academy's first dictionary (and got a third of the way through the alphabet single-handed). It was also Vaugelas who set the intellectual tone by declaring, "Nobody is allowed to create new words, not even the king." What the king thought of this is unknown.

Vaugelas and his fellow academicians valued purity, simplicity and sobriety in language. No matter what their religious beliefs, they were linguistic Calvinists, infuriated by excess rhetoric, quick to damn any stylistic flourishes that displeased them. New words were not the sole target of their wrath: improper words, technical words, peasant words, regional words, and old words that had faded from common usage should all, Vaugelas thought, be expunged. The result would be a modern language, crystal clear, apt for the intellect, a language in which the nation could take pride. He and his colleagues in the academy were not content to describe the language as it existed; they set out to prescribe how it should be improved.

The Immortals' ability to control the destiny of French was never as great in practice as it appeared in theory. New words kept on emerging, and not all the low ones died out. But the academy helped strengthen the position of French across Europe, and it served as a powerful role model for other countries and languages. Reformers who dreamt of rationalizing and modernizing their own idioms looked to Paris with envy. None more so than the English. "The peculiar study of the Academy of Paris," wrote Daniel Defoe, "has been to refine and correct their own language; which they have done to that happy degree, that we see it now spoken in all the courts of Christendom, as the language allowed to be most universal."

The sentence comes from *An Essay upon Projects,* Defoe's first full-length book. His success as a novelist (with *Robinson Crusoe* and *Moll Flanders* among others) lay far in the future. In 1692, the year when he probably began the *Essay,* he was a young, impatient, well-traveled businessman with an intimate knowledge of debt and a thirst for social reform. He called for changes in England's bankruptcy laws; he wanted women to have access to higher education; and he hoped to see the birth of an English academy. "The work of this Society," he stated, "should be to encourage polite learning, to polish and refine the English tongue, and advance the so much neglected faculty of correct language . . ." Much of the polishing, refining and advancing would take the form of purgation, because Defoe also aimed to eliminate "all those innovations in speech, if I may call them such, which some dogmatic writers have the confidence to foster upon their own native language, as if their authority were sufficient to make their own fancy legitimate." New words were a confidence trick.

GoldenPalace.com, noirbettie and Shinan Govani don't have to worry about whether their verbal imaginings are "legitimate." But three hundred years ago, even a political dissenter like Defoe was convinced that an academy should govern English. The reputation of its thirty-six members "would be enough to make them the allowed judges of style and language; and no author would have the impudence to coin without their authority . . . 'Twould be as criminal then to coin words, as money." Later writers concurred. Jonathan Swift may not have wanted to imprison writers for the crime of creating words, but he too looked forward to an English academy and, in his *Proposal for Correcting, Improving and Ascertaining the English*

Tongue (1712), he suggested that if only the language could be "refined to a certain standard, perhaps there might be ways found out to fix it for ever."

The anxious rhetoric of Defoe and Swift reminds us that alarm about the state of English is nothing new. "Our language is extremely imperfect," Swift wrote; "its daily improvements are by no means in proportion to its daily corruptions"; even worse, "it offends against every part of grammar." Latin for him offered a linguistic ideal against which English fell miserably short. Then as now, the hunger to stop change in its tracks gave proof of the unease that change provoked. Seeing no reason for any tongue to keep on altering, Swift cited Chinese and Ancient Greek as languages that had remained stable over many centuries. Admittedly, English could never be perfect. But "I am of opinion, that it is better a language should not be wholly perfect, that it should be perpetually changing." This was, we should recall, the same Jonathan Swift who in his novel *Gulliver's Travels* would coin a host of words. "Yahoo" and "Lilliputian" are still current; not so the delightful "splacknuck." Swift did not always practice what he so vehemently preached.

Neither did Samuel Johnson, the great writer, talker and man about London who, in 1755, completed the first major dictionary of the English language. In the absence of a London academy, it required a man of heroic stubbornness to undertake such a task, and Johnson was ideal for the role. He was by temperament a curmudgeon, one who looked on the present with some dismay and who peered into the future with foreboding. Though he was glad to define rare polysyllables like "amnicolist" and "adespotic," he choked over "tiny" ("a burlesque word"), "cheery" ("ludicrous"), "lesser" ("a barbaric corruption of less") and "shabby" ("a low word that has crept into conversation and low writing; but ought not to be admitted into the language"). Perhaps an academy could serve as a bouncer, tossing "shabby" and its ilk into the cold? Johnson knew the arguments in favor of one, but he disposed of them in a couple of subordinate clauses: "If an academy should be established for the cultivation of our style, which I, who can never wish to see dependence multiplied, hope the spirit of English liberty will hinder or destroy . . ."

Even today, an academy may be tremendously useful for a language. It can create a standard out of several feuding dialects; it can give weight and respectability to new coinages; it can reduce the chances that speakers will simply borrow or steal foreign terms. Yet thanks to its spirit of freedom —

or thanks to nothing more exalted than its vast bulk — English continues to roam wild. David Crystal has called it "a vacuum-cleaner of a language, sucking in words from wherever it can get them." The notion that limits should be put on its growth may seem downright absurd.

∽

When Samuel Johnson began to organize, classify and define words, he was an idealist. He believed that a successful dictionary could "retard, if not re-pel" a language's "tendency towards degeneration" — as if there were some golden age of speech from which the eighteenth century had fallen away. He hoped that a dictionary "should fix our language, and put a stop to those alterations which time and chance have hitherto been suffered to make in it without opposition." Those hopes were dashed. Eight years of hard labor on the dictionary made Johnson a realist, and by the time its 2,300 closely printed pages were published, he knew that any lexicographer would be foolish to imagine that "his dictionary can embalm his language, and secure it from corruption and decay." So the vigilance of language academies in France and Italy must be in vain: "Sounds are too volatile and subtle for legal restraints; to enchain syllables, and to lash the wind, are equally the undertakings of pride, unwilling to measure its desires by its strength." Johnson went on to give some cogent reasons why languages in-evitably change. Trade, learning, fashion, literature and translation all ar-rive flush with newness, and all undermine the verbal stability he had once aspired to establish. He didn't mention immigration.

But in our time, hundreds of millions of people live outside the coun-try where they were born. And what struck Johnson as a deluge of new words in the eighteenth century seems a mere trickle by the standards of the twenty-first. Languages now scoff at restraint; they defy attempts to hold them in. Yet without such attempts, we would be lost in a delirium of signs and sounds. Which is, I suspect, why the ideal of "the Dictionary" lin-gers. It functions not only as a symbol of linguistic expertise but also as an embodiment of moral rectitude. Johnson told a friend that in preparing his dictionary he refused to cite "any wicked writer's authority for a word, lest it should send people to look in a book that might injure them for ever." As he knew, words have power. He called them "the daughters of earth."

Dictionaries continue to represent, in many eyes, an authority above and beyond the whims of circumstance. The Bible once enjoyed such authority, as the Qur'an still does across large stretches of Asia and Africa. But whether or not they call themselves Christians, most people living in the West today don't believe in the factual, word-for-word truth of the Bible. (You might say that our society's attitude to the Word has morphed from "Let us pray" to "Let us play.") Dictionaries have even begun to take over one of the Bible's historic roles — we have faith in their verdicts. When we swear to tell the truth, the whole truth and nothing but the truth, we might well place our hand on a *Webster's* or an *Oxford*. It's as though dictionaries tell us what we mean. One recent study noted that over an eight-and-a-half-year span, the members of the U.S. Supreme Court resorted to "the dictionary" 146 times in their written judgments. In fact they publicly referred to several dictionaries.

The great divide in the dictionary world has always been between those who prescribe and those who merely describe. Noah Webster, the greatest of American lexicographers, was a noted prescriptivist: in his *American Dictionary of the English Language,* he told his readers which words they should use, and which they would be smart to avoid. A nation brimming with newcomers was glad of his advice: if you didn't speak English as a mother tongue, you could follow Webster's rules with confidence. His work functioned as a teaching aid, a handbook of verbal etiquette; it improved and helped to standardize a nation's private spelling. In his 1833 updating of the King James Bible, he not only replaced much of the archaic vocabulary ("kine" gave way to "cows," "trow" to "suppose"), he also made the sacred texts more suitable for polite society. And so "whoremonger" became "lewd person," and "testicles" turned into "peculiar members." Instead of spilling his seed, Webster's Onan "frustrated his purpose."

Yet in his word-compiling, Webster struck a different note, one that goes against his image as a stern bowdlerizer. "The business of a lexicographer," he wrote, "is to collect, arrange, and define, as far as possible, *all* the words that belong to a language, and leave the author to select from them . . . according to his own taste and judgment." (That phrase "as far as possible" gave him sufficient leeway to leave a few offenders on the outside.) More than a century later Philip Gove, the editor in chief of *Webster's Third International Dictionary,* followed the master's lexicographical precepts rather than his somewhat inconsistent practice, opening the book to four-letter words and eliminating the old editorial comments like "erroneous," "poetic," "improper" and "jocular." "For us to attempt to prescribe the language," Gove wrote, "would be like *Life* reporting the news as its editors would prefer it to happen." He was roundly condemned for moral laxity.

There are judgments, even so, in Gove's version of the dictionary, just as there had been in all previous editions. When I looked through the latest incarnation of *Webster's Third,* published in 2002, I noticed that its first definition of "feminism" is, surprisingly, "the presence of female characteristics in males." "Womanly," in its pages, means "marked by qualities characteristic of a woman, esp. marked by qualities becoming a well-balanced adult woman." But "manly" gains a fuller explanation: "having qualities appropriate to a man: not effeminate or timorous: bold, resolute, and open in conduct or bearing." Lexicographers can never entirely escape from their society's beliefs. Yet beliefs are in perpetual motion.

Today, as in the past, the selection and definition of words vary from one dictionary to another. The variations are occasionally glaring. This is so obvious a point that I hesitate to mention it — except that, if you think about it for long, it's enough to undermine faith in any single dictionary as the arbiter of truth. Consider the verb "table." The *American Heritage Dictionary* (fourth edition, 2000) defines it as "to postpone consideration of (a piece of legislation, for example); shelve." But in the *Compact Oxford English Dictionary* (third edition, 2005), the same word means to "present formally for discussion or consideration at a meeting." "Table," when used as a verb, has two senses, almost diametrically opposite in their meanings. Many dictionaries mention only one. "Liberal" has subtly different meanings in American and British dictionaries; when it comes to "neoliberal," the differences are drastic. "Entrée," a main course in New York restaurants and dictionaries, is a light second course in London and a first course in Montreal.

Apart from their everyday use in schools, offices and legal chambers, dictionaries are crucial to a pair of competitive mental sports: Scrabble and spelling bees. One reason why these activities are now so popular is that here, if nowhere else, the language is forced into order. Rules are rules. Mistakes are mistakes. Relativism is unthinkable — either a contestant has made a word that conforms to the dictionary or she has not. Her sequence of letters can hold no more ambiguity than the digits on a watch. Scrabble players currently obey the third edition of Merriam-Webster's *Official Scrabble Players Dictionary* — unless they live outside North America, in which case they take their marching orders from the *Collins Official Scrab-*

ble Dictionary. Webster's Third is the official dictionary of the immensely popular National Spelling Bee in the United States — but an invited participant each year is the winner of the New Zealand championship, which relies on the eleventh edition of the *Concise Oxford English Dictionary.* Why do such details matter? Because for some words, spellings as well as definitions vary. *Webster's Third,* for example, accepts no variants for "paralyzingly," while Oxford insists on "paralysingly."

Spelling bees reward contestants who are blessed with elephantine memories and nerves of steel. The events make irresistible TV. What they suggest about language, however, is open to question. In a formal competition, each word arrives with an exact meaning and spelling. It's a prescriptivist's idea of heaven. Context and nuance are irrelevant; all that matters is correctness. This works fine in the artificial setting of a spelling bee, but it's not so helpful when language spills out into the world. Streets, classrooms, bedrooms and locker rooms all require a word to be combined with other elements of language, not kept in an isolated compartment. In the hothouse environment of a spelling bee, neglected terms like "degringolade" and "pococurantism" are legitimate, while useful expressions like "foshizzle" and "googlebomb" are not. It's by a purely arbitrary right that *Webster's Third,* or any other dictionary, exercises the power to decree what's an acceptable or unacceptable morsel of speech. But real life does not obey hothouse rules. Real language is expressive, creative, bursting at the edges — and fraught with ambiguity.

⌇

That's what I think, anyway. But lots of people disagree with me. A word's publication in a dictionary — it doesn't have to be among the many that use the name Webster's — offers tangible proof of its acceptance. If your favorite dictionary lacks a particular expression, you may refuse to believe the expression is real. A word's arrival in a dictionary, like a graying athlete's election to a hall of fame, signifies lasting success. The word has "made it." It has earned a secular kind of immortality. This explains, perhaps, the curious tale of "bouncebackability."

One day in 2004, Iain Dowie, then the manager of Crystal Palace, an English football club (soccer team, if you prefer), was talking about his squad's resilience. One of the less fashionable teams in London, they often found themselves a goal or two down. But the players refused to give up, and would battle hard to equalize. As Dowie explained in an interview, "Crystal Palace have shown great bouncebackability against their opponents." An off-the-cuff, oral expression, "bouncebackability" soon became chic in print. Political columnists as well as sportswriters began to use it. An article in *The Scotsman*, describing the leader of Britain's Conservative Party, said, "As a former cabinet member of Major's government, Michael Howard has an even harder job ahead of him. He has to show he has enough bouncebackability to get him into Number Ten."

A Sky-TV sports show, *Soccer AM*, mounted a campaign to promote the word. Dowie was credited with being both a savvy manager and a sharp word coiner. A website sprang up, bouncebackability.biz, featuring a choice of red and blue T-shirts on which the word was prominent. The site contained a link to an online petition, asking the editors of the *Oxford English Dictionary* to welcome "bouncebackability." The petition gathered more than 5,400 signatures. Enthusiasm dwindled only after the term muscled its way into the *Collins Living Dictionary*, and was named a "word of the week" by the *Macmillan English Dictionary*.

I couldn't help noticing that four of the first six comments attached to the petition had spelling mistakes in them. "Can not belive this is not encluded," wrote one of the signers. "itsadisgrace," said another. "should replace useless words like 'inpromtue,'" suggested a third. Although this hardly inspires confidence in the lexicographical talent of the signers — or the spelling skills of the British public — it suggests that "bouncebackability" had gathered a brigade of partisans who wouldn't normally care about the fate of a word. "Well done to Iain Dowie and Soccer AM for making this word possible!" wrote one starry-eyed fan.

The petition succeeded — with an ironic twist. In 2006 the *Oxford English Dictionary* announced it would accept the word. But unlike *Macmillan*, which had already named Dowie as the source of "bouncebackability," the *OED* coolly pointed out that this wasn't a new expression at all. "It's actually a pretty venerable word," remarked Graeme Diamond, the head of New Words at the *OED*. Indeed it appeared as long ago as 1961 (Diamond perhaps has a briefer notion of venerability than many of us do). Even more distressing to some of the word's proponents, its origins involve baseball. The first known reference, praising the comeback power of the Cleveland Indians, was made by a reporter for the *Times Recorder* in Zanesville, Ohio.

While Sky-TV was trying to push "bouncebackability" into the dictionary, another campaign was being waged to pry a term out of it. This would prove a harder task, because while democracy — or is it mob rule? — may help words slither into a large dictionary, it's much more difficult for anyone to extract them. Even so, the British Potato Council, representing about four thousand farmers and processors, decided that "couch potato" should leave the *OED*. The council's head of marketing, Kathryn Race, explained: "We are trying to get rid of the image that potatoes are bad for you." The potato people asked the dictionary makers to replace the offending phrase with "couch slouch," and in June 2005 they staged a demonstration near the offices of Oxford University Press. Potatoes are "inherently healthy," they declared.

But it would take a shocking change of policy for the dictionary to banish "couch potato," which appears to originate in the America of the 1970s. Like the Hotel California of that storied decade, the *OED* is programmed to receive. Once you've arrived, you can never leave.

∽

I was quietly pleased that the couch potato and bouncebackability campaigns, which had dozens of competing dictionaries to choose among, targeted the *OED*. For when I was a university student, I spent three memorable years in Oxford. Like so many young people before and after, I wandered the city with a college scarf wound around my neck, gaining or pretending to an intimacy with Oxford's cheap restaurants and floor-to-ceiling bookstores, its pocket theaters and back-lane pubs. The magisterial name *Oxford English Dictionary* gave me confidence that as an aspiring poet, I'd arrived in the right place. If this was where words made their home, surely it was also the heart and soul of the language?

Oxford was changing in the late 1970s, and students — no longer required to sport the academic gown — had begun to live in areas of town that in earlier generations they seldom visited. A trio of takeaway Indian restaurants were what occasionally drew me to Walton Street. They crowded together on the east side of the narrow road, twining its way north from the city center to the red brick terraced homes of Jericho — once a Victorian slum, now more likely to shelter artists than factory workers. The rock bands Radiohead and Supergrass played some of their earliest gigs in a Walton Street pub called the Jericho, before the owners unwisely changed its name to the Philanderer and Firkin.

On its west side, the street is dominated by the imposing stone edifice that houses Oxford University Press. Books have been emerging from Oxford presses since 1478, but OUP is a relative newcomer — this building arose as recently as the 1820s. Its size and splendor create an impression, perhaps justified, that the press carries as much political and intellectual weight as any of the ancient colleges. In fact it's the largest university press in the world. It boasts a private quadrangle, one that passersby can barely glimpse from the street. As a student, even though at joyful or drunken moments I felt I owned the city, I never ventured inside the Jericho quad.

In previous centuries, this was a place that spawned hobbits and orcs, slithy toves and frumious bandersnatches. Yet despite the presence of such ardent word coiners as J.R.R. Tolkien and Lewis Carroll, Oxford has long held a reputation for linguistic conservatism. It is the home, Matthew Arnold wrote, of "lost causes, and forsaken beliefs, and unpopular names, and impossible loyalties." Of peculiar words, too. Even now, a student who arrives at some Oxford colleges quickly learns the arcane meaning of terms like "scout" and "sconce," "battels" and "eights." Not every dictionary includes them. But they're all to be found in the grandest word-hoard this language (or any other) has yet produced: the *Oxford English Dictionary*, better known as the *OED*.

Its affiliation with Oxford, and with that university's press, is a matter of luck as well as judgment. The dictionary was born in London, and it would have grown up in Cambridge under different initials if Cambridge University Press hadn't spurned the project. In the 1870s, before the still juvenile dictionary and its newly appointed editor, James Murray, moved to Oxford, the idea of producing a vast dictionary on historical principles — one that would trace the development of every word that had been written down as far back as the Early Middle English of the twelfth century — stood in danger of becoming a further lost cause. The Académie Française had tried to create a French dictionary on similar historical principles, but their effort was abandoned before the end of the letter A. English, unlike French and Italian, had no academy to guide and constrain it. By the Victorian age, the language already had an international reach, an unusually fat vocabulary and a thousand-year-old history. How could any dictionary contain it?

The task was impossible, which makes the result all the more astonishing. Perhaps the single outstanding reason for the *OED*'s success was that Murray, a barbigerous genius and an extremely canny Scot, built up a network of devoted, assiduous informants around the world. They lavished years on the unpaid search for words — not just the retrieval of obscure and archaic ones, but also the early appearances and complicated usages of very common ones. ("Range" is much easier to spell than "rarefication"; it's also much harder to define.) So whereas Samuel Johnson defined about 43,000 words — Noah Webster pushed the total up to roughly 70,000 — the *OED* surpassed those numbers in its first few letters.

It was published in agonizingly slow installments; Murray refused all blandishments to release anything that fell short of his exacting standards. Yet he couldn't entirely ignore the Delegates of Oxford University Press — his employers. In 1896, annoyed at the ponderous pace, they told him: "It is a waste of time and brain to give . . . any serious attention" to "the latest specimens of Journalese, or the newest Americanisms." But even then, the old distinctions between acceptable and unacceptable words were breaking down. After thirty-six years on the job, Murray died in harness in 1915, late in the letter T. If his rate of productivity seems a little plodding, consider that the *Deutsches Wörterbuch*, begun by the Brothers Grimm when Murray was a boy, remained unfinished until 1960. The *Svenska Akadamiens Ordbok*, Sweden's equivalent to the *OED*, has suffered an even more prolonged gestation. The first volume was published in 1898; nobody knows when the last will appear. As of 2007, Swedish lexicographers had yet to trudge as far as U.

X, Y and Z having already been delivered, the *OED*'s final installment (*wise* to *wyzen*) appeared, as luck would have it, exactly a century after the publication of Webster's *American Dictionary of the English Language*. By 1928 the total of defined words had reached nearly 415,000. The dictionary's official biographer, Simon Winchester, calls it "this most magnificent and romantic of enterprises." Romantic, in that sense, is almost a synonym for quixotic. No sooner was the dictionary complete than work began on a supplement, one that would attempt to capture all the terms which had emerged since the *OED* began its long unveiling; the first installment (*a* to *ant*) had been published in 1884. "Absquatulate" had unaccountably been missed, as had "acarologist," as had "absinthe" used as a synonym for sagebrush — and there were plenty of new-minted terms too, such as "aeroplane." So many, in fact, that the 1933 supplement ran to 867 pages.

But English would not stop expanding. Four more supplements came out in the 1970s and '80s, adding an extra 50,000 words — a larger number than had held the entire language in Dr. Johnson's version. These supplements, for the first time, welcomed slang into the *OED*. By 1989, the advent of computer technology allowed the press to combine the original *OED* and all its supplements into a twenty-volume "second edition." Each complete set weighs 150 pounds and eats up four feet of shelf space. Soon the whole dictionary became available on a searchable CD-ROM. Even so, it was felt to be inadequate, partly because none of the original entries had ever been revised, and partly because of the continuing explosive growth of English. And so the press — whose fame and fortune now seem indissolubly linked to those of the great dictionary (along with its many offshoots: the *Concise*, the *Shorter*, the *Primary*, the *Pocket* and so on) — committed itself to creating an altogether new, third edition.

∽

On a bright morning in late winter, I walked up Walton Street to enter Oxford University Press. Dictionary makers occupy a good part of the premises. I was early for my appointment with Edmund Weiner, the deputy chief editor of the *OED*, and I dawdled past the little shops along the way. Terms that would have baffled the early editors were now an everyday affair. At an all-sausage restaurant with the punning name The Big Bang, one dish featured "a grain mustard mash served with a stilton jus." ("Jus," in English, had been obsolete for hundreds of years until a late-twentieth-century revival.) The menu outside a venerable Indian restaurant promised dishes like Bombay duck, puri and paratha, none of them explained, along with others that still require translation: *nira mish, shabzi massalla, keena nan*. In linguistic terms, the empire keeps striking back.

Weiner proved to be a slim, middle-aged man wearing a blue shirt and, not surprisingly, glasses. His office, located in a new wing overlooking a bare inner courtyard, was dominated by a pair of high-powered computers. I thought of James Murray, who toiled away in an iron shed he called the Scriptorium, where millions of yellowing quotation slips filled pigeonholes stretching the length and breadth of the building. Murray and his assistants overcame a host of difficulties: the slowness and complexity of the task, a persistent shortage of money, the uncomfortable working conditions and some painful quarrels with the university. The lexicographers of today's and tomorrow's third edition are better paid, better housed and better respected. Yet in certain ways Murray enjoyed an advantage over them: he understood what his sources could be, he was clear about the nature of his mission, and he knew in what shape it would eventually be fulfilled.

Edmund Weiner, by contrast, seemed weighed down by doubt. Work on the new edition began to appear in 2000 with a revision of the letter M, and the finished entries are continually being updated online — but, he admitted, "we've stopped talking about a completion date, because so many things are uncertain." Will the new *OED* be finished in the 2020s? Or is that too optimistic? "I hope it's not as late as the '30s, because lots of us won't be here to see it." An honest answer, but not one with the ring of confidence.

In any case, what will there be to see? Nothing heavier than a CD-ROM (or whatever item of technology may have superseded it), nothing more substantial than the flickering entries on a screen? "It's not decided," Weiner said, "what happens in X years' time." All the new entries that wealthy subscribers now pay to read in a quarterly electronic version, along with the multitude of their unwritten successors, could eventually be printed — if that's what Oxford University Press chooses to do. It could also decide that the dictionary has grown so obese, it must remain forever electronic: not so much out of print as never in print, and beyond the reach of the technologically illiterate and the poor.

"There's something slightly nebulous about an online form," Weiner said with more than a hint of wistfulness. "Whereas a book, hopefully it will never go away. Will it?"

I couldn't offer much reassurance. I love the printed word, but I don't enjoy the prospect of trees dying to provide the tens of thousands of oversized pages a single copy would demand. When I asked if the *OED* still aspired to give readers what Simon Winchester, with pardonable exaggeration, called "the meaning of everything," Weiner managed to avoid a straight answer. "We maintain the mission," he said, "even though we know that in many areas, it's now impossible to fulfill. With the revisions to the second edition, we actually upped the ante — the essentials of World English are covered. Though we probably don't cover Singapore English, for example, in proper detail." The historical introduction to the first edition spoke with guarded pride of "a complete English dictionary" — not that its coverage of regional forms was anything like complete. The early editors were happy to neglect both dialect and slang. They left it to others to notice that left-wing texts and working-class sources were also seriously underrepresented.

"The language is expanding so fast," Weiner continued, "this may be an impossible mission. But we haven't drawn back from any frontiers we were pressing on before." It's a careful and revealing statement, for it implies that the *OED* fully understands there are some linguistic borders it will not push against. Murray and his far-flung volunteers never had to think about language as it was pronounced in films and on television and radio; they relied on the published word. But today the *OED* makes regular use of screenplays, television and radio scripts, even advertisements. Unscripted talk on radio and TV is harder to handle: how do you prove the existence of a word you suspect you just heard? Still, in the twenty-first century, that's not the lexicographers' main challenge.

"The Internet," Weiner said slowly, "poses problems." He closed his eyes and rested his head on his right hand, as though suffering from a migraine. "We tend to avoid citing the Web unless we feel we really have to. What we've tended to cite are newsgroups and discussion groups — they guarantee to archive them for a long time. We've occasionally taken quotations from websites. But we don't like doing that."

When the *OED* documents a word, it wants the result to be checkable. That's difficult to achieve with language on the Internet, which is ephemeral by its very nature; its words survive at the mercy of webmasters and search engines. Much of what appears online is also unreliable. Apart from the Internet's innumerable factual and verbal errors, it also contains vast quantities of specialized vocabulary that mean nothing to outsiders. "If we send a LMS from a GSM to any RIM," a contributor to an Indian discussion forum wrote in 2005, "it does not come to the RIM at all. It disappears totally. Ideally it should come in one single LMS or alternately, it should come in different packets of 160 chrs. However none of the reliance phones — mobiles or FWPs is able to receive any LMS at all." Online dictionaries of technical terms could doubtless help me make sense of all that. But should the *OED* try to keep pace? At what point should it, and other dictionaries that aspire to fulfill a comprehensive mandate, incorporate such jargon into their work?

There's a further issue. Countless times every day, teenagers chat or e-mail or post an electronic message in which words take on a fresh meaning or a wildcat spelling. Can this be of any conceivable interest to the heirs of James Murray? Maybe not. The *OED* likes to wait until a word is well established before granting it admission. Yet, as a dictionary that abides by historical principles and wants to know the origin of all its entries, how can it ignore one of the most widely used means of written communication in the world? Online messages are, you might say, the primordial linguistic slime out of which words flirt, mate, hatch, quiver, evolve and (sometimes) mature. The heart and soul of the English language no longer inhabit Oxford; they hang loose in cyberspace.

Weiner sighed, gave a rueful smile, and went back to the work he'd been doing when I arrived: splitting one of the *OED*'s existing entries, about a West African tribe, into two. The tools have changed beyond recognition since the heroic labors of Johnson, Webster and Murray, but the basic trade of a lexicographer remains the same: endless finding, endless defining, endless refining.

A key difference in their work is philosophical. Samuel Johnson set out not only to "ascertain the meaning of our English idiom," but also to "preserve the purity" of it. Noah Webster believed as a matter of moral duty that his dictionary should help forge a language proper to the United States. Until the twentieth century, most lexicographers considered it their duty to say how the language should be used. Even James Murray and his Oxford colleagues had, in Weiner's judicious words, "a certain prescriptive mentality. But I think they were better than their principles. You can find judgments dotted around the dictionary, though they're often in minor corners." The *OED*'s definition of "prick" in its anatomical sense, for example, comes with the warning phrases "now low" and "a vulgar term." By contrast, a guiding principle of the dictionary's twenty-first-century editors is to make as few prescriptive judgments as possible. They don't intend to dictate how the language should be used — if lots of people choose to say "mitigate against," the contested phrase will be included despite the purists' insistence that "militate against" is correct. Questions of appropriateness seem almost insignificant when set against the language's sheer bulk.

❦

Edmund Weiner wasn't the only lexicographer I met at the *OED*. I also spoke to Graeme Diamond, the young boss of New Words who had so delighted and dismayed the proponents of "bouncebackability." Outside the arched entrance to the building, where crocuses and snowdrops basked in a mild unwintry sun, an old-fashioned telephone box advertised a "Runaway Helpline" with "24 hour confidential freefone." I'm old enough to wince at the spelling. But Diamond, a tall, short-bearded man dressed in black, seemed relaxed about the changes sweeping over English. What good would fear do — to him, me or anyone else?

His unit contains a handful of people in both Oxford and New York. But not all of their work is devoted to finding and defining neologisms. They also work hand in hand with the current "revision project," noticing meanings that are absent from the existing entries and, Diamond explained, "parachuting in to fill the gaps." Take a quick look at the new version of life in the letter M, and you'll realize that some of these gaps were surprisingly broad. Along with definitions for terms that arose in the twentieth century — "machete," "minikini," "mudbugging" and the like — the third edition includes older words that were unaccountably left out. "Manslot" (found in Old and Middle English), "morrow-while" (first recorded in 1225), "misnurture" (1540) and "Manitoba maple" (1887) are among them.

Where Dr. Johnson looked for his examples in classic literature, the *OED*'s editors now find grist for their mill in publications like *Cosmopolitan* and *Discount Store News*. In 2007 they sought the help of the British public in tracing the origins of common terms like "wolf whistle," "Bloody Mary," "marital aid" and "loo," all of which slipped into the language discreetly enough to puzzle lexicographers. "People would be wrong," Diamond warned me, "if they thought of us typically reading something in the paper one day and sticking it into the dictionary the next. We want to resist putting ephemera in, because the *OED* never takes anything out. If it's been recorded in the dictionary already, it will stay there."

In the *OED*, accordingly, the voices of southern England, perhaps especially the dialect of Oxford, may always be overrepresented. But here, as in so many other ways, the Internet has hugely expanded the possibilities. Local words like "ziggy" — a sports term in Detroit for the firing of a coach — were once confined to a single place; now the Internet makes them available to anybody. *Depanneur*, to name but one, recently migrated across the Atlantic and landed on the website of *The Guardian*. No English-speaker in Montreal visits a convenience store, a corner shop, a 7-11 or a neighborhood grocery; instead we head to a depanneur — a term from Quebec French originally referring to a tow truck, or something that helps you when you're in a fix.

"So," I asked, "is 'depanneur' likely to make it into the *OED*?"

Diamond looked uncomfortable, as though he were trying to find a polite way of saying "Not on your life!" "Theoretically, yes, that could get in. It always sounds a bit brutal, but in the scale of things now, one million English-speakers is not a lot."

"There might be a lot fewer speakers for some Dorset dialect word," I said.

"Not everything in Dorset dialect would get in either."

Somewhere in OUP's vast buildings, Diamond said, is a room full of the original quotation slips. Venture in, pick up an old scrap of paper, and you might be staring at "the unreadable writing of some reverend from the nineteenth century. And that tradition does still carry on. Recently we had quite a correspondence with a man who is obsessed with cream teas — in the West Country, especially, they have a whole vocabulary. That exceedingly detailed knowledge is still feeding in."

Despite the growth of a computer-produced corpus of the English language, dozens of volunteers in several nations continue to read for the *OED*. "The really prodigious ones," in Diamond's words, are paid. One of his colleagues decides what fields of experience the dictionary has underrepresented in the past; he then chooses books in those fields and distributes them to people who will read for language, not just meaning. The readers work through the pages, highlighter at the ready, and when they notice a word used in an intriguing way, either figurative or literal, they mark up the text. I was thinking that the process sounded refreshingly old-fashioned until Diamond added that the highlighted books are returned to the *OED*'s "data capture department." If a usage passes muster, an editor will work on the word in "Pasadena" — a system of electronic editing whose letters are said to stand for "Perfect All-Singing All-Dancing Editorial and Notation Application."

Some of the trickiest questions that editors face involve loanwords from foreign languages. World English overflows with them. Malaysian English, for instance, contains hundreds of Chinese terms. "The difficulty always is," Diamond said, "are the words being used in a bilingual context where the writer can expect the readers to code-switch, so that it's really Chinese being used in an English context? At what point does it become English? There's no hard-and-fast answer. One of our principles would be, is it being used outside the region? Another would be just the sheer weight of evidence." Sometimes lexicographers make the wrong guess about new expressions: in 2000, when Random House published a new version of its

Webster's College Dictionary, its editors included obscure phrases like "stork parking" but omitted the junk-mail meaning of "spam." Paradoxically, the nature of the *OED's* mission — its high-minded inclusiveness, its thirst to be complete — makes the work ever harder. Dictionaries given over to specific niches — Irish terms, let's say, or Formula One racing — may have an easier time accepting new words *because* they have so much less to accept.

Before I met him, I had imagined that Diamond's job would be, so to speak, to gather up smart young words that were roaming the countryside and to welcome them into a permanent home. Now I was starting to see him differently: as a gatekeeper, whose chief role was to stand guard beside an overcrowded building and keep words out. He took my metaphor and ran with it: "It's a bit of both, I'm afraid. There's a 'come one, come all' invitation. But we do have a door policy. And it's not in the way words are dressed — it's to do with how many mates they can bring along. The invitation is for all. But not all of them get in."

The more the merrier: I understand. But I still think you'll find more mates buying six-packs of cream ale in a depanneur than nibbling tea biscuits in Lyme Regis.

～

To measure how far we've traveled since the age of Defoe and Swift, we need only look at the annual awards that twenty-first-century lexicographers give out for "word of the year." Far from trying to embalm the language, Dr. Johnson's heirs rush to embrace the new: they seek and celebrate examples of language change. The media, always keen on appearing up-to-the-minute, happily cooperate — although much of the general public, I suspect, remains suspicious. "Embedded" (YourDictionary.com, 2003), "adultescent" (*Webster's New World College Dictionary,* 2004), "podcast" (*New Oxford American Dictionary,* 2005) and "truthiness" (*Merriam-Webster,* 2006) are a few of the recent champions. Despite their fast-track approval by reputable dictionaries, not all of these words will survive. The American Dialect Society plays a similar game; in 2003 its winner was "metrosexual." Within a year, "retrosexual," "technosexual," "übersexual" and other variants were swarming about. Language is endlessly promiscuous.

The best place I know to watch the promiscuity in action is the website UrbanDictionary.com. It calls itself "a slang dictionary with your definitions. Define your world." The invitation is essential — for the charm, along with the risk, of Urban Dictionary is that any visitor to the site can act as a lexicographer. Mere seconds after arriving, a twelve-year-old boy can deliver a "thumbs up" or "thumbs down" verdict on definitions that may involve complicated, unrealistic and degrading sex acts, along with many other definitions that are simple, realistic and nonviolent. Urban Dictionary requires neither payment nor registration; it asks no questions. The combination of power, fun and anonymity may help to explain why it has grown to be among the most popular sites on the World Wide Web.

Urban Dictionary sprang to life in 1999, in the quasi-rural setting of San Luis Obispo, California. (It moved to Silicon Valley six years later.) The site's presiding genius, a software engineer named Aaron Peckham, was an eighteen-year-old freshman at the state university of Cal Poly when he created the site. Originally he meant it as nothing more elaborate than a parody of the rather staid and formal Dictionary.com. In one typical month, the "words of the day" at Dictionary.com included "homily," "corpulent," "doyen" and "coterminous" — not the most edgy or vibrant terms you can imagine. Peckham's site, by contrast, thrives on edginess and may never define "coterminous." Its guiding principle is that the only true authorities on language are the people who use it: Urban Dictionary is both populist and collaborative. The site's growth was at first relatively slow, but by January 2004 it had welcomed about 300,000 definitions; two years later, the figure was up to 1.5 million.

If you're baffled by the lyrics of popular songs — why should a woman sing "My milkshake brings all the boys to the yard"? — Urban Dictionary is a good place to look for an answer. Or, in the case of "milkshake," more than thirty answers. The most frequently defined word on the site, as of May 2007, was "emo" — no fewer than 4,225 explanations had been sent in. Some of the definitions are witty: "sport," for instance, being "the name your dad calls you by that makes you feel like a total loser." "Fo shizzle my nizzle" (one of several possible spellings, all of which the site accepts) has dozens of explanations, my favorite being "a shortened form of the phrase 'Indeed, that is a prodigious idea, my African-American brother!'" Among the entries for "suicide" are clever ones like "the quickest way to answer life's biggest question," "something which should always be the LAST item on your to-do list," and "your way to say to God: 'You can't fire me! I quit!'" But the definitions go on and on, eventually arriving at this (I will quote less than half): "me im a suicidle person because of my bf he is so evil but i love him so much but i really dont think he cares about me oh well i should just die and get on with my nonexistence . . ."

By May 2007, about 1,650 definitions were reaching Urban Dictionary every day. It's impossible to determine whether the bulk of those entries are the work of young-at-heart people with a genuine love of slang and a fascination with the language, or of adolescents full of grudges, prejudices and hormones. (It's possible, I realize, to belong to both categories.) Peckham believes that just over half of all visitors to the site are between eighteen and twenty-five years old, with another 10 percent being under eighteen.

Before he instituted a review system for each new definition, the site was plagued by fake definitions of extreme obscenity. One for "girl scout" involved rape, torture and murder. In an effort to reduce the chances of such entries appearing again, tens of thousands of visitors to the site have agreed to serve as volunteer editors. The guidelines they are sent call for a definition to be rejected if it's racist, sexist, sexually violent or nonsensical (also if it's nothing more than an ad or a friend's name). Almost anything else remains acceptable: swearing is kosher, misspelling is fine, and ferocious attacks on famous people are welcome. When I e-mailed Peckham with questions about the site, he summarized the guidelines this way: "Publish stuff that would be relevant for a large audience. Don't discount something just because you disagree with it."

To get a more intimate look at how the system works, I signed up as a volunteer editor. All I needed to provide were an e-mail address and a username; nobody asked if I had any qualifications. Here, I thought, would be language at its rawest. And I was right, unfortunately. One of my first batch of words — doubtless it seemed hilarious to the adolescent who dreamt it up — was "BLUUUUUUGGHBTHLTH": "Occurs when an obese man falls out of an aeroplane, opens his gigantic, all-devouring mouth as a parachute but it opens so wide he accidentally EATS THE WORLD." (Thumbs down.) One boy — I won't repeat his name — was defined as "an extremely small penis." (Thumbs down again.)

A harder choice arrived a few days later, in the form of "romanian." The definition was well written and unpleasant: "(adjective) A person with Romanian-like qualities. Hairy, lazy, and having a strong sexual attraction to cattle." I'll spare you the noun's definition, which is longer and nastier. One of the examples went as follows: "You are so Romanian! You haven't had a job in 3 years! And stop trying to rape the horse!" Peckham's guidelines left me in doubt as to which direction my thumb should move: "Publish racial and sexual slurs but reject racist and sexist entries." What's the difference between a racial slur and a racist entry? In the end I voted to accept the definition, feeling much guilt as I did so (it appeared on the site, but has since been removed). While "romanian" has few definitions, terms like "islam," "god," "jew" and "american" attract all the verbal warfare you might, alas, expect. Peckham takes pride in the democratic spirit of Urban Dictionary — and on a purely verbal level, democracy can be tough to distinguish from a vicious brawl.

To read Urban Dictionary's nearly three hundred definitions of the commonest four-letter word in the language was a deeply tedious experience, enlivened only by a surprising number of entries propounding the absurd idea that the word is short for "fornication under consent of the king." (The word "was" appears in the above sentence because early in 2007, a few volunteer editors removed most of the entries for some commonly defined words, "emo" included; Peckham has changed the site's policy so that editors no longer have such power.) A mark of its success is that Urban Dictionary fast became self-referential. To "urban up," the site tells you, means "To seek out the definition of a pop-culture, urban, obscure, or other word on UrbanDictionary.com." The most popular definition of "lonely" is this: "An adjective describing one who finds him or her self looking up words such as 'lonely' on urbandictionary.com because he or she misses his or her loved one, or has not yet found one to be named as such." Like so many websites, Urban Dictionary can become an enclosed world. Yet does society have enough shared places that encourage verbal play?

"No savvy lexicographer ignores Urban Dictionary," Grant Barrett has written. "Its visitors might seem like a million chimps trying to hammer out Shakespeare, but among the useless words are gems that do indeed deserve to be on the permanent record." The problem lies in finding them. Barrett himself is an extremely savvy lexicographer, with a thought-provoking blog on language and a day job at Oxford University Press in New York. He shows genuine respect for what Peckham has accomplished: "Every entry contributed to an online dictionary is a love note to the English language." Yet he also warns that if the making of dictionaries were left completely to the public, "what we'd have would be sexual, scatological, and nonce terms and a slew of racist comments about our neighbors. The entries for boring but needed terms, such as prepositions or helping verbs, would languish." Who would bother to define "despite" when you can have fun defining (or inventing) "desperbation"?

Urban Dictionary may, in the end, be a prisoner of its own principles and a victim of its own success. On a forum discussing the site, one volunteer editor wrote in to say, "I am sure when I first started reading UD, the quality of the definitions was much better. The site is completely losing focus of being a dictionary for legit, real slang and becoming a message forum for teens to gain popularity by making up stuff." The sheer supersize of Urban Dictionary may well be making it less and less user-friendly. It's as though the website is gulping down dozens of pickle-ridden cheeseburgers a day, along with a ton of fries, colas and donuts (a word that on the website gets more than fifty definitions, has several spellings, and generates dozens of compounds) — not forgetting those milkshakes, of course.

"I will work on this project forever," Peckham told me in November 2006. He was still in his mid-twenties, and he still had no paid staff. "Why would I want to stop? The site is exciting and alive, and growing faster than ever. There are always new opportunities and new interesting content to read. Each submitted definition is a glimpse into somebody's life. And, a lot of them are lol funny." That's text-messaging talk for "laugh out loud," in case you were wondering — although "laugh online" and "lots of love" also have their advocates. Among the dozens of definitions for "lol" on Urban Dictionary are ones that claim it means "look out lover" or "let's order linguini."

Does it matter if the site posts definitions that are obviously fake? "You can't tell users what to do," Peckham replied. "I mean, that's one of the biggest things I've learned from this project. Fighting so many users and telling them how to use your creation is useless, because there are just too many of them. Personally I think it's better to embrace and support their use — or misuse — of whatever you created." He admits that he can't enforce the guidelines: "I simply don't have the time or energy to pull people aside and say, hey, stop doing that. That would grow old quickly." It's a revealing instance of the word "old."

"Urban Dictionary's all about software to help people understand each other," Peckham explained. Across the Atlantic, Graeme Diamond might say the same about his work with the ever-changing *OED*. Put aside their obvious differences, and you find the two men confronting the same issue: how can readers and speakers make sense of a language exploding like a supernova?

3
Throw Away Your Dictionaries
Asian English

THE ENGLISH — well, most of them — seem reconciled to the idea that the future of English does not rest in their hands. New Zealanders, Australians and Canadians never thought it did; Africans and West Indians have seldom thought it could. But I wonder how many Americans have come to terms with the notion that the long-term future of their principal language may lie across the Pacific Ocean, on a continent where only a handful of people speak it as a mother tongue.

Why is that a likely prospect? On occasion, size matters. Asia is the home of more than three in five human beings. And as the global use of English continues to increase, more and more of its speakers are bilingual or multilingual Asians. In some parts of the continent English may remain irrelevant except among the local elite. But in other countries it has put down sturdy roots, and has altered in the process. Microsoft, Hollywood, Wall Street and the Pentagon remain powerful presences, and they speak American. Yet the more widespread and accepted English becomes in a given society, the more it turns into something other than just a foreign language flashing cursors, DVDs and stock options.

English is hard to resist and easy to transform. It has an incredible talent for fusion. Over the past few decades, the language as spoken in eastern and southern Asia has grown into a complex of idioms beyond anyone's control or full understanding. In Malaysia, for example, the blend of English with Chinese languages and Malay is widely known as Manglish. English-speakers in China are said to speak Chinglish. The South Korean equivalent goes by the name of Konglish. And so on. These acts of hybridization pay tribute to the power of English outside its usual homelands. But the names, whether scornful or cute, can be misleading. Their similarity obscures a subtle but essential distinction between the new variants of English spoken in nations that were never part of the British Empire (Japan and Korea, for instance) and the forms evolving in places where Britain acted as a colonial ruler (such as India and Malaysia). Konglish and Manglish are different types of idiom; Manglish plays a richer, deeper role in society and attracts a broader range of speakers.

Even so, it's possible to draw a few general conclusions about the changes happening to English in the Far East. All across the region, its grammar and vocabulary are undergoing major change. The vocabulary picks up fresh words from local tongues; so the colloquial English spoken in Manila, say, brims with Filipino terms that mean nothing in Bangkok. Old or new, these terms are deployed in a radically simplified grammar. "Long time no see" and "no go" are veteran examples; originating in China, the phrases have joined the English mainstream. Phonetic changes can be equally striking. What Britons and Americans think of as familiar words soon become unrecognizable in their new home. In Konglish, the term for pancake is *hat-ke-i-keu*. Say it out loud. Does it sound vaguely familiar? Its four syllables started off as the English word "hotcake."

These varieties of the language began humbly — fractured English being propped up by loanwords from local sources — but time, distance and repeated usage are transforming them and giving them fresh significance. Different countries have arrived at different stages in the process, a process that, in a small way, any act of trade or travel is liable to affect. As the writer Kyo Maclear points out, "Whenever you track moments of cross-cultural encounter (whether it be the 'happy' encounter of tourism, or the more traumatic encounter of conquest) you will find that language changes. It witnesses. It testifies to these transactions."

Admittedly, it's sometimes hard to distinguish witness from sheer error. That may be particularly so in South Korea, a nation that has embraced learning English as a quasi-religion. Simon Doubt, a young Canadian who taught for several years in a provincial Korean city, explained to me that "knowing English has become a way to improve your social status. Koreans take social hierarchy very seriously (living in Seoul, for example, and having a big apartment are social indicators), and if people have the money to afford English schools and tutors, they take that opportunity . . . Shop owners are keen on displaying signs in English to show that their shops are trendy, modern and sophisticated." Yet much of the English on display falls short of sophistication. To prove the point, Simon e-mailed me photos of a coffee shop called Hello Beans and a store named Baby Sale.

Social status is only one of the reasons why English has become so widespread in the Far East. As the dominant verbal currency across a far-flung region, it allows communication between people and societies who share no other tongue. A Chinese businessman in Manila, a Filipino maid in Hong Kong, a Japanese software engineer in Jakarta and a Sri Lankan construction worker in Seoul all benefit from some functional skill in English — indeed, knowledge of English is now an official requirement for foreign employees in Malaysia. But to make themselves understood, such nomads seldom need to speak "correctly." Plenty of stay-at-home citizens also benefit from a modest proficiency in English — think of the working life of a hotel clerk, a police officer, a reporter or a taxi driver in any large city. And then, of course, there are Asia's students, tens of millions of them, whose hungry attentions to English fluctuate between the formal register of the classroom and the colloquial, anything-goes realm of the Internet. English, many of these students believe, puts them in touch with the future.

ᦉ

The linguistic future takes on a different cast in South Asia, where formal English has a long history — Robert Clive launched the British Empire in India decades before the American Revolution, and his language embedded itself in schools, courts, the army and the labyrinthine civil service. In turn, hundreds of expressions from India found a way into English and other European languages. Every time you say "shampoo" or "bungalow," "mango" or "calico," "pundit" or "thug," you're using a word that began life in India.

A subcontinent where more than eight hundred languages are spoken each day, India has always been an administrator's nightmare. Its population far exceeds the number of people living in the entire Western Hemisphere. The commonest language in the capital, New Delhi, and in several northern states is Hindi, an Indo-European tongue, part of the same vast family as English. But most people in the southern states speak a language belonging to the Dravidian family (Kannada, Tamil, Telugu and the like). English acts as a crucial counterweight in South India, where, as Salman Rushdie has noted, "the resentment of Hindi is far greater than of English . . . English is an essential language in India, not only because of its technical vocabularies and the international communication which it makes possible, but also simply to permit two Indians to talk to each other in a tongue which neither party hates."

More than sixty years after independence, English continues to be one of India's official languages. It's also the preferred language of most of the generals and politicians who rule Pakistan. In both countries, the ability to speak grammatically correct English is linked to social class. But as the Pakistani broadcaster Masud Alam found when he returned home after fifteen years abroad, "To the common man, English is still a wild horse he'd like to mount every now and then but one he cannot tame."

Ambitious young Indians see English as a passport to material success. In the past decade, call centers have proliferated in several major cities, and, as the 2006 documentary *Bombay Calling* makes clear, most employees earn a starting salary more than four times the average national income. The film follows a group of young workers who receive lessons in cultural training and accent change — they chant phrases like "He's an American guy" — before cold-calling potential customers in Britain, Australia and the United States. Most of these customers will have no idea that they're speaking to people in India. The pressure is intense: "How can there be people out there," says an angry manager, "without one sale for consecutive two three days?" Some of the workers head off to a restaurant after work one night. Fatigue and pleasure loosen their tongues, which revert to Indian pronunciations. "Ve rock," a young man explains, "or ve suck."

I spoke one day to Sarah Power, who works as a language and accent coach at a Microsoft support center in Bangalore, a fast-growing metropolis in South India. Software engineers come there from all over the country, so the workforce is full of different accents, nuances and interpretations of grammar. "One thing that happens here at call centers and support centers," she told me, "with Indian agents translating from their native languages to English, is the repetition of a word in order to emphasize it. This can sound very odd or rude. The customer will ask something and the agent will confirm that he's heard the customer by saying 'OK, OK, OK.' It sounds like a brushoff, but the agent feels that he's just really saying OK. This goes for 'no' as well. If the customer says, 'So should I click this right now?' the agent might say 'No, no, no, no, no,' five or six times in a row, just to emphasize that he should not — but of course the customer finds this rude and disconcerting. And it happens with 'fine' too. The customer will say, 'I'll check the number and get back to you in a minute,' and the agent will say 'Fine, fine.' It's difficult to convey to an agent the impression these things have on North Americans."

Apart from the United States and perhaps Britain, India has the largest number of fluent English-speakers in the world ("perhaps" hinges on the exact meaning of fluent). But virtually all those speakers — unlike the majority of Americans and Britons — are bilingual or multilingual. Under the sway of local languages, English has taken on phonetic and grammatical qualities that are accepted in the Indian subcontinent but may seem wrong elsewhere. Let's take a quick look at a celebrated poem by the Bombay writer Nissim Ezekiel (1924–2004), "Goodbye Party for Miss Pushpa T. S." I realize that its impact comes from delicious exaggeration. But, as with any caricature, the poem's exaggerations are grounded in truth.

"Friends," the speaker begins, "our dear sister / is departing for foreign / in two three days . . . // You are all knowing, friends, / what sweetness is in Miss Pushpa." The progressive *ing* form of a verb is common in Indian English; so is the syntactical use of familiar words ("foreign," "two three") in new ways. "Coming back to Miss Pushpa / she is most popular lady / with men also and ladies also . . ." Speakers of Indian English are prone to omit "a" and "the," and they place a heavy emphasis on words like "also" and "only," using them later in a sentence than is normal in Standard English. "Whenever I asked her to do anything, / she was saying, 'Just now only / I will do it.' That is showing / good spirit . . . Pushpa Miss is never saying no." In many Indian languages, including the Bombay-area Marathi that Nissim Ezekiel spoke, the order of words is more flexible than in English. So "Miss Pushpa" is "Pushpa Miss" also.

Despite its playfulness, "Goodbye Party for Miss Pushpa T. S." is quite conservative in terms of language. In more than forty lines, Ezekiel includes no words that are unique to India; he merely juggles words from Standard English. Writers in the twenty-first century are likely to push the language further.

One day in Montreal I met Anita Rau Badami, a well-known novelist who was born in South India in the 1960s. Her father was a railway engineer, and during her childhood the family moved frequently. Though she emigrated as a young woman, most of Badami's fiction continues to be set in India, and her own rich voice retains its Indian cadences and lilt. Her answer to one of my early questions — "What's your first language?" —

made me realize how different her native country is from most of Europe and North America: "I have three first languages, actually: Hindi, Bengali and English. My parents spoke English to each other. You fluidly move from language to language without really thinking about it. My first language? I don't know." In much of Africa, too, children naturally grow up speaking several languages; Aboriginal children in Australia once did the same. But in the so-called developed world, that's a startling concept.

The Hero's Walk, Badami's second novel, is set in Toturpuram, a fictional city on the Bay of Bengal. She avoids naming the state or the dominant local language, allowing words from both Tamil and Kannada to appear in the text. Badami narrates her story in a fairly straightforward way, using internationally proper English; most of the Indian expressions appear when the characters speak to each other. "After one month," a Hindu priest tells the parents of a newborn child, "bring him to the temple for a special puja that will clear any lingering shani kata circling his future." "Now, if she had died *before* her husband," a woman named Nirmala says, "it would have been better for her. She would have gone to Yama-raja as a sumangali in her bridal finery with her wedding beads around her neck and kum-kum on her forehead."

Many of Badami's Indian readers can't understand the southern words — as she admitted to me, "someone from North India won't have a clue." Yet the author doesn't use expressions like *shani kata* and *sumangali* just to be difficult. They give a rich sense of local color. More important, without the use of words like that, no novel could possibly be true to the vibrant linguistic flux that is India today. Some degree of language mixing is essential for any novelist to convey the felt truth of Indian speech. Badami also plays with the rhythms and syntax of Indian English, as when Nirmala pleads with her husband, "Will you write to her, but?" Later she asks, "Why you suddenly require a sweater? This morning only you were grumbling hot hot hot, and now you behave as if you are going on a yatra to Gangotri." Like the local expressions, the adapted syntax reflects the daily conversations of tens of millions of Indians. "English is a porous medium," Badami told me. "You can pull through all kinds of threads from other languages."

In India, you've been able to do so for centuries. As long ago as 1886, British readers were delighting in a *Glossary of Anglo-Indian Colloquial Words and Phrases,* better known as *Hobson-Jobson.* The phrase sounds English enough, but it's derived from the Shiite Arab lament "*Yā Hasan! Yā*

Husayn!" Introducing the glossary, the authors quoted a sentence that "might easily have passed without remark at an Anglo-Indian mess-table thirty years ago" (in the 1850s, that is): "The old *Bukshee* is an awful *bahadur*, but he keeps a first-rate *bobachee*." The italicized words all come from the Urdu language. In the 1960s, when V. R. Ragam compiled a *Pilgrim's Travel Guide* for South Indian readers of English, he advised them to bring the following items to the Himalayas: *amrutanjan, agarbattis, dhavali, baniyans, pandari bag, setuvu, odiyams, japamala, dhup powder, kumkuma, kundi, asanam* — along with diarrhea pills, indigestion pills, malaria pills, dysentery pills, "List of departed souls and their Gotras" and "Rotten cloth pieces 4."

From the most elegant saris to scraps of rotten cloth, India has a way of reconciling opposites. It's only fitting that English and Hindi have entered a loose union called Hinglish, one that is understood by hundreds of millions. Other fused and flourishing idioms in India go by names like Benglish, Punglish and Tinglish. The government prefers not to sanction Hinglish, yet major businesses are now making use of it. Pepsi's "Ask for more" campaign became, in Hinglish, *Yeh dil maange more*: "The heart wants more." Coke responded with the slogan *Life ho to aisi*: "Life should be like this." "My grandfather's generation grew up thinking, 'If I can't speak English correctly, I won't speak it,'" an advertising executive named Sushobhan Mukherjee told the *Christian Science Monitor* in 2004. "Now, power has shifted to the young, and they want to be understood rather than be correct."

Mira Nair's film *Monsoon Wedding*, released in 2001, gives a good sense of the mixture of languages that characterizes India. The wealthy Punjabi couple at its heart live in Delhi, where their daughter is about to marry a young Indian engineer with a job in Houston; guests fly in from Melbourne and Dubai. Language switches at high speed among Hindi, English and Punjabi, the young people preferring to speak English but willing to change as needed. The words are mirrored by the musical score, which darts from traditional ghazals and Punjabi bhangra to jazz and global pop. A subplot, involving the budding love between the family's housemaid and the head caterer, occurs mainly in Hindi. But even here, English words and phrases ("fridge," "thank you") push through. Likewise, the caterer talks to the bride's father in Hindi, tossing in English phrases like "millennium-style" and "old-fashioned" to impress his client.

On her trips back to India, Anita Rau Badami notices "a deliberate attempt to speak this mixed lingo — it's become trendy, and it never used to be. When I was growing up, you either spoke English or some other language. And if you did speak the mixed language, it was just for fun. It was nothing to be proud of. But now it's taken over, with English threaded through *everything,* including what the laundryman and the auto-rickshaw fellow say. The only difference is that students from the posher universities use more English and less of the other languages. So the proportion varies."

Her words made me long to hear Asian English in action. I needed to see for myself how it interacts with other languages. So I began to look for a place on that huge continent where Standard English is both a national and a profoundly foreign tongue. A place that has developed a colloquial form of English unique to itself. A place where the use of words is keenly debated, yet where cultures and languages mingle freely. Before long I boarded a plane to Singapore.

ࢵ

In a shop on Orchard Road I bought a postcard of Orchard Road. "Shop" may be a misnomer. The card came from the largest bookstore in Southeast Asia: a branch of Kinokinuya, a multilingual Japanese chain, which takes up much of level 3 in a mall named Ngee Ann City. For six straight years, the mall won a Singapore Tourism Award in the category of "Best Shopping Experience: Shopping Centre." That prize says a lot about Singapore, an island city-state that enjoys roughly the same relationship to malls as Manhattan does to skyscrapers. Faced in marble and granite, seven levels high, Ngee Ann is, as its website proudly declares, "a city-within-a-city that . . . has a gross area of more than 2 million square feet." Orchard Road, the retail heart of Singapore, pulses with shopping centers — indeed it pulses with little else — but Ngee Ann is unavoidable.

I arrived in early February when, in readiness for Chinese New Year, scarlet sashes adorned the stone lions guarding the main entrance to Armani, Calvin Klein, Christian Dior, Crystal Jade La Mian Xiao Long Bao, and other high-priced boutiques. A plaque above a lion's head said that the "Ngee Ann City Topping Out Ceremony Was Officiated By" — followed by the names of a couple of worthies. The language on the plaque is English, sort of. The language in the street is another matter. Some people call it Singapore Colloquial English or Singapore Vernacular English; others use the term Singlish; still others ignore or despise it.

A persistent sheen of difference from Standard English meant that everywhere I went in Singapore, I did a verbal double take. This is not a city where words can be taken for granted. Singapore's directness can be unnerving: strolling near my hotel, I passed Super Servants, "the helpful maidshop." An ad in a store window declared, "Changeable sponge available for different perfume flavor to suit your desires." Listening to Singaporeans, it's useful to be a changeable sponge.

The postcard did not show Orchard Road looking like the marble-faced future incarnate. The photograph on it dated from 1910, and featured a pair of oxen dawdling down a broad track. Trees along the pathway were a remnant of the fragrant pepper and nutmeg plantations that gave the street its name and its first wealth. Hidden from view are the mansions — now, like the trees, demolished — that belonged to rich Peranakan: merchants of Chinese origin, also known as Straits Chinese, who adapted swiftly to the British Empire. Their legacy to present-day Singapore and Malaysia is both economic and linguistic. The Peranakan exemplified fusion long before fusion became a cultural cliché: their food and clothing were Malay, their religion and social networks were Chinese, and their speech mingled Malay with the southern Chinese idiom of Hokkien. Baba Malay, this language was called — though *baba* usually refers to boys and men, *nonya* to girls and women.

Emerald Hill Road, which rises above the hurly-burly of Orchard Road, suggests what the Peranakan aspired to. Its houses, built early in the twentieth century, are in an architectural style called Chinese Baroque. One morning I walked up the slim street, past a collection of ornate, brightly painted, two-storey homes with carved doors and sloping tile roofs. At nine-thirty the shutters were already closed against the equatorial heat. A wary cat with a lopped-off tail dashed past a plaster lion and disappeared behind a forecourt wall. The houses told a story of privacy and ostentation. I passed a very Singaporean sign: "Be Considerate. Pick up your dog's poo. It is an offence not to."

This was the setting of Singapore's most influential play, *Emily of Emerald Hill*. Its author, Stella Kon, knew the district intimately; she based the one-woman piece on her grandmother, Polly Tan (also known as Mrs. Seow Poh Leng). The playwright grew up in Oberon, the extended family's house high up Emerald Hill, with a tennis court on the lawn near papayas, rambutans and star fruit ready for picking in the garden. In the 1980s Kon wrote a monologue about a fearful child bride who grows into a stubborn dowager, blind to the damage she inflicts on her family. By then the old homes survived in a time warp. War, Japanese occupation, the tense end of colonial rule, a brief union with Malaysia, the economic boom that followed independence in 1965 — all these transformed the island's character. Nothing here stays still for long: Emerald Hill Road now boasts a Spanish bistro, a Belgian bar and a Japanese restaurant, past which blue-uniformed children march to and from Chatsworth International School.

Unlike most plays set in Singapore, *Emily of Emerald Hill* treats the nation's history both seriously and personally. But that accounts for only a fraction of its impact. More remarkable is Stella Kon's treatment of language: the way that Emily, remembering or creating the past, uses terms like *achar, blangah, chuchu* and *manjah* — Baba Malay words, dropped without explanation into an English-language play. In India nobody would blink at the literary use of local expressions. But this is not India. "Sometimes," Emily imagines telling her dead son Richard, "you take Mother out for a drive to makan angin" — take her out to "eat the wind"; that is, a breath of air. Words from other Asian languages stud the text: *cheong sam,* a woman's gown, is Cantonese; *tambi,* a Tamil word, means brother or young man; *ah soh,* Hokkien for sister-in-law, can refer to any older woman. Kon's English is embedded in local experience too. When Emily talks of procuring "love letters," she means nothing more scandalous than long wafers, a delicacy at Chinese New Year.

Immensely popular in Singapore and Malaysia, *Emily of Emerald Hill* went on to be produced in Melbourne, Hong Kong, Honolulu and Edinburgh. The play's success helped reinforce an idea that would remain controversial, even radical, in the early twenty-first century: that the daily speech of Singapore is nothing to be embarrassed about; that the country's vibrant mixture of English and Asian languages should be a source of pride. Government leaders still look on it with shame.

❧

Its language debate is among the few things Singapore has no interest in exporting. I had drinks one evening in the grandiose, whitewashed Cricket Club with an obese lawyer of South Indian origin who kept me waiting a few minutes outside the ladies' powder room before ushering me into the bar. His English was impeccable both before his first double whisky and after his third. When he'd downed it, the man peered over his goatee and confided, "Profanities come to me most easily in Hokkien." "Profanities like what?" I asked, the picture of innocence. He meant phrases like *I giah lum pah chut lai tom to'teng*: "I take my genitals out and bang them on the table."

The particulars are unique to the four million people of Singapore, yet the issues underlying the debate are the same ones confronted by English-speakers in a host of postcolonial settings. Kenyans and Pakistanis, Jamaicans and Nigerians all ask themselves: Does English belong to us? What values should it reflect? How important is it to adhere to foreign ideas of correctness? Can a government shape the way a language changes? If you want to be global, can you also be local, or should you try to minimize local expressions? To grasp why Singapore has become a prime testing ground for questions like these, and perhaps for the future of English across Asia, it's helpful to understand a little about the country's past.

Three in four Singaporeans are of Chinese origin. By the late nineteenth century the Peranakan, who had traded in the region for generations, were far outnumbered by new Chinese immigrants, drawn to a port city that thrived on the rubber business. Very few of these migrants were fluent in Mandarin, the language of China's government; instead they spoke such regional idioms as Hokkien, Teochew, Cantonese and Hakka. These languages are written in the same characters as Mandarin, but their grammar, phonetics and oral vocabulary are different. (If you call Chinese a single language, logically you should argue that Spaniards, Italians and Portuguese all speak the same tongue.) Indians also arrived in Singapore, mostly from the Tamil-speaking south. And because the loud city stood at the tip of the Malay Peninsula, it attracted thousands of Malays. Add in the older people who spoke Baba Malay and Kristang (a fading creole derived from Portuguese and Malay), and you glimpse the linguistic complexity the governing British faced.

Their solution, of course, was to ignore the Asian languages swirling around them and to run the place in English. But after the Second World War, as the empire withered, Singaporeans faced a hard choice. Should their common language be Malay? The Chinese majority thought not. Should it be Chinese? The Malays and Tamils weren't happy about that — and anyway, which version of Chinese would it be? In the mid-1960s the island suffered race riots in which Malays battled Chinese. After Singapore gained independence the prime minister, Lee Kuan Yew, attempted to shape the country in his own image: demanding, rational, hard-driving, intolerant of gum chewing and other vices. He ran the country for more than thirty years, and would exercise power as a behind-the-scenes "Minister Mentor" into the twenty-first century. As a law student at Cambridge University he had been known as Harry Lee. He spoke English with aplomb. So, he decided, should his people.

At first Lee backed a policy of four official languages: English, Mandarin, Malay and Tamil. If any of them carried extra clout it was Malay, the "national" language. Singapore's national anthem is still in Malay: *Mari kita rakyat Singapura / Sama-sama menuju bahagia . . .* But Malay also came with unwanted baggage: the failed union with Malaysia and a long association with Islam, a religion most Singaporeans had no desire to embrace. Lee sensed a need to strengthen Singapore's uncertain identity and to keep the nation ultracompetitive. He launched a "Speak Mandarin" campaign in 1979, aimed at encouraging unity by discouraging diversity; the campaign succeeded in curtailing the use of other Chinese tongues in the nation's homes. But eight years later the pendulum swung back: Lee decreed that all children, regardless of their ethnic origin, would be educated in English. Schooling in Mandarin was abolished.

Since then, English has functioned as Singapore's main language, with Mandarin a comfortable second. A logical decision? Perhaps. Except that many Singaporeans, even now, don't speak Standard English and have great difficulty with Mandarin. They talk to each other in what has, inevitably, become known as Singlish — the helter-skelter language of the streets. An impromptu creole that adds Malay, Tamil, Hokkien and other Chinese languages onto an English base, Singlish defies the government's urge to regularize and purify. Compared to its closest relative, the Manglish of Malaysia, it contains more words from Chinese languages and fewer from Malay. Of all the English-based idioms spoken in the Far East, Singlish may be the most distinctive.

In the Ngee Ann City bookstore I picked up the *Coxford Singlish Dictionary,* a treasure house of risky language discreetly tucked on a "local authors" shelf. The book came packed with phrases that outsiders find inexplicable: *Wah lau, kena do one hunlet puss up, gun poon si, man!* Say that again? "Wow, doing one hundred pushups is so tough, it can even kill a cow!" The book (it's not a dictionary in the way Noah Webster conceived of the term) includes a wicked parody of travelers' phrase books. Arriving in a

London hotel, a visitor might be asked, "Did you have a pleasant flight?" The equally polite inquiry in Singlish: *Your plane, how?* A waiter at an upmarket London restaurant would say, "Good evening. Do you have a reservation?" The Singlish equivalent: *You got early-early call, not?*

Your language, how? To start the new millennium, Singapore launched a Speak Good English movement, complete with annual reminders and exhortations. "I believe we should all make the effort," said Prime Minister Lee Hsien Loong (the son of Lee Kuan Yew) as he inaugurated the 2005 campaign, "and consciously speak good English — at home, at work, or in social gatherings. Speaking good English does not mean using bombastic words or adopting an artificial English or American accent. We can speak in the normal Singapore tone, which is neutral and intelligible. But speak in full sentences, with proper sentence structure, and cutting out all the 'lahs' and 'lors' at the end of each sentence."

Cutting out, that is, the shortcuts, slang, tones and verbal tags that Singlish has borrowed from other parts of Asia. And eliminating, perhaps, the hundreds of Chinese and Malay phrases in local speech, as well as the singular usages of English terms that baffle outsiders. In Singapore, "blur," "extra," "fetch," "send" and many other common words don't mean what you'd expect. Phrases like "very what one," "up the lorry," "went rounding what" and "catch no ball" are even harder to figure out. Idioms like these are not hangovers from the colonial era. They suggest how a language lives and breathes.

∽

Yet all this is an improvised, unsanctioned way of speaking, and it exacts a psychological toll. A Quebec linguist, Alain Polguère, who spent several years in Singapore recalls "a profound suffering on the cultural level — a lack of desire for Singaporeans to affirm themselves. The English spoken there is stigmatized constantly." Lee Kuan Yew has called Singlish "a handicap we must not wish on Singaporeans." Trying to make "Good English" a competitive sport, the government has set up interschool spelling bees and Scrabble matches. It regards Singlish as bastardized — as though a spoken idiom unwashed by foreign approval is, by definition, illegitimate.

Outside the government, too, there are Singaporeans who want no part of an idiom so unstable, so rough-and-ready. Arthur Loke is among them. A cultivated gentleman with salt-and-pepper hair, large brown eyes and the most direct of gazes, he runs the law firm that bears his name from the twenty-third floor of one of Singapore's landmark developments, Suntec City. "A new futuristic city," the PR people call it, comprising five office towers, a shopping mall and the national convention center. "Futuristic," in this sense, means tall enough to intimidate and ugly enough to fit into any North American metropolis.

The simplicity and classic restraint of Arthur's private office matched his voice: soft, mellow, well modulated, tinged with a British intonation that managed to seem unaffected. So did his very name, which gives the calculated impression that Arthur's background is English, not Chinese. Decades ago he attended the same private boys' school as Lee Kuan Yew: "We were given all the privileges because we spoke the colonial masters' language." By contrast, "The language spoken by some of my secretaries is not really close to standard English. Singapore English is less standard even than the English of South African blacks. The language here is so mangled, it's unbelievable. Clients" — did I detect the faintest of shudders at the word? — "very often come to me speaking in their patois English, but you can speak the way I do and not have to go down to their level. Even some lawyers speak very badly." Law, of course, is embodied in language; it can hardly function without a common understanding of words. Perhaps lawyers have a professional interest in applying a brake to language change.

As a lawyer and intellectual-property agent, Arthur does business in China and prides himself on knowing how to maneuver through the system's intricate subtleties. He regrets not being entirely fluent in Mandarin, the language of his Saturday golf games: one of his fellow golfers, a Taiwanese entrepreneur, speaks little English. But, Arthur added, "the Mandarin here is horrible — it is not standard Mandarin. They have not taught the subject well. People say things in a very kitchen style." In its disorderliness, Singapore's spoken English is matched by its spoken Chinese. His is a nation, Arthur believes, where people grow up "feeling hatred for the Chinese language."

I thought he was exaggerating until I met a native Mandarin-speaker who recently took up an academic post in Singapore. Although she declined to be quoted by name ("People in Singapore are very easily offended"), she confirmed that her mother tongue has a low status in her new country. To her chagrin, she finds it easier to hold a Mandarin conversation in a "wet market" than an office or a classroom, even with colleagues of

Chinese origin. Singapore has been dubbed "the air-conditioned nation" — Lee Kuan Yew once told the *Wall Street Journal* that the air conditioner was the most significant invention of the last millennium — and other languages do best on this tropical island in places where air conditioners are absent. Tamil flourishes, for instance, in the narrow streets of Little India. I had a meal there one night in a vegetarian restaurant where the only utensil is a diner's right hand. It's a favorite hangout of Dougal Simmons, who teaches English for the British Council. Earlier generations of British expats would not have learned martial arts from Asian masters, nor have preferred Little India to the Cricket Club. But Dougal is one of a new breed, fully aware of the ironies of his job.

"We spend most of our time," he told me, "trying to teach standard British grammar to people who never use standard British outside the classroom." He paused and took a swig of Tiger beer. "In class you teach students to say 'Turn off the lights,' not the Singlish 'Off the lights' — they use 'off' and 'on' as verbs. Then at the end of the class their mum comes in and says to the kid, 'Eh, you lah, off the lights for teacher!' So I don't think the kids retain much of the grammar we teach, 'cause they never use it except for an hour a week." Dougal watches their struggles with sympathy, not annoyance: "Singlish is a highly functional language, and we point out that it's fine to use it outside class, as it is to speak in Cockney. But if you need to take exams that are marked in the UK, or send letters outside the country, try to learn standard English!"

High school students here still have to pass Britain's GCE (General Certificate of Education) exams, a requirement that strikes a blow for Standard English — how could a London examiner tell *cheena gherk* from *cheong sam*? The requirement appears to smack of colonialism, yet to some Singaporeans Standard English is a means of escape, even liberation. Testimonials from parents and students appear on the local website of the British Council, whose mandate is both to teach the language and to promote the culture of the United Kingdom. A happy mother explains, "I come to the British Council because I want the children . . . to speak Standard English"; a student praises a course by saying, "The activities helped me to rack my brain."

The racking council has many rivals. Look up "educational consultants" in the yellow pages, and you'll find listings for more than two hundred companies, many with names like Outspoken Effective Communications Consultancy or Vocal Tones Speech and Language Consultants. "Vocal tones," in all likelihood, means without Chinese tones. The desire to excel in foreign exams may be among the strongest restraints on English change across much of Asia. The *Straits Times* regularly bulges with ads from universities in Britain, Ireland, Australia and the United States. For teenagers in Singapore and many other countries, GCE and SAT are acronyms that can make or break a life. Long years of wrestling with the language are worth it (or felt to be worth it) when they lead to an admission letter from a Western university.

English can buy a seat in the departure lounge. Standard English, that is.

∽

When he celebrated a "neutral and intelligible" tone and "proper sentence structure," Prime Minister Lee was discreetly sniping at the way his people speak. Singapore English is a moving target, of course, and it covers a broad range. A Singapore version of the *Times-Chambers Dictionary* appeared in 1997, and some East Asian words edged in. But the dictionary makers, wanting to maintain an acceptable international standard, excluded hundreds of others. *Kampong* (a traditional village) was acceptable. *Kiasu* (a quintessential Singapore expression, evoking not so much a desire to win as a morbid fear of losing out) was not.

Vocabulary is only the start. The local divergence from Standard English extends to the structure of sentences and the sounds that words make in a mouth. One of the most basic elements of any language, the verb "to be," is changing in Singapore: it shows up when you might doubt its usefulness ("My mother is stay here what") but vanishes when you're expecting it ("He very sad"). Prepositions are in flux — I passed a sign outside the YMCA that read, "Volunteer or donate to help the people at Sri Lanka." Some elements of Singlish recall Indian English, such as the appearance of adverbs like "already" and "only" when a sentence is about to conclude. Here, as in India, words are repeated for emphasis. I talked to a young Singaporean woman whose father had phoned her after the December 2004 disaster to say: "Eh Ming Ming ah, don't go to seaside seaside places because tsunami can come anytime." But the influence of Chinese syntax allows Singapore English to roam even further from its parent than Indian English does. Sentences like "That magazine on the sofa, take come here" are common. To ask a question, just make a statement and add "or not?" — "Come on Friday, can or not?" "Love letters, got or not?"

In search of greater clarity in these matters I caught a taxi to the NIE, otherwise known as the National Institute of Education, a place mandated by the government to promote "social cohesion and racial harmony in school." Lubna Alsagoff, who heads the English Department, had warned me to tell the driver I did not want to go to NUS or SMU, better-known universities. The driver got lost anyway. Rightly or wrongly, he sped past a private preschool called EtonHouse. "We specialise in standard English, Mandarin, Japanese," said a big notice board. Classes begin when children are eighteen months old. Behind the explicit "standard" lies an unspoken word: power.

Lubna, an attractive woman in early middle age, of mixed Chinese and Arab ancestry, oversees a department of more than sixty professors. While she talked, I sipped an iced mocha in the library's elegant café, looking over verdant parkland three floors below: "When I was young, the common language in Singapore used to be a Malay patois. But now it's been replaced by Singlish. I speak it, and I'm proud to say I do. I like the intensity of Singlish. But I'm constantly trying to update, because the young are changing the language so fast." She nodded toward Max, the café manager, adding that Singlish alone permits her to converse with him: "Singlish includes; Standard English excludes. Half the people in Singapore don't speak English well. Singlish is all they have. For them, Singlish isn't a colloquial form — it's their highest level. Without it, I couldn't bridge the gap that is caused by my education. The more languages you command, the better communicator you are. I need Singlish to be able to communicate."

You might think, and the government surely hopes, that with English now dominant in Singapore's classrooms, Singlish will wither away. Lubna has her doubts. Children are the future of any tongue, and the children of Singapore put pressure on each other to use Singlish. Her son went to an international kindergarten with a lot of foreign classmates, and was bullied in school the following year because he spoke Standard English. He finally confessed to his parents, "My schoolmates think I speak funny." The boy learned Singlish fast.

As Lubna explained, Singapore wants to promote English as both a global language — her metaphors were a lifeline and a gateway — and a common language. It's intended to arrive without cultural baggage. To profit from English while staying aloof from the supposed moral corruption of the West, Singapore has tried to seize hold of the language as though it were merely a tool. Amid the nation's mishmash of races, religions and histories, English is meant to be a neutral instrument. Yet can a people thrive if their common language is bland and culture-free? Singlish embodies the zest and tenacity with which Singapore's residents have made English their own — and the government's neutrality policy helps to explain why the slang-packed hybrid has emerged with such force. "It's necessary for teachers to use Standard English in the classroom," Lubna concluded, "but I think it would be a mistake for the government to try and stamp out Singlish. It would drive it underground, and you don't want that."

That night, I ate dinner at a hawker center: a Singapore institution, best imagined as a cluster of outdoor food stalls on a grand scale. Jung Goh, a radio producer, had asked me to meet him at the Newton subway station's "control tower." This turned out to mean the ticket office. We wandered the nearby rows of stalls, ordering curried sardine *mutabak, bak kut teh,* carrot cake and other dishes, then sat down and waited for the hawkers to bring over our food. Carrot cake, a mainstay of local cuisine, is a fine example of Singlish, being devoid of carrots — a savory, steamed cake made with white radishes, it also contains eggs and green onions. Blame a mistranslation from Mandarin, which has similar names for carrots and radishes. I drank Heaven and Earth. In Singapore that's not a metaphor; it's a jasmine tea trademarked by Coca-Cola.

Dinner, for Jung, was an exercise in code-switching. He talked to me in Standard English about the government's belated attempt to foster the arts and his own belated effort to learn Mandarin. When he pulled out his (to use the local term) handphone to call a friend, he spoke a Singapore version of English I could easily follow: "She used to teach English, is it? No stress lah." But when he addressed the hawkers, his Singlish was so broad I had trouble grasping anything he said.

If broad Singlish began to appear in the nation's leading newspaper, the *Straits Times,* it's a safe bet the editors would soon be fired. The paper practices self-censorship in both language and politics; its ideal is a reassuring shade of gray. Even so, local color seeps through. During my stay in Singapore, I found various examples: "Christopher Lee is also a poster boy for aunties." "We don't want maids who are so blur they are unable to communicate with their employers." A student wrote an opinion piece quoting a taxi driver who had asked him, "Boy ah, SMU has less support from gahmen is it? Is that why you all must pay more?" Even the chief justice, forgetting the prime minister's advice, was quoted as saying, "People say the courts are very efficient. I don't think so lah."

↝

Singapore has a secret. It's this: the place does *not* mirror Lee Kuan Yew. If it did, Singlish wouldn't exist. A language, any language, embodies the character of the people who shape and speak it. An idiom as swift and makeshift, as lithe and haywire as Singlish could never have grown up in a city with perpetually hunched shoulders and eyes glazed from overwork. When the world arrives in Singapore, it sees that the Convent of the Holy Infant Jesus has morphed into a shopping mall — but it seldom notices that at the heart of the mall stands Father Flanagan's Irish Pub.

One day I asked a Singapore critic and poet named Kirpal Singh if the language of the streets reflected his country, and he enthusiastically agreed: "Singlish is very colorful, very rich, very vibrant. It's fundamentally idiomatic — and it's also an absolute slut. It takes words and phrases from wherever it can. It's basically Singapore writ large." The government needs an idiom apt for Suntec City, and that's fine — some of the time. But the people need an idiom fit for the Newton Hawker Centre.

When a person moves from a formal to an informal idiom, Kirpal prefers to say "she switched to Singlish" or "he changed to Singlish" — the common phrase "slipped into Singlish" implies a fall, an error. "The arbiter of language," he told me, echoing Aaron Peckham and Urban Dictionary, "should be the people who use the language." Kirpal once served on an examining board beside a distinguished Englishman who marked as wrong the sentence "When I saw her, I saw blur." "To me," Kirpal said, "that's perfectly legitimate. It's a very imagistic, metaphoric statement. So I argued with the Cambridge examiner who had given it a zero."

"Did you win the argument?"

"I won the battle but I lost the war. The examiner changed his mind. But the government never asked me to be on an exam board again."

Kirpal favors a middle ground in his country's linguistic battlefield. That ground belongs to a "glocal" idiom: educated Singapore English. Glocality is a concept put forward by the linguist Anne Pakir, who has proposed that varieties of English could maintain strong local differences yet still be widely comprehensible to people in other countries. Indian English, in these terms, is glocal; Konglish is not. "I'm not an out-and-out supporter of Singlish at the written level," Kirpal explained, "and I don't think it has the power to be a glocal language. But Singapore English does! It's not slovenly or sloppy. I think that ten, twenty years from now, Singapore English is going to develop into a very powerful mode of expression."

Whether he's right may depend, to some degree, on the authorities' attitude to a language that refuses to stay still. Will the government realize that words can't always be controlled? Or does its response to Talking Cock augur a new era of repression? Singlish can be spectacularly profane, but "talking cock" does not have obscene connotations; it means lighthearted or meaningless chatter. And when, in 2000, a group of young Singaporean expats in the United States decided to establish a website devoted to the gossip, banter and rumors of home, they named the site TalkingCock.com. Its linguistic element — the highlighting of Singlish — is a key difference from American and British models like *The Onion* and *Private Eye*. But Singapore has no tradition of public satire, and Talking Cock annoyed the nation's leadership. Soon they blocked access to the website from institutions under their control. On the computers at NIE, Talking Cock is out of reach.

The government must consider a website more dangerous than a book. For in 2002 it did nothing to stop the appearance of the *Coxford Singlish Dictionary* — the Talking Cock team published it in both Oregon and Singapore. "The beauty of Singlish lies in deliberate wordplay," the editors wrote, "so speakers should approach it with an irreverent sense of humour." Even though the book became an enormous success, many of its creators and contributors have chosen to remain anonymous. The public face of Singlish belongs to a lawyer turned writer and cartoonist, Colin Goh, and his wife, a university professor named Woo Yen Yen. (They also direct films.) The couple now live in New York and return to Singapore for a few months each year. I met them on an April evening in Montreal, patches of ice and filthy snow still disfiguring the roads. Singapore seemed as far away as, well, it is.

As soon as he began to talk about home, Colin grew lively; Yen Yen was quieter, more reflective. "Our real problem," he said, "was the government censorship of the arts. It got so ridiculous — people who wrote sitcom scripts had to submit their work to a government grammarian. We think it's important for people to see their language confirmed in the mass media." His linguistic conviction, or passion, infused a comic strip he eventually began to write in Singapore's afternoon tabloid, *The New Paper.* "Lately," he said, "because we've been so public about Singlish, I think the government has begun to take the point." He sounded unsure whether to be pleased or nostalgic.

Colin was keen to outline the triumphs of Talking Cock. Yen Yen preferred to talk about her family: "For me, one of the saddest things in language change is the way it cuts off communication between generations. I have a grandmother who speaks mainly Hokkien. She can't really communicate at the dinner table because everybody is speaking English. That's sad. You're losing a lot of stories."

Singlish emerges out of that loss. "The government keeps trying to characterize it as a pidgin," Colin said, "but Singlish is more like Cockney — the same wordplay, the rhymes." Where else can you find such expressions as "steady pom pee pee" (cool under pressure) or "Last time policeman also wear shorts" (That's nothing new)? Where else is an arrogant person known as "ya ya papaya"? Colin raised his glass and stared at me in defiance, as though I were about to tell him off. "Singlish," he declared, "may be the only unique thing about Singapore."

☙

All the people who use a language bring a private understanding to it. Whether we live in Karachi or Kalamazoo we mold language in our image every day. "Asia is way behind the West," Nury Vittachi told me, "when it comes to understanding that there is no 'right' and 'wrong' in language — language is about communication, and if you succeed in precise, clear communication, then language is doing its job. When the Singapore authorities make their tirades against Singlish, they are simply showing that they have not kept up with the modern understanding of the place of language in communication."

Vittachi is one of Hong Kong's leading authors and journalists. In April 2003, writing in the *Far Eastern Economic Review,* he caused a stir by suggesting that Asia's new lingua franca is "Englasian" — a blended idiom composed of "vocabulary from English set into syntax from Chinese, Hindi, Tamil and other languages." Singlish, in this view, is not an eccentric love child of English and Hokkien so much as an avatar of a greater, fast-blossoming Englasian. "Throw away your dictionaries," his article declared. "The unwritten language Englasian really is threatening to supplant English as the business language of Asia."

To show what Englasian sounds like, Vittachi imagined a dialogue between a waiter and a customer — a dialogue that could be taking place anywhere in the Far East.

WAITER: You wan'?
DINER: Two piece kari gai, two piece French fry. Faidee-lah.
WAITER: Set?
DINER: Doe waan'.
WAITER: Dring? Chah?
DINER: *(Tilts head diagonally from side to side)*
WAITER: Ching cha, milk-tea?
DINER: No, kopi bring, can or not?
WAITER: Can. And?

And so on. You'll notice how the vocabulary includes some terms that are instantly recognizable ("French fry," "two piece"), others that are markedly different from their English equivalent ("kopi" for coffee, "Ching cha" for Chinese tea), and a few that bear no relation to Standard English ("faidee-lah" is a Cantonese expression meaning "make it fast"). Moreover, the language has been pared to a minimum. "Yes, certainly. Would you like anything else?" uses up eleven syllables. "Can. And?" takes but two. Englasian snaps and crackles.

Vittachi returned to the topic a few weeks after his original article. Readers had reminded him that "the stripped-down, no-frills dialect of the Malaysian Chinese community" is very different from "the flowery speech of speakers of Indian English." Indeed, Englasian — as Vittachi described it — is an East Asian phenomenon that does not really apply to people living in India, Pakistan, Sri Lanka and Bangladesh. So he made up a second dialogue, this time involving a meeting between an Australian entrepreneur, an Indian accountant and a Malaysian investor. "He here already, is it?" asks the Malaysian. "Yesterday already esteemed Australian partner checked in," the Indian replies.

The breadth and verve of today's Englasian help distinguish it from a mere pidgin. Historically, pidgins were contact languages, born when people from two or more cultures had a need to communicate and a hard time doing so. Pidgins have traditionally been stigmatized as broken language, full of inadequacies and errors. Their vocabulary was small, meaning that pidgin-speakers could have difficulty saying exactly what they meant. The opposite of pidgin English, it seemed, was *proper* English. But among the English-based idioms now growing so quickly in the Far East, many of these criticisms seem beside the point. Their potential vocabulary is enormous, not just because of the vastness of English, but also because words from many Asian languages can be tossed into the brew. Vittachi's readers assured him that, compared with Standard English, Englasian was shorter, faster and more fun. It doesn't stumble off the tongue; it careens. And it costs nothing to learn.

It also reaches far more Asians than Standard English can. As Vittachi points out, "If I spoke formal, traditional English, I could communicate, with difficulty, with perhaps one in five of the people I encounter on my travels in Asia. If I speak in simple, Asianified English, I can talk with about three out of five people. This means I have several hundred million more potential friends!" Englasian is spreading so fast, he believes, because unlike Standard English, it can be picked up easily. "There's a huge irony here," he told me. "Academics often write that English is one of the most complex languages on earth. I believe this is completely wrong. English vocab is taking over the world — it is unstoppable. But formal English grammar is a nightmare. On the other hand, Chinese grammar is wonderfully simple. So the simplified English spoken in Asia (English vocab learned from television, mixed with logical Chinese syntax) is actually one of the easiest languages to learn." It is, in Vittachi's phrase, "the front-line language" between different groups, one that is continually evolving to serve the interests of its speakers. Editors be warned. Grammarians be damned.

᠊ᠣᠯ᠊

"Your mouth is your tiger" — so says a Malay proverb. Given the sheer number of people in the region and the tigerish leap of their economies, it's possible that far in the future, Standard English will reflect an Asian norm rather than an Anglo-American one. Think of how syllables are stressed. In Britain, Australia and North America, variations in verbal stress are crucial to how people speak — the rhythm of songs and poems depends on it. But in the Far East, most syllables bear an equal amount of stress. To a Western ear, the result sounds oddly percussive. That doesn't mean it's wrong.

The absence of word-ending consonants can also disconcert. One day in Singapore I overheard a young man talking on his handphone to a past, present or future girlfriend. "You want me to respect you?" he asked. Except that it sounded closer to "Ya wa'me ta respe'ya?" In the unlikely event that an American were to ask "Got or not?" a Singaporean would probably hear "Gawd er nawd?" But an American listening to a Singaporean might hear "Gah'ah'nah?" If this sounds peculiar today, it may seem natural to our grandchildren. Beauty is in the ear of the listener.

Whose mouths contain the future of the language? And will it eventually break apart? The expansion of English in Asia highlights questions like these. Asian executives and political leaders may prefer the stability of an unvarying international language that follows neat rules, but their employees, spouses and children go on using local forms and variations with colloquial extravagance and glee. In a later chapter we'll ask what happens when untold numbers of foreign expressions pour into Japanese. But now let's turn to the robust movement of English across Europe.

4

Your Rule Will Soon Be Here

Global English

A FEW YEARS AGO I wrote that English is "the Wal-Mart of languages." It was an irreverent attempt to sum up the power of English in the contemporary world: its size, its convenience, its phenomenal growth, its ability to overwhelm the competition. The image annoyed a few people. If you cherish your language, you don't want to see it equated with cheap labor and giant parking lots. I apologize for any offense I caused. Perhaps you will be happier if I now suggest — in a similar spirit — that English is the mallard of languages.

Mallards, the most common and familiar duck in North America and Britain, also thrive throughout Europe and much of Asia. Settlers introduced them to Australia and New Zealand, where they now outnumber the indigenous species. Living as I do in Montreal, I admire their nonchalant willingness to stick around through the late fall, even the winter, when less hardy types of duck have long since migrated south. The green feathers on the males' heads are breeding plumage. Foraging near the banks of the St. Lawrence River, the birds seem placid enough. Appearances can be deceiving — male mallards have been observed raping ducks of both sexes, and engaging in necrophilia.

It's not their glossy appearance or their occasional fondness for corpses that leads me to propose a resemblance between mallards and the English language. It's not their loud calls, either. Instead, it's the effect they have recently had on other species of duck. American black ducks, in particular. Bird guides will inform you that male black ducks look very different from mallards (the females are similar). "Our darkest dabbling duck," in the National Audubon Society's phrase, has a milk chocolate color and distinctive white underwings. Or, I should say, it did. If you grab a pair of binoculars and head off to a river, lake or marsh, you may see birds whose markings are intermediate between the two species. Black ducks live in eastern North America, whereas mallards used to breed mainly in the West; but mallards have flourished over the past century, extending their range across the continent. They now breed with the much less common black ducks to such a point that anxious biologists evoke "a breakdown in species integrity."

It's the same story in the South Pacific, where pure forms of the New Zealand grey duck are fast disappearing. The introduced mallards have been far too ready to mate with the locals — in the words of another biologist, "mallards are highly aggressive breeders." This aggression also threatens the long-term survival of the Australian black duck, the Florida mottled duck, the Hawaiian black duck, even the obscure Meller's duck of the Madagascar highlands. These species are at risk not just because of habitat loss, overhunting, pollution and the usual doleful array of environmental suspects, but because they keep getting too intimate with mallards.

On our globalized planet, solitude may no longer be an option — even for wildfowl. Mallard genes are overwhelming the genes of other birds. This loss of biological diversity means that in what we still sometimes call the natural world, one type of duck is becoming ever more dominant.

ᔕᓇ

The mallardlike aspects of English are the main topic of this chapter. We have seen how the language freely absorbs words from elsewhere; now let's turn to its expansionist power. In the absence of genes, English has diffused its vocabulary and syntax far and wide. With its unrivaled dominance in commerce and science, diplomacy and warfare, information and entertainment, it is closer to being a global language than anything the globe has yet known. (Mandarin has far more mother-tongue speakers, but its learners are only a tiny fraction of those who speak English as a second, third or fourth language.) Nicholas Ostler, in his 2004 book *Empires of the Word,* estimated that the total number of English-speakers had already reached one and a half billion. The language exists in a multitude of hybrid forms. They can be a creative force — sometimes.

The encroachments of English were first observed many decades ago. When the Harvard scholar Charles Dunn studied the people of Cape Breton Island, on Canada's East Coast, in 1942 and 1943, he found that "the factor which most distresses the Gaels . . . is the way in which English words and expressions have crept into their mother tongue." Thousands of Gaelic-speakers had left Scotland during the Highland Clearances of the nineteenth century. Settling on the big island, they kept their music, religion and language alive long after emigration had ceased. They were a strong, determined bunch. Yet by the 1940s, as Dunn wrote in his excellent book *Highland Settler,* "they ruefully confess that their Gaelic has become 'half English and half Gaelic.' One hears this apology time and time again in Cape Breton."

Dunn, who was a fluent Gaelic-speaker, didn't altogether blame the settlers. He knew that when they abandoned their crofts and fishing villages on the Western Isles of Scotland, they lacked any words for "banana," "tomato," "prune," "baking powder," "brick," even "stove." All these items had no place in their lives or their language. When such goods and products became available to the Scots in the New World, they simply adopted the English words. They also borrowed terms for most of the technological innovations in the late nineteenth and early twentieth century. Purists tried to spread new-minted expressions like *cagar-cein* ("distant whisperer"), meaning a telephone — but in the realm of ordinary language, purists seldom enjoy much success. Even in the 1940s, most people dropped the word "phone" into their Gaelic.

Reproach entered Dunn's prose only when it came to what he saw as the verbal negligence of the islanders: "You may hear a dignified old Highland lady tell her friend, *Bha upset stomach aice* (She had an upset stomach), when she could name the distress quite as poignantly in Gaelic. On a stormy day, a man will say of the weather, *Tha i tough* ("It's tough"), when there are any number of satisfying Gaelic adjectives with which he could vilify the elements." At the time of Dunn's long research trip, many of the Scottish descendants in Cape Breton still heard and spoke Gaelic every day. But their conversations were more and more surrounded by English on the radio, English in the newspapers, English in the schools, English in the speech of other people on the island. Understandably, English words began to emerge from Gaelic breath.

It seems a natural process. And as Dunn remarked, "No language ever plundered vocabulary so recklessly as the English, and it is only fair that the old pirate should disgorge some of its booty to a needy cousin." What he didn't foresee was that within a couple of generations, Gaelic would be reduced to little more than songs, night classes and summer immersion courses. The daily language of all but a few diehard families would be English. The dialect of English still spoken on Cape Breton includes a few Gaelic elements — words like *feis* (festival) and *ceilidh* (a social gathering, often with storytelling, always with music), as well as phonetic features like the dropping of unstressed syllables. But the needy cousin, to adapt Dunn's image, has become so impoverished that he limps around in the pirate's secondhand clothes.

None of this may come as a shock to you. The only surprise, perhaps, is that Gaelic — extinct in its other North American strongholds — still hangs on for dear life in Cape Breton. By now the old pirate has sailed elsewhere. He spends much of his time in Europe, Rotterdam being among his favorite ports. Is the everyday language of the Netherlands about to become half English and half Dutch?

ॐ

No, not yet. But there are telltale signs that English is infiltrating the country's speech to such a degree that life would be almost unthinkable without it. The website of the Delft University of Technology — Technische Universiteit Delft, I mean — is bilingual. Everything it says in Dutch, it says in English too. But if you go to the Dutch "sitemap," you'll find that many of the pages come with English names. Whether it be Ombudsman or Traineeship, Molecular Science & Technology or Sustainable Energy, Delft alumni netwerk or Studenten highlights, you can read a Dutch text only after clicking on an English (or almost English) name.

I visited the site after learning that the students' union at that particular university gives out an annual Worst Teacher Award — not for pomposity, lethargy, self-promotion or other hazards of the academic life, but for the most flagrant error in English committed by a professor. More and more classes at Delft are being taught in English, and the unhappy recipient of the prize receives a large sausage (*worst* in Dutch). One year the winner had told his students, "I tried to lead you around the garden." It's a direct translation of the Dutch phrase *Ik probeerde je om de tuin te leiden.* But in Dutch, unlike English, the implied meaning is "I tried to deceive you." The professor made a mistake, I agree, but it seems a bit harsh to punish him with a Worst Teacher Award. Unless, of course, the prize goes to show how high the general standard of spoken English now is in the Netherlands.

The vocabulary of Dutch is crowded with English words. This is a plain statement of fact, not a criticism. The leading expert on the English invasion of Europe's languages, Manfred Görlach of the University of Cologne, has written or edited several books on the topic, notably a 352-page *Dictionary of European Anglicisms*. His entries go up to the late 1990s, and it's a safe bet that English penetration will have progressed — if that's the right word — since then. In his dictionary, Görlach was already able to demonstrate how widely Dutch has thrown its arms open to English: first single words, then phrases. *Love-story* has joined the Dutch language. So has *self-fulfilling prophecy.*

English words beginning with *over* seem especially popular in the Netherlands. With *oversekst* and *overhead-kosten,* the Dutch have made a modest effort to transplant the term into their own linguistic soil. But many other words enter Dutch with their English spelling intact. *Overall, overbooking, overdressed, overdrive, overkill, overlay* and *oversized* have all found a second home in the Dutch language. Each of them has perhaps become, to use another new Dutch word, a *statussymbool.* The language, you might think, has gone *overboord.* Yet in many cases the word expresses a new idea (*overkill*) or a new reality (*overbooking*), and the Dutch want to keep up to the moment. Besides, mastery of uncommon English expressions can bring a speaker a modicum of prestige.

The Dutch embrace of English is extreme, but not unique. Görlach and his associates looked at fifteen other European languages while he was compiling the dictionary, and found copious examples of English in them all — even a language as linguistically, culturally, politically and geographically remote as Albanian. (*Llav stori* is an expression there too.) *Pole position* has raced into Spanish and Romanian. *Septiktank* has made a splash in Norwegian. A few years after the Soviet Union's collapse, *big mak* was a mouthful in Russian and Bulgarian. I'm not pulling your leg — or, as the Dutch would say in their own language, I'm not playing with your feet.

Words used to take decades to move across languages. Now they do so within years, if not months or even weeks. "Zap," meaning the use of a remote-control device, is fairly new to English. Yet by the 1990s, in one form or another, it had joined Dutch (*zapper*), German (*zappen*), French (*zappeur*), Spanish (*zapear*), Greek (*zaping*) and several other European languages. So had "zoom," which quickly spawned such variants as *zumirati* (Croatian), *zoomol* (Hungarian) and *súmmlinsa* (the Icelandic term for zoom lens). When such words undergo a significant change, the adaptation is often a sign of health. One of George Orwell's most famous coinages, now used in a variety of contexts, has become *der grosse Bruder* in German and *Gran Hermano* in Spanish. That's fine. But in Dutch, it remains *Big Brother.*

An English word doesn't always keep its English meaning when it enters a foreign language. In recent years Italian has become enormously receptive to English words. Visiting his parents' homeland in 2006, the Montreal poet Carmine Starnino found "an ever-ready willingness to anglicize technical terminology (using 'printer' rather than 'stampante') or to adopt certain catchphrases. 'Okay,' mostly used to express hoped-for approval, is all the rage here, as in '*Quella camica costa solo 200 euros, okay?*'" Many new Italian words end with the English syllable *ing*. But the results may confound English-speakers. It's hard for us to guess that *i lifting* refers to a facelift, or that *i pressing* can mean political pressure.

&

What is it like to see your mother tongue being taken over by foreign words and cadences? What unease and grief can emerge? It's impossible for me, a native speaker of English, to be certain how Gaelic-speakers on Cape Breton Island in the 1940s felt about the process. Perhaps, though, we can gain a better sense of their lived experience if we look back to a newspaper article published in England a century earlier.

History has a long sweep to it; and seen from a historical standpoint, English is a Johnny-come-lately to its current stardom as a lingua franca. For more than a thousand years in Europe, Latin played that role to perfection. Great thinkers like Francis Bacon, Isaac Newton, Baruch Spinoza and John Milton still wrote in the language as late as the seventeenth century. When Latin had fallen into terminal decline, French took over. During the Enlightenment, any European aspiring to be a soldier, scholar, diplomat or trader, or even to tour the continent's great cities, needed to know an *asperge* from an *auberge*. English began to exert its dominance only with the signing of the Treaty of Versailles at the end of the First World War — a symbol that the United States would henceforth be a major power in global affairs. But on June 28, 1848, when a correspondent for the Manchester Guardian wrote an unsigned article about the riots that were alarming Paris, he (it's very unlikely to have been a she) could assume that the vast majority of British newspaper readers would understand French.

"A sanguinary and obstinate insurrection has outbroken in Paris," the report begins, "in consequence of the determination of the government to clear the ateliers nationaux." The publicly funded workshops, that is. This, the opening sentence — the lead, we'd say now — contains an untranslated phrase in French as well as several Latinate expressions, one of which ("sanguinary") recalls the French word *sang:* blood. As the report goes on, more French words push their way in. Troops have been ordered "to diminish the number of ouvriers," and to achieve a "dispersion of the attroupement." Workers forced to leave their homes were supplied with money "and with feuilles de route." To prevent any further violence, "the gendarmerie . . . gathered on the open square before the Hotel de Ville," while "the Palais de Justice was guarded by the garde mobile."

I'm struck by the blatancy — the unapologetic use of so many French words without translation or explanation. The article also contains several *faux amis:* false cognates, or expressions that sound similar in the two languages although their meanings are different. Such words set perpetual traps for writers, translators and interpreters. (The other day I picked up a bilingual brochure from a tree-pruning firm in Montreal that offers *sinistre assurance,* or disaster insurance; in English, alas, the company is promoting "sinister insurance.") False cognates suggest not only the close and intertwined histories of French and English, but also the separate paths the two languages eventually took. And so, in 1848, readers in Manchester learned that workers from different parts of Paris had the idea of "forming a junction." One group marched off "to the quay of the Hotel de Ville." Three words in these brief phrases — junction, quay, hotel — don't mean the same thing in English and French. The *Guardian* reporter was using them in their Parisian sense.

French exerts an even more subtle influence on the article. It involves words of French origin that are (or were) accepted as English expressions, but which take the place of shorter, more common terms. The journalist evoked "apprehensions that tranquillity would be seriously disturbed." And he described a member of the provisional government who refused to meet one of the workers' leaders because "he could not recognise him as the organ of the operatives." "Organ" (meaning spokesman) and "operative" (meaning workman) were acceptable terms in the 1840s, "operative" being a recent transplant from French. If the reporter's phrase sounds vaguely ridiculous to us, it's partly because French and its parent language, Latin, have much less impact on English today than they did in the past. Our language has hitched a ride elsewhere.

It's possible, I realize, that the *Guardian* correspondent in Paris was a Frenchman with an imperfect grasp of English. But even if that were the case, no editor at the newspaper bothered to cut or rewrite his Gallicisms, so the point remains: English readers at the time were expected to understand French. Their language was porous toward Paris. *Ouvriers, operative, hotel de ville, gendarmerie, attroupement, junction, feuilles de route, ateliers nationaux:* perhaps these were among the *oversekst, overboord status-symbools* of their day. To any *Guardian* readers who did not happen to know French, the article must have seemed baffling and disconcerting — even, I suspect, a bit threatening. If foreign words could slip so easily into the English language, maybe foreign ideas could migrate with them.

Now imagine how it would feel if the *Guardian* article and others in the same vein confronted you every waking hour — in offices and bars, in classrooms and department stores, on TV, on the radio, on billboards, on the Internet, in movies, in print. Such is the ascendancy of English.

⌒

But whose English? Speakers of both the American and British varieties have long complained about a transatlantic invasion of their speech. Two of the prime complainers were H. W. and F. G. Fowler, who in *The King's English* (third edition, 1930) insisted they were not out "to insult the American language." They proceeded to do exactly that: "We are entitled to protest when any one assumes that because a word of less desirable character is current American, it is therefore to be current English. There are certain American verbs that remind Englishmen of the barbaric taste illustrated by such town names as Memphis . . . A very firm stand ought to be made against *placate, transpire* and *antagonize*." All three of these verbs, needless to say, would go on to enter daily use in England, along with hundreds of other Americanisms of doubtful virtue. In retrospect the Fowlers' tirade looks silly. Language mavens, those secular descendants of fire-and-brimstone preachers, love to proclaim "Thou shalt not" — but their dictates seldom have much effect.

The Fowlers were contemporaries of H. L. Mencken, whose fat volume *The American Language* drips with unconcealed contempt for Britain and its speech. "To the common people," Mencken wrote, "everything English, whether an article of dress, a social custom or a word or phrase has what James M. Cain has called 'a somewhat pansy cast.' That is to say, it is regarded as affected, effeminate and ridiculous. The stage Englishman is never a hero, and in his role of comedian he is laughed at with brutal scorn. To the average red-blooded American his tea-drinking is evidence of racial decay, and so are the cut of his clothes, his broad *a*, and his occasional use of such highly un-American locutions as *jolly, awfully* and *ripping*."

But in contemporary England, you could go for weeks without hearing anybody say "ripping"; "jolly" seems to be on its way out; and that broad *a* is confined to a rarefied level of society. Americans have also grown fond of tea. What has outlasted Mencken's sour examples is the American habit of using Englishmen as villains in the entertainment business — British actors continue to earn a small fortune playing bad guys in Hollywood. In the 1990s my daughters watched a succession of Disney movies (*The Lion King, Aladdin, Tarzan, The Hunchback of Notre Dame* and so on) whose evil characters dripped malice with an English accent. For evil to speak in any other foreign voice might have brought accusations of racism.

Despite standardizing forces like travel, big business and Hollywood, the differences between British and American English still loom large. I realized this after coming across an article published in *The Guardian* (now based in London, not Manchester) in 2005. The article was 763 words long. It appeared under the headline "BBC governors to be scrapped" — a verb most Americans seldom use. Readers outside Britain may be equally puzzled by "row" (rhyming with "cow," as in "the row between Ms. Jowell and Lord Birt"), "charged with" (not a crime but a responsibility: the "board of trustees will be charged with ensuring . . .") and "Number 10" (London's equivalent of the White House). Phrases like "director general," "public facing role," "media select committee," "governance unit" and "trust structure" may be unfamiliar in other countries. But having lived in England in the late '70s and early '80s, I caught their gist.

Other terms in the article left me shaking my head. What is "plc style"? Is "top slicing" something to fear? Does a "remit" have any relationship to "Nolan rules" or "green paper" (a report, not a type of stationery)? All these expressions belong to the kind of buttoned-up, white-collar language that, in our age of instant communications, might be expected to move toward a global standard. Such a standard — whether or not it's desirable — remains elusive. I found the *Guardian* article unsettling. It made me realize how foreign the language of England had become to me.

Both the Fowlers and Mencken have intellectual heirs. One of Mencken's is Ben Yagoda, a journalism professor at the University of Delaware, who in 2004 complained that British expressions like "go missing," "sell-by date," "run-up," "on holiday," "one-off" and "chat up" have been infiltrating American speech. Yagoda didn't believe any of them should have crossed the pond. "Briticisms have passed their sell-by date," he sarcastically concluded, "and the odor (or should I say odour) is getting a bit rank." More telling, though, is the rapid growth of Americanisms in countries where a British-based English has long been the norm. In South Africa and Malaysia, Nigeria and Australia, hundreds of American words are sweeping their British counterparts away. For the language of power and desire no longer inhabits London. "Garbage," "freeways," "semi-trailers," "real estate" and "liquor stores" have now become part of the Australian landscape (with "liquor stores" displacing "bottle shops"). Similarly, "plea bargain," "arraigned" and "in back of" are part of today's South African English. Older people occasionally object. To no avail.

～

I'd been taking verbal snapshots for months. On a trip to Barcelona, I walked past shops with names like Love Store, Happy Books, Bobby's Free, and Pimp, and saw a huge billboard above the Carrer Mallorca bearing the slogan "Intelligent Design. Today, Tomorrow, Toyota." A festival of French-language music in Montreal featured shows by groups called Groovy Aardvark, No One Is Innocent and Les Breastfeeders. On the front page of an Austrian magazine called *News,* big headlines announced "Das Grosse Interview" and "Exklusiv: Die Story." A German-language brochure that came, for some reason, with my Korean cellphone offered me "Herzlich Willkommen im Samsung Fun Club," with a "Premium-Klingelton Downloaden!" And on a KLM flight I picked up a copy of a Dutch magazine with a full-page ad for the "Flying Dutchman–American Express kaart" and the slogan "Frequent buyers worden frequent flyers." *Worden* is Dutch for "become." The key *woorden,* however, were becoming English.

Snapshots can be revealing up to a point, but they don't tell us what's going on beneath the surface of languages. Which is why Maria Rakusova's e-mails were so much help to me. Maria is a graduate student in Bratislava, the capital of Slovakia. That country split away from the Czech Republic during the "velvet divorce" of 1992, giving national status to a language whose complete alphabet has no fewer than forty-six letters, including both *dz* and *dž.* Slovak, a Slavic language, is a sister of Czech, a cousin of Polish and Ukrainian among others. What gobsmacked me about Maria's messages was her casual reference to "the older generation," by which she meant "my parents' age, born in '60s."

"Since English has become the language number one in business, law, media world and politics," she wrote, "it is absolutely necessary that it is penetrating also to the other countries apart from the Anglophone ones. Although English has not yet exercised a big influence on the sentence structures, it has inevitably enriched our vocabulary, in particular that of the young generation." Music, movies and computers all act as copious funnels of English words; Slovakia has rock bands who sing entirely in English. The four-letter words of my language have also trundled into Slovak — *fak of,* for example. Messages that get transmitted across languages are seldom what poets, teachers or politicians might wish.

Older people in what was then Czechoslovakia — let's not stop to define "older" — studied Russian in school. Today, starting in kindergarten and continuing through high school, Slovak children learn English. But whereas the use of Russian stopped at the classroom door, the use of English carries on beyond the school grounds. Nothing is cooler. Adolescents deploy the language, in a modified form, when they text-message each other. A teenage boy in Slovakia will now address a pretty girl as *beib,* or begin a conversation with *H hany* — hi, honey. She might type a reply with *laf* — love, that is. Even a church is now *čurč.* ("The spelling of English word is Slovakicized," Maria explained. "You put down what you hear, according to our own alphabetical pronunciation.") And so, in the realm of Slovak texting, *Q* stands for question, *BB* for bye-bye — and *D* for the.

In Slovakia, as elsewhere in Europe, English is a crucial language for anyone involved in big business, scientific research or higher education. But in those domains, for the most part, English remains English. When it comes to youth culture, by contrast, English mingles and merges with other languages. "Nowadays wherever you go," Maria said, "you can see signs, posters, graffiti, etc. in strange Slovak-English combination." Students prefer not to repeat the Slovak for "fail"; instead they say *failnut.* The word for shopping used to be *nakupovat;* now it has become *shopovat.* When the young shoppers finally return to their parents, they say *idem houm* — "I go home," that is.

Failnut and *shopovat* are examples of blending at the level of individual words: a microcosm, if you like, of a trend affecting the language on a larger scale as well. Often an English word of one syllable will graft itself onto a Slovak stem. *Fakovat* means to make love, though it's not an expression teenagers should utter in front of their parents or teachers. When a girl wants to announce "I'm blogging" or "I'm making a blog," she'll say *blogujeme*. And when a boy replies that he's using a search engine, he'll say — you guessed it — *searchujeme*. "Words like comp, net, blog, shop are used on a daily basis," Maria observed. "These are international words, anyway."

I was thinking about the way young Slovaks stretch the linguistic boundaries when I came across a slim volume called *Panique à la Pop Academy*, published in France in 2005. A school reader for ten-year-olds, based on the international franchise *Star Academy*, it incorporates some math exercises into the text. (*Star Academy*, despite its English name, was first broadcast in France; the many spinoffs include *Star Factory* in Romania, *Fame Academy* in Germany and *Fame Story* in Greece.) Glancing through the story, I noticed "French" words like *pop-corn, week-end, music-hall, surfeur, star* and *gloss* — as in a stick you apply to the lips. The young characters had names like Ginger, Mallorie and Jennifer. They called themselves Charlie's Angels, exchanged gossip about "Radonna," "Crad Pitt" and "Tom Crise," and learned their lessons from teachers named Monsieur Flexpointe and Mademoiselle Girlpower.

Remember, *Panique à la Pop Academy* was not designed to teach English as a foreign language. It's a French book addressed to French children. Evidently the target audience is more likely to enjoy a tale about the adventures of Mallorie and Ginger than one describing the exploits of Marie and Germaine. The kind of hybridization this book embodies is hard to interpret as a creative force. It suggests that, regardless of the disasters of U.S. foreign policy and the frequent tensions between Paris and Washington, French educators still look on English as a way to keep juvenile eyes glued to the page. Anglicisms make the text seem cool.

Millions of foreign learners of English around the world might now consider the intended audience of *Panique à la Pop Academy* an older generation. "As learners become ever younger," David Graddol predicted in *English Next*, "English teachers of the future may find themselves wiping toddlers' noses as they struggle with an interactive whiteboard, or they may find their classrooms have been moved to shopping malls and theme parks." Among high school students in many countries, a knowledge of

English is already taken for granted — and so, in years to come, "English teachers working with older learners may be remedial specialists."

～

In France, despite the behavior of Mallorie and Ginger, English continues to be perceived and used as a foreign tongue. That may no longer be quite the case in Finland, a country whose own language (a member of the Finno-Ugric family) is vastly different from English. Half a century ago the most important languages in the country — apart from Finnish itself — were Swedish and Russian, with German and French lagging behind; English had only a marginal presence. Now, having surpassed the competition, it serves as an essential second language for Finnish people. Many schools in Finland offer English-language instruction in math, history, science and nearly all other subjects. On television, interviews with foreigners take place in English. It's generally the only language that interviewers share with non-Finnish guests. The task of following English dialogue on TV is passive; viewers don't take part in the conversation. But to join English-language chatrooms, and to write English-language blogs and fan fiction — even if the other participants are Finns — young people's skill in the language must be active and creative.

The linguist Sirpa Leppänen calls English in Finland a "domesticated resource." Her studies of the fan fiction written online by girls in Finland show how teenagers move between their two languages with playful ease. In one episode, written by a fifteen-year-old girl and based on a short-lived American TV series called *Invisible Man*, a girl wakes up in the hero's California apartment and sees him, as she writes in Finnish, "come out of the shower, wearing nothing but a towel. I took a moment to stare at his stomach muscles." The hero, whose name is Darien Fawkes, speaks to her in English: "So, you woke up, huh." The girl replies: "Um? . . . Yeah, I did. Umm . . . so how did I get here?" Then she says to her readers, in Finnish, "I raised my eyes to Darien's eyes and belly." "I found you from the alley," Darien says. "Ouh," she replies, then tells her readers: "Mä olin kyllä nukahtanu kotonani espoossa, Suomessa. En San Diegossa." In other words, she had fallen asleep in her home in Finland, not San Diego. "What are you doing alone in San Diego?" Darien asks. "How old are you anyway?"

And so on. The mistakes in English are small ("from the alley," for instance). Indeed the girl's sheer competence in the language forms an integral part of the imagined, longed-for romance. English is what enables her to carry on an intimate conversation with an American hunk in a towel — for although Darien Fawkes can do all kinds of desirable things, speaking Finnish is not among them. As Leppänen explains, "The everyday lives of Finnish adolescents and young people in modern Finland are heavily saturated with Anglo-American or English-language media and popular culture. Thus, the fact that the Finnish fans write in English could also be seen as a way of participating actively in English-language intermedial, virtual, digitised, electronic and televised popular culture." English is more than just a professional asset; it's a personal force, a social tool.

What impact does all this have on the Finnish language? Leppänen says it is substantial. Finnish was one of the many languages without a word for "please"; now it has ours. It did have a word for "sorry," *anteeksi*; but "sorry" has moved in anyway. So, come to think of it, have "anyway" and "by the way," the result being that even when people are speaking Finnish to each other, they use English words as discourse markers. Lots of other terms have been borrowed, and so have a few grammatical structures, notably what Leppänen calls "the passive, non-personal use of 'you' (*sä*)." None of this arouses much resistance, but some Finns do get annoyed when fixed English phrases and idioms are translated and dropped, word for word, into a language where they don't seem to fit. "In the long run" has given rise to a comparable Finnish phrase, *pitkässä juoksussa,* which many people feel is awkward, if not wrong. Their feeling hasn't made the phrase go away.

Finns still invent many new words that technology requires of them, yet they also know — and use — the English equivalents. A generation from now, a recently coined term like *sähköposti* stands to be either dominant or obsolete. At the moment, it vies with *e-mail, maili* and *meili,* and nobody can say which expression will become the norm. Text-messaging Finns have come up with their own acronyms to express "I love you," "In my humble opinion," "See you" and the like — but they also sprinkle their messages with *ilu, imho* and *cu.* Don't think of these as merely English initials. They are now, like "blog" and "shop," international words. By way of response, the language academies of many countries — Turkey is a good example — have altered their focus in recent years. Having spent the 1930s and '40s promoting Turkish against the incursions of Persian and Arabic, the Turkish Language Association now does all it can to keep English at bay.

Computer technology alters so fast that people in much of Europe use the current English expressions, sometimes making cosmetic alterations to fit the terms into their own language. "In Estonian," Anne Varangu told me, "commands and functions verbally sound as they do in English but are phonetically manipulated in the written version. The result: 'save' becomes written as 'seiv,' and so on." A thousand miles and several borders to the south, at a university in Dubrovnik, Vlasta Brunsko noted that "most Croatians use the English terms. There are Croatian words — not always; for example 'CD-ROM' in Croatian is also 'CD-ROM' — but most people prefer English. I am the best example for this. My software is in English and so are my icons (File, Edit, View, Insert, Format . . .). If you give me PC in Croatian, I wouldn't know how to operate."

"There is a coolness factor with technology, as with aspects of youth culture," explains Brian D. Joseph, a linguist at Ohio State University and the editor of *Language,* the journal of the Linguistic Society of America. "And non-English-speakers who study in English-speaking institutions often find that since they get their technical training in a foreign language, it is very hard for them to talk about that technical stuff in their native language. They have had to learn all the technical jargon in English, the style of discussion, the English standards for presenting ideas — so they default to English for that realm."

For people in eastern Europe a generation ago, the allure of English was not technological but political. Moscow walls in the 1980s were alive with graffiti like QUEEN GROUP THE BEST and KISS FAN (a fan of the rock group Kiss, that is). Russian bands, such as Primus, attracted smaller amounts of graffiti. When a graffiti writer wanted to celebrate Primus, he used English: PRIMUS FANS. But if he disliked their music or their style, he reverted to Russian: PRIMUS GOVNO ("Primus is shit"). English became the language of adoration. After the Soviet Union collapsed, young Russians began to realize that the West was not the paradise of their fantasies. But regardless of politics, the language of rock, and more recently of rap, continues to be an object of European desire. "Dein Herz Schlägt Schneller," a song by the Hamburg hip-hop group Fünf Sterne Deluxe, is awash in English vocabulary (*beats, banjo, skills, sellout, flows, soul, style, X-file, rap, cool* and more). Entire English phrases (*if you need a fix baby*) elbow their way into the lyrics. The song leaves German struggling for air — *bitte bye bye.*

Music is also making the force of English felt across Africa. The great Nigerian musician Fela Kuti (1938–1997) was born with the last name Ransome-Kuti; in midlife he dropped the English Ransome in favor of a Yoruba word, Anikulapo ("he who carries death in his pouch"). Still, he wanted to be understood by a wide audience, so he began to mix English into his songs — the cities and villages of Nigeria echo with more than five hundred languages. In songs like "Original Sufferhead" Kuti blended Yoruba with Nigerian Pidgin English: *E-no dey, government sef e dey? . . . Dodo nko? Ten kobo for one.* This kind of shape-shifting idiom is well suited to mockery and political satire; Kuti was regularly at odds with his country's rulers. Youssou N'Dour, now perhaps the most famous musician in Africa, follows in Kuti's footsteps by using the Wolof language of his native Senegal along with French and English. In his song "Agouyadji," N'Dour makes a remarkable confession: "I used to believe / Those of us who speak Pulaar were inferior . . ." Now he appeals to the Senegalese to work together as brothers and sisters, speaking their own languages. "Agouyadji" is a Pulaar word for a gong that calls people to a meeting; the title may well be an act of contrition.

Yet the song is in English.

∽

Elsewhere on the planet, Chile has seen an explosion of English learning in the twenty-first century. So has Iraqi Kurdistan. As many as three hundred million people in China are now studying English. But the most surprising case of a government determined to make children bilingual involved a country that is located far from any English-speaking nation, lacks any tradition of English use and has a language and culture that could scarcely be more remote from most English-speakers: Mongolia. "We are looking at Singapore as a model," Mongolia's then prime minister, Elbegdorj Tsakhia, told a *New York Times* reporter in February 2005. "We see English not only as a way of communicating, but as a way of opening windows on the wider world." A graduate of two American universities, Elbegdorj came to power promising to transform Mongolia into a bilingual country. He was ousted in 2006 (the reasons had little or nothing to do with language) before his plans attained fruition.

In Mongolia, a government set out to impose a wider use of English on its people. The commoner pattern is for a people to speak more and more English regardless of a government's wishes. Nepal has more than 120 indigenous languages, many of which have been losing ground in recent years to Nepali, the national tongue. The courts, schools and government favor Nepali, but as the writer B. K. Rana observed in the magazine *Ogmios* in 2005, "Everyone in urban areas prefers speaking English in Nepal. Nowadays, urbanite people mix up half English and half Nepali when they speak a sentence. The FM radio announcers mix up nearly 75 per cent English and 25 per cent Nepali words and phrases when they speak aloud a sentence." In a poor country like Nepal, where most people don't have TV sets or computers in their home, radio is a very powerful medium.

Yet English can be a hard language for anyone, not just Mongolians or Nepalese, to master. Its spelling is unpredictable, its pronunciation variable, its vocabulary huge. Its grammar, while deceptively simple, contains a mass of pitfalls, phrasal verbs being the trickiest of all. Unless you've grown up speaking English, it's tough to remember the difference between "stand up for" and "stand up to" — not to mention "stand in" and "stand out," "stand off" and "stand on." Nastiest of all, "stand for" and "stand by" carry double meanings. (English asks its prepositions to work tremendously hard for their living.) While all human languages are at times illogical, English seems to take the unpredictability principle to an extreme. You can stuff a corpse into a body bag but not into a body building; a student body has many students, though a heavenly body does not have many heavens; I can read your body language but not your body clock, let alone your body count. In the face of so many verbal choices, each one needing to be made at high speed, movements are afoot to promote a simplification of the language for foreign learners.

Such schemes have blossomed in the past. The best known of them was Basic English, laid out by the British scholar C. K. Ogden in 1930. Ogden believed that if the language were restricted to a vocabulary of 850 key words, foreigners could master it within a few weeks. The grammar would need to be simplified too, so there would be no place, as in the preceding sentence, for a subjunctive. Ogden's work greatly impressed the novelist H. G. Wells, who predicted that by 2020 almost everyone in the world would be able to speak and understand English. Typically for Wells, the remark was both a gross overstatement and a brilliant insight. He took

Ogden's new creation and ran with it in his fictional history of the future, *The Shape of Things to Come,* published in 1933. In Wells's vision, "One of the unanticipated achievements of the 21st century was the rapid diffusion of Basic English as the lingua franca of the world and the even more rapid modification, expansion and spread of English in its wake." He shrewdly added, "On the whole it was more difficult to train English speakers to restrict themselves to the forms and words selected than to teach outsiders the whole of Basic."

It's possible, by some ingenious manipulation, to translate almost any literary text into Basic English. It's impossible to do so without losing something. (To put the previous two sentences into Basic English would mean replacing twelve words, not just long ones like "ingenious" and "manipulation" but short ones like "into," "without" and "losing.") Other issues arise too. Ogden's choices were culturally specific to the England of his time — "apple," "church," "kettle" and "sheep" all appear on the 850-word list, but "banana," "mosque," "wok" and "camel" do not. And by shrinking the vocabulary of English, Ogden did not necessarily make communication any easier. Many of his words mean several things — because "gift" and "introduce" are absent from the list, the word "present" has to cover both those concepts and also to evoke the moment between past and future. A depleted vocabulary can produce a loss in clarity.

People with a different mother tongue often have trouble catching the exact tone required by their adopted language. Even though he had lived for many years in Los Angeles, the movie director Roman Polanski sounded terribly foreign when he told Martin Amis, "I'm trying to extenuate those contrasts in my character that make me stick out as a sore thumb from my surroundings." For anybody struggling with English, the language's enormous store of proverbs, metaphors, idioms and catchphrases is particularly hard. Their compression of meaning relies on a listener's fluency, allowing no time for explanation. I think of the rural British sayings I grew up with, many of them unrelated to my daily life as a boy in a North American city. Experience taught me what my immigrant parents meant by phrases like "Gone for a burton!" or "Donkey's gallop, short and sweet!" — but would an English-speaker from Singapore or Hong Kong have had the least idea? Conscious of the power of English, and resentful of the advantage that idioms give to people who are raised with the language, the Japanese linguist Takao Suzuki declared: "At present the distance between the native speakers and English is zero, whereas the distance which separates us from English is enormous to say the least. It is just to diminish this horrendous disparity that we should tug English towards us." Tugging, in Suzuki's terms, entails some determined subtraction; it means stripping the language of the colorful images and expressions that native speakers often cherish.

"Dear English speakers: Please drop the dialects," wrote Mikie Kiyoi, a Japanese woman who worked as an executive with the International Energy Agency in Paris. French was a distant second language in her professional life; Japanese was not used at all. "I have to live with this unfortunate fate," Kiyoi added. Still, she accepted fate. What she declined to accept was how her Anglo-American colleagues spoke English in a colloquial, idiomatic fashion that she and other Asians battled to understand. She called this an abuse of privilege. "We non-natives are desperately learning English; each word pronounced by us represents our blood, sweat and tears. Our English proficiency is tangible evidence of our achievement of will, not an accident of birth. Dear Anglo-Americans, please show us you are also taking pains to make yourselves understood in an international setting."

It's not surprising, then, that as the power of English grows, the notion of a logical, easier-to-follow version of the language has lost none of its appeal — an English Lite, if you will. Perhaps the language can be drained of its extraneous elements and refashioned in a depleted form that would somehow encapsulate its essence. One of the successors to Basic English was the unfortunately named Nuclear English, propounded in 1981 by a Professor Quirk. It failed to explode. Yet early in the twenty-first century a new movement along Basic or Nuclear lines began to gain ground, especially in Europe. It's spearheaded not from Britain or the United States but from France, a fact that may help explain why the movement avoids all reference to "English." This new entity goes by the name of Globish.

Its founder, Jean-Paul Nerrière, is a former vice president of marketing for IBM. In 1989, during one of his many trips overseas, Nerrière realized that even in his heavily accented English he was able to communicate more easily with Korean and Japanese clients than were his fellow executives from the USA or Britain. They were dependent on idioms, trapped by culture-specific knowledge, hampered by a huge vocabulary; Nerrière was not. Simplicity and directness, which were all he could offer, were all his clients wanted. A stripped-down version of English, he came to believe, is fated to become "the worldwide dialect of the third millennium." And so he invented, or formulated, Globish. Speaking to Robert McCrum of the London *Observer* in December 2006, Nerrière described it as "decaffeinated English."

Nerrière's decaf language arrives with a vocabulary of 1,500 words, making it nearly twice the size of Ogden's list from 1930. While that's a significant difference (Globish permits you to say "gift," for example, although "introduce" remains absent), ingenious ways still need to be found to replace many common English words that failed to make the cut. A Globish Lord's Prayer begins like this: "Our Father, Who comes to us from above, / Your name is holy. / Your rule will soon be here, / Your will will be executed, in this world, and in the above as well."

The "worldwide dialect" is, as you see, a radically simplified version of living English. That distinguishes it at once from artificial, invented languages like Esperanto, although they spring from a similar desire: to make communication across borders easier. Neither is Globish a pidgin, for pidgins involve not just simplification but also mingling and creative distortion. Dozens of pidgins are or were spoken around the world, many of them based on colonial languages other than English, all of them incorporating local words and pronunciations. The same prayer, expressed in Hawaiian Pidgin English and published in *Da Jesus Book,* is a lot wordier and less solemn: "God, you our Fadda, you stay inside da sky. / We like all da peopo know fo shua how you stay, / An dat you stay good an spesho, / An we like dem give you plenny respeck. / We like you come King fo everybody now. / We like everybody make jalike you like, / Ova hea inside da world, / Jalike da angel guys up inside da sky make jalike you like."

When put into Tok Pisin — a creole, born from an English-based pidgin, that has become the national language of Papua New Guinea — the beloved passage veers even further away from anything recognizable as English. Papua New Guinea is not the only country to use a creole as a national or official language; Vanuatu, Mauritius, São Tomé and Príncipe, Cape Verde, Haiti and the Seychelles do the same. Bislama, an English-based creole that is the national language of Vanuatu, takes its name from the Portuguese *bicho de mar,* or small sea creature — the sea slug, in other words. I can't think of any other language named after an invertebrate. Islands, you'll notice, nurture creoles. They tend to survive poorly on a mainland.

In his recent books *Découvrez le Globish* and *Don't Speak English, Parlez Globish,* Nerrière suggests that his caffeine-free parlance could help rather than hinder the survival of other languages. They will continue to act as the bearers of culture and the transmitters of identity, whereas the task of Globish is merely to convey information. Nobody is likely to grow up speaking Globish as a mother tongue. "I am helping the survival of French," Nerrière told McCrum, because Globish will "limit the influence of the English language dramatically." I admit to skepticism on this point. It sounds like an attempt at linguistic inoculation: giving everybody a disease-causing agent, with the aim of keeping the resulting infection as mild as possible. Nerrière hopes for the exact reverse of what H. G. Wells cheerily predicted: that the diffusion of a simplified form of English would lead to English's further growth.

Globish has in Nerrière an appealing advocate. He refuses the pessimism that afflicts so many writers about the future. His French is jaunty, punchy and open to new expressions — an *Internaute globiphile,* for example, is Nerrière's crisp phrase for a web-surfing lover of Globish. He has the chutzpah to assert that when *globiphones* know how to compensate for their limitations, they are superior to native speakers of English, who are complacent in their certainties and their sense of linguistic entitlement. The long-term future for English as spoken by *angloricains* (another of his favorite expressions; we might say Englericans) is, Nerrière claims, gloomy.

But, like Basic English, Globish has its critics. Nerrière may be a brilliant man but his training is in business, not linguistics, and his choices of vocabulary and grammar rules for Globish are not what most experts would have made. Why should "chairman" appear on the word list when "chair" does not? And why is "estimate" a better term to learn than "guess"? As the young German linguist Joachim Grzega has complained, "The systemic principles for its elaboration are nowhere explained . . . Moreover, Globish shows a tremendous amount of errors and inconsistencies." Nerrière's own grasp of English is less than perfect — at one point he writes "the upteeth time" in place of "the umpteenth time." He also appears to think that "Did you build?" and "She's been putting" are acceptable sentences.

Those are tiny points, but they serve to illustrate how hard it is to get English right. A generation ago the Swedish linguist Pär Hultfors carried out research in the south of England, noting the responses of local people to their language on the lips of foreigners. (His work was published in 1986 under the ponderous title *Reactions to Non-Native English: Native English-Speakers' Assessments of Errors in the Use of English Made by Non-Native Users of the Language*.) Some of the mistakes Hultfors recorded will doubtless remain mistakes: "He drives badlier than his brother," or "Smell on these flowers!" But other "errors" may already be acceptable in many places, perhaps even in Globish: "I was operated last week"; "He told me to not worry"; "I look forward to hear from you." In recent years, Eurospeak, the informal name for the formal vocabulary of the European Union, has become a linguistic force, pushing terms like "additionality" and "comitology" into British English. Phrases like "passport control" (which makes perfect sense in French and German) have become common in Britain — in North America, "passport control" still sounds odd. But if non-native speakers are indeed fated to have a major impact on how English develops, phrases like this will almost certainly become standard.

Joachim Grzega, who has his own idea of standardness, plumps for a linguistically rigorous system he calls Basic Global English, or BGE. It comes with just twenty grammar rules and a vocabulary of only 750 words. Unlike the proponents of Globish or Basic English, Grzega asks learners to find and memorize another 250 words in any subject area they please. That may provide enough of a psychological incentive to make the learning of BGE easier than the mastery of Globish. But for the moment, even if BGE has the steak, Globish has the sizzle. Within three years of their appearance in France, Nerrière's books had been translated into Spanish, Italian and Korean, and had gained wide attention in other languages too.

Confusingly, his key term has also been taken up by a retired engineer in India, Madhukar Gogate, to denote his own version of English, one that dispenses with most capital letters and punctuation marks but aims "to foster world brotherhood." In Gogate's words, "A proper approach is to . . . start a new language, a new script at an informal level. I call that Globish." In fact what he proposes is neither a language nor a script but a simplified spelling system. "One can easily navigate from English to Globish," Gogate writes optimistically on his website. "'hi iz e jauli gud felo' = He is a jolly good fellow. It is easy to teach Globish." *yes vel.*

Gogate, Grzega and Nerrière have all devised a plan to alter how English is used, and all of them have turned to the Internet to propound their ideas. Most important, none speaks English as a mother tongue. They have made it their mission to affect the future character of a language that is foreign to them. (Not many English-speakers could imagine doing the same with Hindi, German or even French.) People have wondered, David Graddol suggests in *English Next,* whether Mandarin or any other language could possibly topple English from its dominant position. "The answer is that there is already a challenger, one which has quietly appeared on the scene whilst many native speakers of English were looking the other way . . . The new language which is rapidly ousting the language of Shakespeare as the world's lingua franca is English itself — English in its new global form." To proponents of this simplified lingua franca, native speakers, whether in their British or American form, are not necessarily a model.

They may serve as an impediment. Their accent may be far removed from that of local people; if they are monolingual, they can't translate to and from local languages; they may, inadvertently or otherwise, bring a heap of cultural baggage. According to the traditional model of language learning, native speakers form an inner circle, one that everyone else has difficulty entering. For most languages, that model still holds true. But for English, Graddol suggests, it's passé: "The 'inner circle' is now better conceived of as the group of highly proficient speakers of English — those who have 'functional nativeness' regardless of how they learned or use the language." Accent matters far less than intelligibility. Cultural references may be totally unwelcome.

In his earlier study *The Future of English?* Graddol emphasized "the growing assertiveness of countries adopting English as a second language that English is now *their* language, through which they can express their own values and identities, create their own intellectual property and export goods and services to other countries." Yet, as we're about to see, the assertiveness of English can still have a profound impact on other nations' values and identity.

5

Hippu Hangu

Language in Japan

THE PAINTINGS WERE FULL of words, English words. "Bella's wedding dress" appeared in the lower left corner of a watercolor entitled *Not Titled Yet.* Higher up was the phrase "one of those thing." The painting also featured an arrow and the numeral 2 but, so far as I could see, no dress. Another painting, *A Feeling of Morning,* included the words "metro" and "alisia." A third, which had no apparent connection to veal stew, said "osso buco" on it. The words were like jagged shards, scattered amid the visual debris. Japanese characters were nowhere to be seen.

"I make mistake," said the painter, Norio Ueno, with a disarming smile. His English was poor, but not so poor as my Japanese. A chunky septuagenarian with thick glasses and a shock of white hair, he led me over to *Rose Garden: Ikaros.* It proved to be a square canvas, largely abstract, without a trace of roses. The word "tone" appears at the top right, "Joseph D" in the middle, "brack wine" below the name — not far from "Ikalos." The painter didn't seem to mind his confusion of *l* and *r;* it amused him.

I saw the exhibition on its final afternoon in a chic museum in Kyoto, the old capital of Japan and, perhaps, its spiritual capital still. Soon many of the pictures would be wrapped up and sent back to Norio Ueno's home on the northern island of Hokkaido — unlike most of Japan's other major artists, he prefers to avoid big cities. Tall and thin, the museum is located in Gion, a Kyoto neighborhood that mixes narrow flagstone streets and beautifully preserved wooden houses with gaudy shops and bars. To complement its modest exhibition space, the museum contains a Zen-inspired sun garden and a tea-ceremony room. Yet the pictures were subversive.

Their titles — *Inscribed by the Wind, The Light of a Dream, Notes in the Water* and so on — hint at the celebrated Japanese pleasure in reverie, transience, shifting identity. But the paintings explode tradition. *Fragments in Cold Water,* painted in 2004, consists of writings and stray shapes against a cool, gray-blue background. The shapes include a large circle, an arrow, a triangle, a line heading nowhere and what may or may not be the stylized head of a dog. Near the middle of the circle is a large capital A. The artist has copied two poems by W. H. Auden, "This Lunar Beauty" and part of "Too Dear, Too Vague," outside the circle, though spilling into it. Farther down, the English goes womlu. In capital letters, Ueno has inscribed SHUT YOUR EYES AND OPEN YOURE MOUTH. (When spelled correctly, these words occur in both *Ulysses* and *To Kill a Mockingbird.*) More lines follow, partly erased and unreadable, beginning with "Sentries ago" and ending with Ueno's signature. It's as though meaning is dissolving, as though language can no longer convey any coherent sense.

With the help of an interpreter, I talked to Ueno about this painting. He said he'd found the poems in a bilingual edition of Auden's work. They reminded him of the French verses by Apollinaire and Aragon that he admired long ago as a student. He hadn't a clue what many of the English words meant. But having grown to love the poems in Japanese, he wanted to reproduce them in the original.

This puzzled me. I asked Yuki Kajikawa, the young woman who directs the museum and had curated the show, why she thought Ueno had done this. It's unlikely, after all, that a painter in any English-language country would fill his or her canvases with Japanese writing, especially if the artist had little idea what the characters signified. She thought for a moment, then replied: "They give a feeling of distance." Ueno comes from a nation where calligraphy has long been valued as an art form, routinely displayed in galleries, museums and private homes. In the eyes of a Japanese viewer, Japanese words in the paintings would impart too much closeness, provide too direct a commentary.

Her answer half satisfied me. It was clear that Ueno made use of foreign words not only as ornament and decoration. At first I thought they conveyed a sense of power. All over the Far East, this is a purpose English serves: it carries an air of authority as well as glamour. But the paintings are forlorn enough to defy such an easy interpretation. Their scraps of grace seem alien to the breakneck, neon-flashing, *Lost in Translation* Japan. Instead they reminded me of an essay by the novelist Kurahashi Yumiko. Writing in 1966, she said: "I abhor the intrusion of the disorder of 'facts' into the world of words I have constructed . . . At an uncertain time, in a place that is nowhere, somebody who is no one, for no reason, is about to do something — and in the end does nothing: this is my ideal of the novel." So is art's job to keep life at a distance?

I looked at the paintings a second time, conscious that Norio Ueno was occasionally looking at me. He was a child during the Second World War, and before moving to Hokkaido he spent years in the ravaged metropolis of Tokyo. That city's suffering in 1945 has largely been forgotten outside Japan. In the words of General Curtis LeMay, who commanded the U.S. air raids, "We scorched and boiled and baked to death more people in Tokyo that night of May 9–10 than went up in vapor at Hiroshima and Nagasaki." Ueno's pictures told a story, I finally realized, of large-scale brokenness — a tale in which cultural invasion, even colonization, played a central role. Ueno took the ideas of rose gardens, mornings and dreams, and shattered them beyond recognition. Then he refilled them with snatches of English. It was as though amid the wreckage of postwar Japan, glowing incomprehensible fragments are what emerged, the world having turned to a foreign language fractured by the memory of light.

‿

The dramatic, almost tectonic shifts in Japanese are the subject of this chapter. Under the influence of English, its vocabulary is altering with cut-and-paste speed. The hybrid speech that many young people now favor in Japan may well embody the most radical incursion English has yet made on another widely spoken language. It suggests the impact that language change can have, not just on artists like Norio Ueno but on a whole society. And it raises the question of whether modernization results in a cultural cost much higher than we like to believe.

To understand the changes, we need to take a look at the singular history and character of Japanese. A good place to begin is with John of Gaunt — for his paean to England in Shakespeare's play *Richard II* applies much better to Japan:

> This fortress built by Nature for herself
> Against infection and the hand of war,
> This happy breed of men, this little world,
> This precious stone set in the silver sea,

Which serves it in the office of a wall
Or as a moat defensive to a house,
Against the envy of less happier lands . . .

British culture, contrary to John's great speech, took shape as an after-effect of repeated invasions: the English Channel proved a meager moat. Nature built a stronger fortress in Japan, allowing its culture to flourish without foreign overlords. On one of the rare occasions when the country faced attack — the Mongols besieged it in 1281 — the invasion was foiled by *kamikaze:* not suicide bombers but a monster storm or, literally, a "god-wind." So whereas English has always been a mongrel tongue, a hybrid of arriving idioms, Japanese (along with the closely related language of Okinawa and the other Ryukyu Islands to the southwest) is what the experts call an "isolate": linguistically, it stands apart. It may bear a distant relationship to Korean; then again, it may not. As far as grammar and syntax — the heart of a language — are concerned, it's enormously different from Chinese. No attempt to link it to any of the big language families — Altaic, Dravidian, Austronesian, Finno-Ugric, Tibeto-Burman and others — has yet proved convincing.

Japanese people have sometimes assumed that no foreigner could ever master their intricate language. As the writer Catherine Bergman once observed, "The theory of the unique race lulled them in childhood, it comforts them when they feel unloved and misunderstood, it justifies them." Yet isolation can be overstated. In fact, Japanese is an astonishingly porous language. Both its language and its culture are inconceivable without Chinese influence. In the first paragraph of this chapter, when I mentioned Japanese characters, I could equally well have said Chinese characters.

Old Japanese was an unwritten tongue. About 1,500 years ago, it's now believed, Buddhist monks sailed to Japan carrying sacred texts that were written in Chinese. In Japan at that time, literacy meant the ability to read Chinese. Buddhism took root and flowered; it gave rise to rival Japanese traditions, Zen being the most celebrated. Chinese characters — kanji — settled down too. They became the script in which, to this day, most Japanese nouns, verb stems and adjective stems are written. But the Japanese didn't just marry their preexisting words to Chinese characters; out of convenience or homage, they borrowed a host of Chinese words, often transforming the pronunciation. As a result, some characters bear related sounds and meanings in Chinese and Japanese; others carry similar meanings but totally different sounds; in still others, Chinese and Japanese sounds and meanings have no relationship at all. Over the centuries, the Japanese also invented a large number of kanji that are unknown in China. The system may be unwieldy, but it works — up to a point.

Because of the differences between the two languages, kanji on their own turned out to be a clunky method of writing Japanese. The language has a mere five vowel sounds, permits almost no combinations of consonants, and relies on some key elements of grammar, such as inflected endings and particles, that are absent in Chinese. A tongue needs to feel comfortable in its chosen script, but Japanese did not feel comfortable in kanji alone. And so, more than a thousand years ago, a pair of local writing systems emerged, katakana and hiragana. They were not usurpers, out to dethrone kanji from a place of honor; instead they became kanji's complement.

Katakana and hiragana look similar to my eyes. But my eyes are not those of a Japanese reader, who can tell at a glance the katakana (its squarish characters are vital for writing recent words of Western origin, as well as scientific and technical terms) from the hiragana (a more rounded script, now used mostly for grammatical chores that Chinese characters are unable to perform). Centuries ago, hiragana was known as women's script, because it fostered literacy in women not previously trained to write. Unlike kanji, both katakana and hiragana are phonetic. They each contain forty-eight signs, one for every basic syllable.

Japanese children have to learn each of these scripts. Today, thanks to the enormous influence of American business and culture, they also need to grasp the Roman alphabet (romaji). It's possible to come across all four ways of writing in a single sentence. The *Asahi Shimbun* newspaper, for example, ran a headline in 2004 that used nine katakana, seven kanji, four hiragana, one Roman letter and the odd Arabic numeral to deliver the stirring news that "Radcliffe, Olympic marathon contestant, will also appear in the 10,000 m." As if all that weren't enough, Japanese texts can be read in different directions. Top to bottom is the most common, but sometimes they move from left to right, and occasionally from right to left.

The difficulties of kanji have, if anything, grown over time. In the 1950s and '60s, aiming to stamp out illiteracy among the masses, the Maoist regime in Beijing decreed that the writing of kanji would henceforth be simplified. But in Japan the characters had already undergone a partial simplification. And in Taiwan the original, complex style remains in force. If we speak of Chinese as a language, we mean the set of characters that knit together several, perhaps many, spoken languages — the written symbols, not the spoken words, are what united China. The changes brought about by time and spelling reforms have led to a linguistic hodgepodge in which any given character can be written in several styles, be pronounced in several ways, and mean a multitude of things.

Despite the simplification of kanji in Japan, the writing of these characters still takes an amount of knowledge and hard work that astounds most Westerners. For example, the word *kinyoubi* (Friday) is written with three characters. The second of the three requires eighteen strokes of the pen. These strokes are supposed to be inscribed in a particular order, not just any old way. In 1981, hoping to limit the number of kanji to a manageable size, the government published a list of *jōyō kanji hyō* — characters for daily use. Most newspapers and magazines try to avoid obscure or archaic words that include nondaily kanji. Even so, the list contains no fewer than 1,945 characters, and hundreds of others can be found in Japanese names.

For all the complications and elaborations of its script, spoken Japanese can be extremely concise. Pronouns are usually implied, not stated. Take the following brief exchange: "Did you go to the movie with Kazuki?" "Yes, I went." In Japanese, this might be rendered as *"Kazuki to eiga e itta no?"* *"Un, itta yo."* A literal translation would read: "Kazuki with movie to went that?" "Yes, went, final particle." Apart from its role as a name, *kazuki* can signify "pleasant peace" or, when written with different kanji, "shining one." Words look uneasy on their own. Context is everything.

All of which begins to explain why the Japanese can appear so opaque to outsiders. "Eloquence is not one of the virtues people have been encouraged to cultivate," Masayoshi Shibatani writes in his book *The Languages of Japan*. "In fact, persuasion of others by means of linguistic skills is largely discouraged as direct confrontation in general is avoided . . . It is the person's ability to arrive at an intended conclusion rather than the persuader's logical presentation that is evaluated. Thus, one who does not get the point by merely hearing hints is considered a dull person." From Periclean Athens to Hyde Park Corner, the European tradition of rhetoric has aimed at convincing a listener by force of logic and argument. Japan's tradition is one that cherishes nuance and tolerates ambiguity, inviting a listener to come up with an implied meaning. If a man says that a woman is *kirei,* is he praising her beauty, her purity or her cleanliness — or some combination of those attributes?

Imagine the difficulties, then, of translating Japanese texts into English. According to Linda Hoaglund, who wrote the subtitles for seven films by the great director Akira Kurosawa, "Japanese and English could not be more disparate languages. Americans find Japanese expressions vague; Japanese find English unforgiving. In Japanese, subject is largely absent, tense often irrelevant. A subject's gender can go unmentioned for whole sentences, and contradictory tenses can share the same paragraph. Social interactions are assumed to be so transparent as to forgo fundamental Western linguistic references. Sentences can be terse if you always know what the other person is thinking." But subtitles mustn't sprawl across half the screen, nor can they continue long after a speaker has finished talking. Writing them, a translator has to balance explanation and implication. When American movies are rendered into Japanese, dubbers and subtitlers face a different challenge: rendering long chains of oaths, curses and expletives into a language not richly endowed with terms of abuse.

Foreigners who strive to master Japanese are often baffled by its remarkable system of *keigo,* or polite speech. Its rules place vocabulary at the mercy of social context. "Will X come to Osaka tomorrow?" seems a simple question. But depending on the setting, the speaker, the person being addressed and the person being asked about, it could be posed in more than twenty ways. Identity in Japanese is fluid, open-ended, almost shockingly changeable. A male teacher might call himself *watakushi* (I, formally), *boku* (I, informally), *ore* (I, intimately or vulgarly), *otōsan* (I as a father, talking to my children), *sensei* (I as a teacher, talking to my class), *ojisan* (I as an uncle, talking to other children) or *niisan* (I as an older brother). The intricacies of *keigo* are not just a question of taste or decorum, like knowing how to address the British monarch or what utensil to wield at a seven-course banquet; they're embedded deep within the language. Yasuto Kikuchi, a linguist at the University of Tokyo, has called *keigo* "the Japanese heart, our way of thinking, our way of behaving, our way of assigning value."

Yet values alter with time, and in time people may come to scoff at traditional ways of thinking, behaving and speaking. "Days and months are the travelers of eternity," wrote the poet Matsuo Bashō in the late seventeenth century. "So are the years that pass by." Today the *shinkansen* —

bullet trains, in the common English phrase — wear an English slogan on the outside of some of their shark-sleek, gunmetal cars: AMBITIOUS JAPAN. Ambitious for what? Early in the twenty-first century a Japanese company introduced Kidsbeer, a nonalcoholic drink with an American-style name. It looks and purports to taste like real beer. In translation, its ad campaign says: "Even kids can't stand life unless they have a drink."

Shut your eyes and open your mouth.

⌇

Kyoto's Japan Rail station, hypermodern to a fault, draws *shinkansen* travelers and local commuters into a glassy complex that boasts a luxury hotel, a museum, a theater, an art gallery, a specialty shopping mall, dozens of restaurants and a big department store. Having arrived there early on a summer evening, I rode the escalators up to a rooftop garden. The eighth floor housed a restaurant called Honey Bee that advertised "Belgium waffles and juicing." Three floors higher, a sign declared EAT PARADISE. Is this a specimen of Japanese English? Asian English? World English? New English? Colloquial English? Weird English? Or just plain wrong English?

All bets are off. All rules are gone. I knew from Montreal's mixture of French and English that when languages exist in close proximity, they begin to merge at the edges. English, as spoken by foreigners in Japan, has developed a startling capacity to soak up Japanese words. Rather than eat paradise, I whiled away an hour by reading the latest issue of an English-language newspaper, *Japan Times.* It contained a short article about teenage misbehavior, written by a *gaijin* named Geoff Botting. His piece was studded with Japanese. I could understand *karaoke* and *manga,* but what of *kyabakura, oppaipabu, enko* and *enjo kosai*?

Karaoke and manga are two of the many dozens of Japanese terms that have made their way into mainstream English. Perhaps those others will follow. Compared to the small quantity of words that English has drawn from Korean, Thai, Vietnamese and other East Asian languages, the Japanese total is impressive. The arts, including the martial and culinary kinds, provide the largest number. But only when a Japanese word expresses a genuinely new concept or object is English likely to borrow it. Manga, for instance, are comic books, but they differ from North American specimens in their size, their seriousness, their variety, their huge audience, their entire look and feel. Likewise, anime is not just a synonym for animated film; it implies a whole aesthetic.

The architectural aesthetic of Kyoto, as seen from its rooftop garden, is one of a steel rush. Having been spared the bombing in 1945, the city failed to escape the boom that followed. It's helpful, peering down, to contemplate the Zen of Mazda. I read a statement in impeccable English by the station's architect, Hiroshi Hara: "The glass shelter over the concourse represents the traditional Japanese aesthetic of a boundary, yet not a boundary. A person traversing the station will recollect the sky. The formalization of the gate is like designing Kyoto's sky." A sky that would soon be awash with fireworks. That evening, once a series of escalators had lowered me to the station's ground floor, I met a young English teacher, Yoshimi Amano, who shepherded me through the pell-mell crowds. We boarded a creaking train for Kameoka, a castle town northwest of the city. It hosts an annual peace festival that bathes the new moon of August in an hourlong rain of light.

Tens of thousands of people had gathered outside Kameoka's little station to watch a fireworks display. In style the fireworks veered from abstract art to schmaltz, from multicolored ribbons and cascades of light to a heart, a star, a snail and a crowd-pleasing cat's head. When Yoshimi strolled off to buy some delicacies from a nearby food stall — August fireworks go with egg-battered octopus — I noticed an old woman in a gray kimono who wore white sneakers and a backpack, and who kept a tight grip on her umbrella. She was, it seemed, the grandmother of a girl aged about ten.

But the girl was not wearing a kimono. Across her chest, a T-shirt read *All Girls Are Born Winners.* Underneath that wholesome message were the words *Juicy Juicy Juicy.* The girl turned away to follow her grandmother, whose umbrella helped her clear a path through the crowd. Another girl, perhaps a year or two older, wore a T-shirt that read *Just Full of the Charms One After Another Which Are on the Market.* I'd be less inclined to think of *Lolita* if it weren't for the persistent emphasis in Japanese porn on the charms of schoolgirls.

When the moon had the sky to itself again, Yoshimi and I found seats on a train back into Kyoto and parted in the vast concourse: a boundary, yet not a boundary. Once you start reading other people's clothing, it's hard to stop. Hard for me, anyway. A young blood in the station sported a T-shirt with the slogan *The Sea Roars a Lullaby.* Another T-shirt mysteriously declared: *Happy Endless Bivis.* I walked back to my hotel past the vending machines, cars, lit-up shops and darkened temples of Kyoto. The hotel elevator contained a sign with an unappetizing picture of cornflakes, yogurt and tea above the inscription *Have Freely About Free Breakfast Ser-*

vice Self-Service. In smaller type, the sign announced: *Carrying Out Out of a Breakfast Corner Should Withhold.*

For decades, sentences like these went by the name of Japlish; but because of the implied or perceived insult in that expression, another name has recently come to the fore: Engrish. Websites are devoted to it. Engrish, unlike Japlish, can refer to gnarled gobbets of language from all across East Asia. But there's a risk: the more you revel in Engrish, the more you make fun of Asians. And the fun can turn to scorn. Why do they make such blunders anyway?

There are, as it happens, three good reasons. The main one is that English often functions simply as a design element in Japanese products. The words are not intended to carry any precise meaning — or rather, the meaning they're out to convey is that the product in question is hip, cool, ultranew. If you're manufacturing a T-shirt, the sea may as well roar a lullaby as murmur a pandemonium. A second reason is that in matters of grammar and phonetics, as well as vocabulary and social context, the differences between English and Japanese are huge. Each language makes it onerous for speakers of the other to write and pronounce correctly. And third, some apparently inexplicable errors can be traced back to mistranslation. Why would a Japanese package of coffee have the name Ease Your Bosoms? The answer, almost certainly, is an inept rendering of the English phrase "Take a load off your chest."

On the rare occasions when Westerners adopt an Asian script, we're likely to get things equally wrong. In the 2007 movie *Alpha Dog,* Justin Timberlake plays a mean young thug, out of sync with the world around him. His meanness is signaled by the quantity of his tattoos. But surely the filmmakers didn't intend the biceps of Timberlake's left arm to be decorated by the Chinese characters for "ice-skating." Ah, the Mysterious West. A few years ago, an English teenager paid ninety pounds to have his arm tattooed with the characters for "love, honor and obey." The tattoo artist must have hated his client. When the teenager strutted out of the shop, he had no idea what the characters said. Eventually he found out: "Basically, this is an ugly boy."

⌇

The world sees Japan as a proud and confident nation. It's renowned for taking other people's crazy ideas and figuring out how to make them work.

Its trains and cars have become a byword for efficiency. Yet as far as language is concerned, Japanese people have often felt uncertain, vulnerable, ill at ease.

The humiliation that followed Japan's surrender in 1945 doubtless bears some responsibility. In his short story *"Amerikan Sukūru"* ("The American School"), Kojima Nobuo evoked the dismay that a shy teacher felt upon visiting a school during the U.S. occupation and hearing a cluster of American girls as they chatter away in English: "He concluded that he and his colleagues were members of a pathetic race which had no place here. Listening to these mellifluous English voices, he could not account for the fear and horror which the language had always inspired in him. At the same time his own inner voice whispered: It is foolish for Japanese to speak this language like foreigners. If they do, it makes them foreigners, too. And that is a real disgrace."

Yet Japan's linguistic doubts go back much further. The linguist Takao Suzuki observes that unlike other peoples, such as Arabs and Persians, "the Japanese have consistently held an extraordinarily negative view of their own language." In the 1880s the country's first education minister wanted English to become the national language. Decades later the revered novelist Shiga Naoya urged his compatriots to switch over to French, which he believed to be the most refined tongue in existence. To become sufficiently cultured, or democratic, or modern, or successful, such voices have called on Japan to discard its own way of speaking.

Today they may be doing precisely that. Not since the wholesale importation of kanji and Chinese vocabulary more than a millennium ago has Japanese been so swept up by change. For every *bonsai, honcho, sashimi* or *tycoon* that has made its way into English, hundreds of words — even entire phrases — have pushed the other way. A recent movie, set in contemporary Japan and aimed at local audiences, had the title *Shall We Dansu?* And a best-selling guidebook, published in Japanese, was called *How to Sex.* The onrushing tide of English means that in Japan, nature is no longer a fortress, nor the silver sea a wall.

In 2005 a source in the Tokyo Metropolitan Police told a journalist that officers were having an unusual problem with teenagers. Rebel behavior wasn't the issue; it was rebel language. "Half the time, they couldn't figure out what kids were saying. So staff began compiling a list of jargon." The list comprises hundreds of new words — many of them adaptations of American phrases, shortened and given a Japanese ending. Adolescent verbs may be particularly hard for the police and other outsiders to grasp. *Famiru,* for example, now means "to go to a family restaurant"; *operu* (from "operation") is "to undergo cosmetic surgery"; *biniru* means "to go to a convenience store" (a *konbini,* that is); and *rabiru* (think of the English word "labyrinth") signifies "to be trapped and unable to act."

Terms like these flummox most people over twenty. Yet they fit a long-established pattern of Japanese wordmaking. For decades, the Japanese have been adept and assiduous at gathering English words and morphing them into something else, producing terms that are new to both languages. The result is known as *wasai eigo* (Japan-made English). Occasionally, as with "love hotel" (*rabu hoteru*) and "salaryman," these coinages will find a way back into English. Many of them are wonderfully inventive and revealing. *Amerikan koohii,* for instance, is a favorite term for weak coffee. *Haroo waaku* (from "hello work") is a job center; *herusu meetaa* ("health meter") means a bathroom scale; *soopu rando* ("soap land") is a brothel. Speakers of English have no idea what these phrases mean — to the chagrin of many Japanese.

The new vocabulary fits into an underlying structure that accepts change slowly. Japanese phonetics has no place for *l* and *v*, which explains the consonant pattern of *rabu hoteru.* Traditionally the language also had no *f,* but it seems more relaxed on this point; many f-words have now entered the lexicon, such as the sports term *foabōru* ("four ball," or a base on balls). Of course, similar phonetic adaptations occur in other languages. The Swahili word for a traffic island is *kiplefiti* — from the English instruction "keep left." But a Swahili noun beginning with *ki* normally becomes *vi* in the plural. And so if you need to talk about more than one traffic island in Swahili, you say *viplefiti.*

Often it's possible to tease out a long filament by which meanings are pulled to life. Take the recent Japanese coinage *enu jii.* Its origins go back to the most vexed and perplexing of Americanisms, "OK." Despite much labor and testy speculation, nobody is entirely sure whether OK started off as the Choctaw word for "indeed," *okeh;* the Haitian rum port Aux Cayes; the Scots affirmative *och aye;* the term for "yes," *waw kay,* in the West African tongue of Wolof; or (the favored candidate of most historians) an abbreviation for the facetious "oll korrect." Whatever the source of OK, people in Japan decided that its opposite must be "no good." In English, the initials of

that phrase are NG. And the Japanese way of pronouncing NG is *enu jii* —
now an accepted term. Similarly, a woman who works in an office — not a
concept for which Japanese had much use prior to the late twentieth century — could be pictured as an "office lady" in English, hence an OL, and
thus, in present-day Tokyo, an *oo eru.*

Aside from this hypermodern overlay, Japanese belongs in no known
language family, and its ancient history remains in shadow. Japan's centuries of solitude meant that within living memory, the language held few
European or American words. A study dating from the 1920s found only
162 such terms that had entered Japanese, more than 40 percent of them
originating in Dutch and Portuguese. (They included *moga* and *mobo*,
short for *modan gaaru* and *modan boi;* modern boys often sported *roido*,
the kind of horn-rimmed glasses worn by the actor Harold Lloyd.) Then
the floodgates began to open. A similar study carried out in 1964 put the
Western-word total at nearly three thousand, English being the source of
the overwhelming majority. Since then the number has burgeoned: fifty
thousand would be a guess. A conservative guess.

Insecurity is one reason why this linguistic invasion has grown to such
massive proportions. But an equally important cause may be phonetic: the
Japanese language works with a very small number of sounds. It's said to
have a total of just 112 potential syllables (Mandarin has about four times
that number, while English boasts at least 3,500). In Japanese, therefore, to
borrow is easier than to invent. Spoken aloud, the Japanese word *kō* can
mean "child," "flour," "individual," "big," "arc," "sin," "price" and "the late"
— not to mention assorted other meanings when it functions as a prefix or
a suffix. Each sense of *kō* demands a different written character. "So in their
speech," Takao Suzuki explains, "the Japanese are heavily dependent on the
graphic image of the word that is stored in their minds. This means that
unless the Japanese know how the word is written, it is often difficult for
them to understand what is said."

The foreign terms serve a purpose, of course. Without a traditional
way of saying "public involvement," Japan may as well accept *paburikku
inborubumento,* even though it's such a portly mouthful. But words like
that can be a chore to remember. Because they're written in the syllabic
script of katakana, not in the traditional kanji, no graphic images of them
are stored in anyone's mind. When they enter the language, foreign expressions often become both cryptic and bite-sized. Dozens of recent bor-

rowings involve the syllable *kon,* thanks to their origin in English compounds that happen to include a "co" sound. A personal computer is a *pasokon,* remote control is *rimokon,* an air conditioner an *eakon,* a mother complex a *mazakon* . . . Not surprisingly, older people struggle to understand what they hear on TV and radio. Words plucked from Western sources have proliferated so much that the language no longer feels theirs.

Chikara Kato, a linguistics professor at Sugiyama Jogakuen University, told the *New York Times,* "We Japanese have an inferiority complex over language which has turned into a dangerous longing. As a result Japanese youngsters are taking a distance from Japanese and favoring katakana words. If you go into a clothing store that caters to young people, you'll find that everything is in English." When the *Times* reporter did precisely that, he found girls wearing *shadoh* (eye shadow) and *hippu hangu* (hip-hugging jeans). Unease about terms like those provoked Prime Minister Junichiro Koizumi to appoint a top-level panel on the language in 2002, its mandate being to analyze freshly borrowed words, advise the media which ones to avoid, and invent Japanese words that could be used instead.

Whether the panel will have any real effect is an unanswered question. Before its work began, Suzuki asked a senior official of the National Police Agency why its campaigns for traffic safety used convoluted, English-based words. Could ordinary people grasp the meaning of *sukuranburu kōsaten* (a scramble crossing, or pedestrian-friendly intersection) or the *kīpu refuto* (keep to the left) campaign? Almost certainly not, the official admitted. But, he went on, "it is easier to get government funding for new projects if they have English names." Bureaucrats in Japan have been almost as eager as teenagers to grab hold of foreign expressions. Instead of throwing light on a subject, these terms can obscure. One of the most flagrant examples is *gurobaru herusukea apurikeishon purojekutto* — a global healthcare application project. In 2004 the National Institute for Japanese Language surveyed thousands of people about the meaning of significant loanwords; it found that *gabanansu* (governance) was understood by only 7 percent of respondents.

Peter Carey, in his subtle, deceptively jaunty book *Wrong About Japan,* describes an exchange he had in a Tokyo Starbucks with a teenage boy named Takashi. The boy, who dresses and behaves in an ultrachic style, asks Carey if he wants some *miruku.* "The *u* ending suggested an English word recently adopted by the Japanese, but in the case of milk, that made no sense at all, so I asked Takashi was there no other word for milk." "Of course," the boy replies, but "miruku is more modern." Carey persists, and is told that the old word is "not so hygienic." What does hygiene have to do with language? "'The other word is *gyuunyuu.*' He wrinkled his nose. 'It means liquid from udder. Miruku is better.'" In truth, the literal meaning of *gyuunyuu* is "cow breast." How could it compete with *miruku,* which not only sounded contemporary and hygienic but was also the name of an anime hero on TV?

Among all the words of Western origin that have penetrated Japanese, the most interesting (or maybe the most dangerous) are those that embody foreign ideas. There may be little point in complaining when new items of technology arrive in English, but what of an English word that displaces a long-standing Japanese concept? A traditional household, for instance, was an *ie:* a multigenerational affair that implied the presence of dead great-grandparents and unborn great-grandchildren, as well as family members still alive. A *hōmu,* by contrast, excludes the ancestors and future descendants, and implies less control on the part of the husband's mother. (*Hōmu* can also refer, oddly enough, to a railway platform.) The concept of home changes with the word. English-speakers can glimpse the effect of this phenomenon if we think of the difference between "cuisine" and "cooking," or between "trio" and "threesome." It's for such reasons that language change can have a profound effect on society at large.

Characters and sounds are the travelers of eternity. So are the words that pass by.

৯৯

The bar was down a flight of stairs beside a paved alley that ran off a side street somewhere in the middle of Tokyo — a metropolis of about thirty-five million people, if you include Yokohama and other adjoining cities. Seen from a skyscraper at night, the place resembles a giant sliver of silicon, its endlessly flashing microchips pressing out on all sides to the horizon. Tetsuo Kinoshita led me to the bar; otherwise I would never have found it. Having exchanged e-mails with Tetsuo, I was expecting to meet a mild-mannered, courteous editor and translator. He was, indeed, courteous to a fault, though to my surprise he was also tall and black-bearded. Inside the bar, two others were waiting for us. Yukio Matsuda, an elderly gentleman in a suit and tie, used to work in Australia as an executive with the Mitsui trading house; he has also translated Dylan Thomas's poetry into Japanese. Brian Miller, shaven-headed and intense, is a former musician with the Phoenix Symphony who has lived in Japan for more than twenty years, running a communications firm while translating poetry and Zen texts into English.

Yukio Matsuda was the first to talk about language, and as he did so his genial expression darkened. He explained how difficult it has become for young people to master kanji: "In order to lighten the burden of learning, the numbers of kanji that pupils had to learn were decreased. In the old days, by learning one Chinese character, we could come to know more words." For example, *da* in Chinese means crude or inferior. Many Japanese words were made with its help, such as *dabora* (tall tale) and *dasaku* (crude work). "So," Yukio continued, "if people learned more Chinese characters, they could have more vocabulary. But alas, people's vocabularies today are very poor because of learning less kanji. Now people are forced to use new, queer words and expressions."

I sipped a beer and munched my way through a small plateful of raw broad beans — a Japanese equivalent of chips or peanuts — wondering if the other men at the table shared his pessimism. Surely people have the choice of using or ignoring "queer words"; nobody insists on them. Tetsuo and Brian belong to a different generation than Yukio Matsuda, and they seemed less dismayed at the changes affecting Japanese. Many of the old formalities and subtleties are falling by the wayside, Brian noted. And probably this is inevitable, as the tradition of lifetime employment weakens and Japan's workforce becomes more mobile. "At a company where everyone has been there forever and will remain forever," he said, "people have a keen sense of their exact place in the pecking order. Relationships are less complex and less nuanced in a corporate organization where people come and go. Language becomes simpler too." Tetsuo was nodding: "My great-grandfather would be shocked to hear me speaking to my teacher or to government officials. The officials used to be called *okami,* meaning 'what is above.' Now they are just called 'civil servant.'"

Yet Tetsuo had a fear of his own. "We're losing the ability to write kanji with our own hands," he said. "When we use a keyboard to write Japanese, we type the alphabets that represent the sound of words. Then, by pressing the Selection key, we see on the display the Chinese characters that fit the sound. Generally the word-processing software guesses the right one for us

— software understands the context." I wanted him to stop so I could absorb this idea, but Tetsuo carried on: "In this way we don't use our hands to write letters. It has been twenty years since I began to use a computer. I haven't any trouble reading Chinese characters, but on the rare occasions that I write something with my own hand, I often feel at a loss. The vague images of characters sit in my mind, refusing to get clearer no matter how I try."

Internet sites give step-by-step demonstrations in how to write kanji. But, like so many other activities, it becomes harder the less it's practiced. Yukio Matsuda confessed his anxiety that tomorrow's children will lose the ability to read and understand traditional texts. The language is changing so fast that Japanese books written a century ago, even a half century ago, have become a challenge for the young to read. If that's the case, I suggested, Japan might decide to abandon kanji altogether and move to a phonetic alphabet — early in the twentieth century, after all, Turkey switched from the Arabic alphabet to a modified Roman one. But Brian shook his head: "Kanji are absolutely essential to Japanese." He believes that the tremendous number of homonyms in the language makes the Turkish approach impracticable.

Brian's own concern about Japanese was of another kind entirely: its rush to embrace the language of his homeland. "One of the saddest things is the profusion of quasi-English in Japanese. It aborts the development of people's vocabulary skills. Communication suffers as a result." I asked for an example, and he told me about a woman in his editorial and design office who revels in quasi-English. She uses the new word *bakku* as a verb meaning "to return" or "to give back." Unfortunately she dispenses with the context that would clarify the meaning — she'll say simply *kore bakku* ("this return"), when what's needed is a longer and more specific phrase like *Okyakusan ga kore wo tousha ni modosu* ("The client returns this to us"). "That can leave a troubling uncertainty about who is to give and who is to receive," Brian explained, "not to mention what, where and how. Of course, the Japanese language allows for clarity, even with imported words. But using imported words of uncertain meaning is a symptom of laxity."

In the past, Japanese people would unquestioningly have followed the linguistic rules that Brian has taken so much trouble to learn. Rules were not an issue; the hierarchies and deferences of national life were echoed in the language. Much of the literary effect of *The Tale of Genji* — written in the eleventh century and said to be the greatest of Japanese novels — depends on this layering of verbal nuance and social structure. Courtly etiquette was so refined that the author (a woman, or perhaps more than one woman, whose identity is unknown) could not name her characters, alluding to them instead by titles such as "the Third Princess" or "the Heir Apparent." But deference is becoming a quality of the past. Does the language still need its many words for subtle gradations of bowing? Teenage girls, Tetsuo said, often avoid speaking of themselves as *watashi* (I, for a girl). Instead they use *uchi,* an Osaka dialect term — or, more radically, they describe themselves as *boku* (I, for a boy).

The men's love of Japanese was clear, their concern for it palpable. I admired them all. Yet as a taxi whisked me back to my hotel in the warm, humid night, I couldn't forget that we four had a combined age of roughly 220. We are not the heirs apparent of language, nor even its guardians — a role that older people often aspire to fill. The aspiration leads to grief. For languages, like teenagers, love to run free. Among Japan's *yuusu* (youth, I mean), two of the country's leading *konbini* chains go by the slang names of *an-pan* and *bun-bun* — the first from "A.M., P.M.," the second from the English numbers "SeBUN-EreBUN." The language, it sometimes appears, has hooked itself up to an irony drip: *zenbei ga naita* (literally, "the entire United States wept") now means "nothing important." Word by word, phrase by phrase, the new expressions may seem charming, or exasperating; but what matters is the sheer scope of change. The price of novelty may be a severe distortion of the language. *M4,* in the slangy Japanese that *yuusu* speak, means an appointment to meet someone at 4 P.M. at McDonald's — a postmodern tea ceremony, you might say.

Expressions like this probably won't last. A few decades from now, *M4* could well mean something totally different in Japan — or it might mean nothing at all. But that's not the point. What matters is that the genie has fled the lamp. Something new is bubbling up in the malls and arcades, clubs and cyberspace that young people inhabit in Japan. It's casual, unpredictable, impolite. It draws on English as a minute-by-minute inspiration, but it's not a slave to English — some of its coinages are purely Japanese and wonderfully subtle. Consider the worldwide symbol of Disney: a new Japanese phrase meaning "to visit Tokyo Disneyland," *nezumi shibaku,* literally means "to flog the mouse."

These usages are unsanctioned and unfettered. Turning the *keigo* sys-

tem of polite speech on its head, they offer young people the chance of social redefinition. In twenty-first-century Japan, few girls and boys are political rebels. But the way their generation chooses to speak Japanese is an act
of revolt. It stands as a defiant refusal to be bound by the rules of the past
— an assertion that the young enjoy the power to remake language in their
own image. Likewise, when teenagers around the world think of Japan,
they don't imagine the serenity of Buddhist temples. They think of the latest video games and wildly extravagant manga, of mutant atomic monsters,
of anime set in technological dreamworlds where flashing buildings pum-
mel the clouds high above a swirl of traffic that screeches to a halt for a
saucer-eyed, button-nosed child.

⌇

They think of the future. In the *Matrix* trilogy, the computer code that im-
prisons human beings in a simulated world is visualized as shimmering,
downward-flowing lines of green characters. Many of those characters are
mirror images of katakana. "Japan has a special place in the virtual future,"
the writer Kyo Maclear observed in 1997 (two years before *The Matrix* appeared). "In its embrace of technology as passion and lifeblood, and its extensive association with science-fiction imagery in which humans fuse with
machines, it is taken to foreshadow the coming age." Even a futuristic
movie like *Blade Runner,* set in a decayed Los Angeles, pays homage to Japan. We meet Rick Deckard, its hero, ordering food at a Japanese noodle bar in one of the film's "dirt-infested ghettos, crowded with techno-
equipped Asian peasants peddling spices and software." But, Maclear notes,
Blade Runner also keeps showing "the image of a digitalized *geisha* re-
fracted on a giant screen banked right off the expressway." Hers is one of
the rare smiles in the film.

The most sustained literary attempt to conceptualize the wired world
to come has been made by the cyberpunk movement: imagine film noir in
a collapsing future, with hackers replacing private eyes in the leading roles.
Cyberpunk authors — William Gibson, Neal Stephenson, Pat Cadigan and
others — have drawn repeated inspiration from Japan. One of the most influential novels in the genre, Gibson's *Neuromancer* (1984), begins in Japan
before the action plunges into cyberspace. Its wounded protagonist, Case,
used to live and hack in the Sprawl — somewhere between Boston and At-
lanta, that is. Then, after his nervous system was sabotaged, he moved to an

industrial city on Tokyo Bay: "Synonymous with implants, nerve-splicing, and microbionics, Chiba was a magnet for the Sprawl's techno-criminal subcultures."

When Case meets the woman who will become his partner in heroic crime, he describes her as "street samurai." The novel's first few chapters are full of Japanese words, nonchalantly mixed into English: yakitori, sarariman, manriki, gaijin, shuriken, yakuza, zaibatsu and more. Gibson also tosses in a variety of Japanese names, both corporate (Hitachi, Nikon, Kirin, Mitsubishi) and geographical. "'Bitch,' he said to the rose tint over Shiga. Down on Ninsei the holograms were vanishing like ghosts, and most of the neon was already cold and dead." To equip his readers for virtual reality, the author first needs to immerse them in an imagined Japan.

Gibson went on to make an earthquake-ravaged Tokyo the principal setting of his 1996 novel *Idoru*. The title refers to a young woman idolized for her beauty by people of both sexes. But the idol in the novel has neither flesh nor blood; she is an aggregation of software. Gibson was prophetic only briefly, for in the very year the novel was published, Japan's first "cyber idol," Kyoto Date, released a single called "Love Communication." She was a virtual girl with an invented history — her parents ran a sushi bar that was a favorite hangout of U.S. troops from the nearby Yokota Air Base — and by downloading a program called PlayKiss, anyone with a computer could strip her naked. Kyoto Date sang in a mixture of English and Japanese. Up to a point, she could communicate. But she could not love.

A decade later, Alejandro González Iñárritu's brilliant movie *Babel* cut back and forth between California, Mexico, Morocco and Japan. In all four settings and in all four languages, its characters struggle to communicate with each other and with the forces of authority. The Japanese scenes focus on Chieko Wataya, a teenage girl living in a Tokyo skyscraper and coping with the shock of her mother's suicide. Chieko is profoundly deaf. Out of emotional and sexual frustration, she starts to behave in ways both dangerous and pathetic. The language that others share is denied Chieko. Its absence casts her adrift in an unreadable city as luminous and vertical as lines of shining text.

Any vast city, I suppose, and any spoken language could have worked for this section of *Babel*. But there's something uniquely fitting about Iñárritu's choice of Tokyo and Japanese in a movie about the noise and violence of postmodern life and the silence at its heart. How can Chieko make herself heard without a voice? How can she love if she can't communicate? Must she adapt by becoming something that's foreign to her very nature? In an extreme form, Chieko's is the pain that countless Japanese people have felt as they watch the lips of others chattering away in a foreign alphabet, an alien set of codes. To the outside world, their culture is unspeakable. "Never," writes Takao Suzuki, "has it occurred to the Japanese that their language could be an asset in the international arena."

6

Radiante

Languages in Los Angeles

I WAS SITTING IN a faux-Scots diner called John o'Groats, sipping a weak coffee, waiting to meet a friend of a friend and reading a free newspaper. Sex ads usually sustain such papers, and *LA Weekly* had its share. But as I flipped the grimy pages, the allure of another trade seemed unavoidable. Some of its display ads were for procedures I could imagine, more or less: lip augmentation, breast augmentation, breast reduction, laser hair removal, skin tightening, nose improvement, tattoo removal, acne scar revision, nonsurgical facial sculpting . . . Other procedures sounded risky, even terrifying: vaginal rejuvenation, gastric banding, skin tag removal, facial fat grafting, female corrective surgery, chemical peel . . . Then there were the terms you won't find in most dictionaries, terms that left me flummoxed: mesotherapy, pulsed light treatment, spider vein sclerotherapy, Brazilian buttock lift, radiance . . . *Radiance?* Los Angeles, I realized after scanning the eighteenth display ad for cosmetic surgery in the paper's first 45 pages, is a city of radiant images constantly being reshaped.

"Mark? Good to meet you." Douglas Brayfield's arrival prevented me from finding out what miracles of healing commerce might lurk on page 46. The Mexican waiter led us to a table across the room from a map showing "Scotland of Old." A psychotherapist by trade, Douglas deals with many clients who, like himself, have reinvented themselves in LA — he's also a poet who has written lyrics for musicals. "LA is more future-oriented than any other city in the States," he remarked over an augmented omelet. "People come here to remake themselves — to shed the past and start over. And not just once, but many times. Nothing stays the same; everything's in a constant state of flux. No one's status remains fixed. It can change on a dime. And often does, both up *and* down. That's why it's so exciting here. It's a dreamer's and a schemer's paradise."

Above his left shoulder, I noticed, was a display about the *Bluenose* —
a sailing ship from Nova Scotia that won race after race in the 1920s and
that still adorns the Canadian dime. Maybe John o'Groats was owned not
by Scots but by Canadians? There are, after all, said to be one and a half
million of us in southern California. The woman at the cash register set me
straight: "No, no, the owners are Germans. But they had a fish-and-chip
shop. And they decided to continue the theme."

Douglas emerged blinking into the spring sun. The traffic along Pico
Boulevard was steady but not alarming. Even so, he shook his head: "In the
next decade, they're predicting another five million people here. It's not a
pretty picture." From his home in the upscale suburb of Santa Monica, it's
sixteen miles to Downtown (in LA, that word is always capitalized), and the
drive often takes him more than an hour. "If they're too far away," he said,
"people don't *do* friends." This is, notoriously, a place where existing is
commuting. Cars here become not just an extension of home but an extension of self. "It's the sense of touch," a Los Angeles cop tells his partner in
the opening scene of *Crash,* which unexpectedly won the Academy Award
for best motion picture of 2005. "Any real city, you walk. You know, you
brush past people, people bump into you. In LA, nobody touches you.
We're always behind this metal and glass." The policeman is inside a car as
he speaks. "I think we miss that touch so much that we crash into each
other, just so we can feel something."

Outsiders can be overwhelmed by the sheer immersity of LA — the
way its astonishing range of peoples, landscapes and weathers, its five
counties and hundreds of municipalities, make it feel more like a country
than a city. During my weeks there, the *Los Angeles Times* ran a front-page
story about a merger between WB and UPN to form the new CW television
network. The article had nothing to do with personalities, programs or
finances, nor even the merciless rise of acronyms; it was about the misery
of a long commute. WB managers wanted the corporate headquarters to be
in the San Fernando Valley; their UPN counterparts were equally keen it
should be located in West LA. "Between West LA and Burbank in the Valley," one top executive said, "it's the two ends of the world."

Wherever CW finally pitched its multibillion-dollar tent, its managers
would doubtless go on speaking a unique brand of English that has evolved
over the past few decades in and around Hollywood — a hilly enclave
whose mystique belies the fact that it's home to just a fragment of LA's vast
entertainment industry. Agents and producers no longer bark out, "Have

him return a call"; they shorten the phrase to "Have him return." What I mean by "making a call" is now, in Hollywoodspeak, "rolling a call." The conversation completed, nobody "hangs up" — you jump or hop off the line. And you don't have many friends, either; in Hollywood, you're more likely to have frenemies. Over pasta and sparkling water one day in Beverly Hills, I asked a vice president of finance for an independent production company if she was aware of using such novel forms of language. "I guess so," she replied with a doubtful look. "Being in the midst of it, you get immune to it." People live in nonstop rewrite here. Language lives in nonstop rewrite.

That's one of LA's worlds, one of LA's idioms. There are many others. Jump or hop in your car in the morning, drive for a day, and by nightfall you'll have passed most of the major languages and ethnic groups on the planet. A recent PBS documentary, *Los Angeles Now,* makes a remarkable claim: "Once the whitest city in America, Los Angeles is now the most multicultural city in the history of the world." Maybe there's a trace of exaggeration involved; I don't know how you measure the accuracy of a statement like that. Still, what other cities might find problematic or unsettling is simply routine in LA. Some of its public high schools provide classes in Korean and Tagalog. Orange County — part of the suburban lurch or slither of Los Angeles toward the south — is said to be home to more Vietnamese people than anywhere outside Vietnam, and their language is taught in several of the county's high schools. This is not the O.C. of brazen, beach-blond beauty that Fox taught the world to imagine.

One day, having rolled a call to the University of California, Los Angeles, I picked up a copy of *u.c.l.a. slang 5,* an invaluable 98-page guide compiled by linguistics students in 2005. Some of the terms, like slang anywhere, are highly local — USC, for instance, is said to stand for "University of Second Choice," whereas UCLA has the edgy sense "University of Caucasians Lost among Asians." Many other words — "buzzed," "flake," "Mary Jane," "raunchy," "sucker" and the like — seem to have been around forever, or at least since I was young. Isn't that the definition of forever?

The liveliest expressions were the newest: morsels of raw language that had gone unharvested in earlier gatherings of campus slang. Many of them show not just what's being said in the halls of UCLA, but also what's being spoken by young Americans in general. "Dumb fine," for example, now means really attractive; "mad beef" means a conflict or problem; and if you have to defecate, you "drop the kids off at the pool." One of the commonest words in the book is "pimp," which has shed most of the negative connotations it still holds in mainstream society. A twenty-first-century pimp can be any man or boy successful with the opposite sex, the male equivalent of a "pimpette" or "pimptress"; and as an adjective, "pimp" is a casual synonym for stylish ("Those shoes are pimp"). As a verb, "pimp" has split into a trio of meanings: to wear, to speak to, and to make something stylish. (The last of these explains why an offshoot of the enormously popular MySpace website has the address pimp-my-profile.com.) I don't suppose I'll ever ask "Will you pimp those shoes?" — but then I'm not an undergraduate at UCLA. If I were, I might lounge around saying "A pimp pimp pimps pimpettes."

"Dumb fine" and "mad beef" show that other adjectives are also breaking loose from their traditional chains of disapproval. The process has already turned "wicked," "sick" and "bad" into terms of youthful praise. In *u.c.l.a. slang 5*, "sick" can mean either great or disgusting; "bad" carries a negative sense as a noun, but a positive one as an adjective; and "wicked" is unambiguously positive. "Tragic," similarly, has lately moved from the mournful to the sarcastic, and may be hurtling on toward the jubilant. At the Urban Dictionary website, the liveliest definition of "tragic" is "An expression of incredulity. Similar to 'Oh my god!,' 'No way!' . . . but perhaps most akin to 'I can't bear to look,' said while jostling for the best view." The entry comes with an example: "That nerd is really going to ask a cheerleader out — tragic!" It's not exactly *King Lear*. A second definition on the site points to an even more radical departure: "A common new adjective to describe a particularly good feeling or sight." To prove his point, the contributor added: "Yo, that bitch was tragic, dawg."

Pamela Munro, the linguistics professor who edited *u.c.l.a. slang 5*, has been collecting campus slang for more than twenty years. It's possible, she told me, to trace a history of pop culture through its impact on the language — "In the eighties the four main characters of *The Flintstones* all gave their names to slang. A 'Wilma' was an ugly girl, for example. The one that lasted longest was 'Barney.' Now, none of that survives." There is in every language a time to get, and a time to lose; a time to keep, and a time to cast away. In its words as in so many other facets of life, LA is especially talented at getting — and at casting away.

~

I hadn't dipped my feet in the Pacific Ocean for years. Which is as good a way as any of explaining why I found myself in Venice Beach one Saturday morning, standing beside a stall where a man was selling "handmade magnetic therapy jewellery" near a poster of Mullah Bush, the World's Most Dangerous Terrorist. Fifty yards up the boardwalk, another man sat cross-legged while grasping a homemade sign: "I Will Work 4 Marijuana." "That's right, I said marijuana," he announced as I strolled by. Pigeons whirled above the golden sand beyond a head shop offering bubbler pipes and Zippo flasks. Next door to Sexetera, a little boy wearing a tie peeked out from Shul on the Beach. Such incongruities, sometimes noticed, more often unremarked, have become integral to our sense of life in the present and to our projected image of the future. They are part of how we define and comprehend change. A century ago, porn shops were furtive and synagogues did not line a beach.

I walked on up to Santa Monica, passing a store on Main Street called Natural High — California Lifestyle Boutique and spurning an opportunity for "Personalized Herbal Consultations." Outside a café a block farther north stood a handwritten placard: "Raw Food Is Our Love-Letter to the World." You can't make this stuff up, I thought. What on earth was the "Therapeutic Prom" that the Santa Monica Civic Auditorium would soon be hosting? But opposite the global headquarters of the Rand Corporation, outside Santa Monica's swan-white City Hall, about forty people — mostly men, mostly dark-skinned, mostly dark-clothed, mostly hauling dark bags or suitcases — lay on the municipal grass, or wandered slowly across it. Los Angeles may be, in Pico Iyer's words, "the world capital of illusion, a kind of terminal of dreams"; it is also America's capital of homelessness, with at least twice as many homeless people as New York and more than ten times as many as Chicago.

The walk from Venice Beach had left me thirsty, so I found a Jamba Juice outlet and ordered a "Brazilian açai berry juice blend, infused w/ guarana, mixed with raspberry sherbet, soymilk, strawberries, blueberries, ice" to all of which was added, ostensibly for free, a "Vita Boost™ — 100% D.V. of 20 essential vitamins and minerals." What arrived in a plastic cup was thick, purple, chilly and expensive. I sat down to absorb it — "drink" seems the wrong word — beside a bulletin board advertising a Dharma Lecture by the Abbot of Chung Tai Zen Center in Houston, Texas. Maybe when incongruities pile up as thick as açai infused w/ whatever, the result is a well-known blankness, that inimitable SoCal glaze. If you're prone to metaphor, you might call LA the incubator of our future selves.

One evening in the following week I was loitering outside Frank Gehry's magnificent galleon in Downtown, otherwise known as Disney Hall, when I noticed a car atop a stairway by the main entrance. It wasn't obvious how the car had got there. I climbed the twenty-seven steps and found it was a 2006 Acura, "Official Automotive Sponsor of the Los Angeles Philharmonic." A panel set into the metal and glass said this: "The sophisticated AcuraLink™ satellite communication system receives data via the cutting-edge XM NowTraffic™ service, and updates are reflected on your screen." Even if you can understand this sentence, you're free to doubt it. For such is the language of bullies — language used not to communicate but to intimidate. It doesn't stoop to explain; instead it aims to dazzle by a pseudoscientific welter of trademarks, polysyllables, clichés and acronyms. "The RL with real-time traffic! Once you experience it, there's no turning back." Maybe that depends on the traffic.

My concert was still an hour in the future. Dusk fell on the vacant sidewalks and a *Blade Runner* frisson came over me. I suddenly remembered that in one of her early novels, Alison Lurie called this "the nowhere city." From somewhere beyond the shining skyscrapers down Bunker Hill, I heard the rumble of helicopters. I waited to cross Grand Boulevard for a view across the Civic Center's sunken park toward City Hall: an incarnation of an older future, familiar to millions in the past as the *Daily Planet* building of Superman's youth. A panhandler on the far side of the road — the only other pedestrian in sight — pressed the traffic button for me, and bellowed "Praise the Lord!" when I'd succeeded in crossing over. In Europe a park like this would be alive with people on a mild spring evening. Here the only sign of human or animal life was the pair of mallards swimming in circles around a fountain, refusing to admit they were lost.

After a couple of weeks in the city, I could easily sympathize. In its endless sprawl, its lack of planning, its creativity, its unpredictability, its gift for absorbing and transforming anything from anywhere, its erasure of boundaries, its flair for improvisation, its glamour, its power, Los Angeles bears an uncanny resemblance to the English language. New peoples are to one as new words are to the other. So Koreatown now has a burgeoning population of Bangladeshis? That's fine. And nearly half of the inhabitants of Glendale are Armenian? Terrific. And LA contains so many expat Iranians that it's sometimes called Tehrangeles? Great. The city's international airport, LAX for short, is the Ellis Island of our time. What's the problem?

Perhaps there isn't any problem. As Salman Rushdie once observed, "To migrate is certainly to lose language and home, to be defined by others, to become invisible or, even worse, a target; it is to experience deep changes and wrenches in the soul. But the migrant is not simply transformed by his act; he also transforms his new world. Migrants may well become mutants, but it is out of such hybridization that newness can emerge." Such is the perpetual hope, the spangled promise, of LA.

Until its supply of fresh water peters out, maybe the city can go on coping with an unending influx of newcomers. In her nonfiction book *Where I Was From,* Joan Didion persuasively argues that California's present mistakes and delusions are rooted in history. The criminally high rate of incarceration, the miserly funding of schools and universities, the breathless pace of growth: all these have been part of California life for generations. "Only recently," Didion writes, "did I come to understand 'change' itself as one of the culture's most enduring misunderstandings about itself." In 1881, the centenary of its founding, Los Angeles had just eleven thousand residents. In the following decade, the population grew 500 percent. Growth became a local pleasure and a civic duty. To boom was normal. It has been that way ever since.

"But there are so many foreigners all over Los Angeles," Gina Nahai said to me one day in a café near Rodeo Drive. Though she was born and brought up in Iran, she has lived in southern California for decades, and as a proud resident of Beverly Hills, she clearly excluded herself from the category of foreigner. Her four novels, all written in English, have been published in at least seventeen languages. Gina is slight and stylish (I refuse to call her "pimp"). "The interesting thing about LA," she remarked, "is that so many other languages here have not only survived but thrived." Farsi, Kurdish and Armenian are good examples. In each of those languages, actors and producers in Los Angeles make TV and radio shows that are hugely popular in the origin lands. During the 1980s and '90s, videocassettes from the city were sold in remote Iranian villages off the backs of trucks, cars, mules and donkeys. Then, just as DVDs were starting to render VHS technology obsolete, satellite dishes did the same to trucks and donkeys.

LA entertains the world; it also consumes the world. On a bright

Sunday morning, bypassing the nearby L. Ron Hubbard Life Exhibition, I wandered around the Hollywood Farmers' Market. One of the farmers was busy promoting his "Italian dandelion" and "Japanese cucumber (similar to Persian)." Customers had lined up in front of another stall to buy "wheatgrass juice" and "beanlicious humus." I think they wanted "hummus," though in the farmers' markets of California almost anything is possible, even "famous Aebleskiver from Solvang." This may be the only state in which a fruit grower would dangle "eccentric citrus" not as a threat but a promise.

Food is one of the easiest routes along which foreign words (*aebleskiver*, for instance) move into a language. Consider the advent of boba. I'd been hanging out at a Thai café in West LA that sold delicious iced coffee, and the first time a waitress asked me if I'd like some boba, I didn't know what she was offering. She meant a few spoonfuls of chewy tapioca, molded into plump bubbles that lurk beneath tea or coffee and need to be sucked up through a wide plastic straw. They taste sweeter and perkier than I've made them sound. Boba emerged in Taiwan in the 1980s, became a craze in Japan in the '90s, and entered North America in — where else? — a suburb of LA. Soon after I returned home from California, I ran into boba for the first time in Montreal. I hasten to say that I'm using the word in its American sense. In Taiwanese slang, *boba* are large breasts.

༄

Everything I've written so far about Los Angeles is true, as far as I know. But everything I've written so far is also profoundly inaccurate. If you think of LA as a room, it would be fair to say that I've been deliberately neglecting an elephant sitting by itself in the corner. Lots of Angelenos choose to do the same — they behave as if the elephant weren't there, or they pretend it's no bigger than a mouse. But soon I think they won't have a choice. The elephant is not aggressive. It just keeps on growing.

༄

Let's talk some more about food. While I was staying in the city, *West* (the Sunday magazine of the *Los Angeles Times*) carried a fine, quirky article by Dagoberto Gilb about how in the past couple of generations, Mexican food has become Americanized. Apart from words like "tortilla" and "taco," which are now so familiar it's hard to imagine any English-speaker in North America not understanding them, Gilb deployed the following terms: *masa, serranos, carne picada, queso fresco, rajas, huevos rancheros, árbol, espinaca, hongo, pozole, taquería, menudo, lengua, machacado, carne guisada, chicharrón, caraitas, manteca, limón, hijole, lonche, chalupa, fideo, grito* and *cochinita pibil*. All these words, remember, appeared not in some scholarly journal but in a mainstream magazine, one that aims to deliver an up-to-the-minute portrait of life in LA.

Gilb also used the phrases *N'hombre, que pinche desmadre!* (not translated) and *lo barato sale caro* (translated), and he finished his piece with a joke: *el perro caliente*. This is not a Spanish phrase — yet. But to catch the point, you have to know that *perro* is a dog and *caliente* means hot. Gilb was making a bilingual pun in a single language. On the magazine's cover was the word *chalupa*, untranslated. Editors are paid to know their readers. And what these decisions suggest is that the Americanizing of Mexico's food goes fork in fist with the Mexicanizing of America's language.

My elephant in the room, of course, is the phenomenal growth of Latin-American communities, cultures and languages in southern California. A few numbers are perhaps in order. Figures from the California Department of Education show that in 2005, in Los Angeles County alone, more than 561,000 children were classified as "EL": they had a mother tongue other than English, a language in which their skills were deemed inadequate for success in school. Of that total, almost 504,000 spoke Spanish. The combined figure for all other languages was only 57,000.

If you add in the numbers from Orange, Riverside, Ventura and San Bernardino counties — what might be called "Greater Los Angeles" or "the LA sprawl" — you find more than 823,000 Spanish-speaking children who were said to be struggling with English. The five counties also contained 461,000 Spanish-speaking children who had moved up from EL to "FEP": in other words, they once had trouble with English but now spoke it fluently. The total number of residents in LA County exceeds 10 million; Latinos are very close to (indeed, they may already form) an absolute majority. In today's Los Angeles Unified School District, roughly 73 percent of children are Latin American by origin; blacks, whites and Asians make up the remaining quarter.

I mentioned this last statistic to a woman whom I met over lattes at a museum. "Yes, but that's just the public system," she replied, as though private academies could somehow transform the picture, or as if children in public schools don't matter. In her world — the 2006 movie *Friends with Money* gives a fair idea of it — Mexican Americans are scarcely visible. You see them as janitors, cooks, waiters, gardeners, garage attendants, maids, construction workers, nannies, cashiers, chauffeurs, street cleaners, busboys — in short, you don't really see them at all. They form the unobtrusive backdrop of your life. You certainly don't listen to their voices.

There are regions of LA where the "you" of the previous sentences would never set foot. The 2000 census credited the city of Maywood, a few miles southeast of Downtown, with 28,083 people. More than 27,000 of them were Latino. Longtime black areas like Watts and Compton now have Latino majorities. With their *farmacias, discotecas* (music stores, not dance halls) and shops devoted to the lavish costumes for girls' *quince años* celebrations, entire blocks of Downtown sound and look more like Guadalajara than Seattle. But the pulse of the Latino community still beats in East LA — not so much a neighborhood as a *barrio.* One morning when I visited the East LA Market — more properly, El Mercado del Este de Los Angeles — I heard amid the bright disorder of its modest shops not a single English word. *Churros* were piled high in the food stalls. The basement was a jumble of hats, socks, baby shoes, discount blouses and Mexican magazines. Travel agencies offered cheap flights south. Western Union offices awaited clients needing to wire money in the same direction; each year, migrants are believed to remit more than $20 billion to Mexico from El Norte.

If governments are sometimes reluctant to admit how widely Spanish has spread in the city, businesses have no such compunction. Near the *mercado* a Miller Lite billboard did not bother to translate *Exige más.* Yet the majority of ads and corporate signs in the barrio used a blend of languages — the informal code-switching or verbal hodgepodge that many people call Spanglish (a term others loathe). A McDonald's billboard was an English-free zone but for the phrase "double cheeseburger." Driving through East LA, I passed the 5 de Mayo Bakery, not far from the Divino Salvador Pupeseria & Restaurant. Names can deliver a pointed signal. Aztlan Auto Sounds is presumably a business specialized enough to need some non-Latino customers, but to Latinos the word *Aztlán* sends a message. The legendary homeland of the Aztecs, it also refers to the territories the United States seized from Mexico in the nineteenth century. *Aztlán* now acts as a codeword for Chicano pride, power and resistance.

A quick note on terminology. I'm avoiding the label "Hispanic," which has a colonial ring to it, and which is applied *to* Spanish-speaking people in the United States while rarely being accepted *by* those people. Many Latin Americans prefer "Latino." But with its Mediterranean overtones, that word too is questioned by people — especially from Mexico and Central America — who proudly claim an indigenous heritage. At least 60 percent of all Latinos in the United States, and an even higher percentage in California, are Mexican American — their numbers dwarf those of South Americans, Central Americans, Cubans, Dominicans, Puerto Ricans and Spaniards combined. A lot of Mexican Americans call themselves Chicano, and I'll use this word from time to time in the pages that follow. But Chicano too is a problematic term, for it excludes other Latinos. No label is satisfactory. Nor do all Latino immigrants speak Spanish as a mother tongue. "It's a privilege to be a linguist here," Pamela Munro had told me, "because LA has the largest population of speakers of indigenous languages in the Americas." She didn't mean the speakers of California's Indian languages; most of those languages have already expired, or linger by death's door. Instead she meant "this huge influx of speakers of Mexican and Guatemalan languages," an influx that fills California even as it creates ghost towns in job-poor states like Oaxaca and Michoacán.

Whatever name they prefer to use, Latinos have often complained of being overlooked and ignored by America's cultural mainstream. "It seems as if we don't exist," the musician Lalo Guerrero pointed out in a witty song from the 1980s, "No Chicanos on TV." Guerrero noted that the trio of babies pictured in Huggies diaper commercials are black, white and Japanese. "Chicano babies also pee" — yet they're not to be found onscreen. Thinking about that song, I remembered my first, glimmering awareness of Chicano culture: how every Sunday night, growing up in western Canada, I would watch *The Ed Sullivan Show* on our black-and-white TV set, hoping that Herb Alpert & the Tijuana Brass would be among the guests. Songs like "The Mexican Shuffle," "Spanish Flea" and "Tijuana Taxi" were so catchy — and so unlike every other kind of music I knew — that I never thought to wonder if the slender, trumpet-toting Alpert had the least connection to Tijuana or anywhere else in Mexico. He was in fact a Los Angeles Jew who led a band, made up mostly of Italian Americans, without a single Latino member. In retrospect the act smacks of impersonation, of Negro minstrelsy. Yet in their desire to shape an image and their willingness to invent an identity, the Tijuana Brass were quintessentially LA.

Latinos are now a lot more audible and visible — even in TV commercials — than they used to be. But there are still subtle boundaries beyond which their voices do not reach. The 2004 movie *Spanglish* is a case in point. The film explores the not-quite-expressed love that develops between its hero, a trendy LA chef called John (Adam Sandler), and his gorgeous Mexican housemaid, Flor (Paz Vega). But in a typical Hollywood movie with a PG-13 rating, it would be too bold, too transgressive for the pair to spend even a single night together. All that the filmmakers permit John to do is drive Flor to his restaurant and cook her a sumptuous private meal. Besides, the film's title is misleading. John, his wife, his daughter, his son and his mother-in-law share their lives with immigrants (the housemaid and her daughter), yet the Anglo characters seldom utter a word of Spanish. Some critics praised *Spanglish* for its courage in presenting a modest amount of Spanish dialogue without subtitles. But what the movie shows is a Chicana already fluent in English and her sultry mother gradually becoming so. Neither of them uses a mixed language; the mother speaks good Spanish or slow, uncertain English. Linguistically speaking, *Spanglish* is a copout.

～

A generation after the triumphs of the Tijuana Brass, Los Angeles became known for a very different kind of music: gangsta rap. Its knife-in-the-face lyrics originated here in the bravura strut and thrust of Ice T, N.W.A. and other performers of the late eighties. One of the groups that personifies gangsta aggression, but also ventures beyond it, is a quartet called Cypress Hill. Their official website defines the music as "pioneering Latino hip-hop rock fusion." Cypress Hill has a song called "Latin Lingo" that defends and praises fusion of the linguistic kind. A line that begins with three words in English ends with three words of Spanish, the rhyme word ("fresca") leading into: "Here homes, have a hit of this yesca." "Yesca" is one of the countless slang terms for marijuana, a substance the group exalts in many of its songs. When other people "clown on" (make fun of) Cypress Hill's language, the band responds by announcing "straight up, it's called Spanglish." What's refreshing, even liberating, is the lack of apology.

"Yesca" does not show up in *u.c.l.a. slang 5*, but other Spanish words do. Most of them are recent borrowings. To be *enfuego* means to be doing well; *vato* signifies guy; a *frijolero* is a Latino; *esa* and *ese* are, respectively, female and male members of Latino street gangs. Such terms represent a critical shift: until the past few years, Spanish lacked the glamour — or Chicanos lacked the confidence — to act as a source of campus words. Latino students are still far fewer at UCLA than you'd expect. But in linguistic terms they're finally becoming audible.

It's as though Spanish-speakers, at long last, have stopped hiding, pretending or feeling ashamed of their tongue, and have begun to make use of the manifold resources at their disposal. Until the late twentieth century, the language was often excluded from America's public domain. Now Los Angeles contains a multitude of Spanish-language TV stations, newspapers, magazines, websites and radio stations — the radio is especially popular. The rest of the country appears to be following suit: the area around Portland, Oregon, not known as a hotbed of Latino culture, now contains ten radio stations that broadcast in Spanish (as late as 2003, it had only three). Growth on this scale alarms the proponents of movements like English First. Its executive director, Jim Boulet, Jr., has demanded the quick assimilation of all immigrants into the dominant language. "Treat Hispanics like Americans," he has said — as though they weren't American already. A favorite Chicano response is that their people didn't cross the border; the border crossed them.

The desire to move beyond cultural and linguistic borders — to make them all but irrelevant — lies at the heart of *Living in Spanglish: The Search for Latino Identity in America,* a 2002 book by the New York poet and journalist Ed Morales. He admits on his fourth page that to most people, "Spanglish is an ugly word. In its most literal sense, Spanglish refers to a bastardized language, an orphan, a hybrid, a mule — in short, a pathetic, clumsy creature incapable of producing viable offspring." Having got that out of the way, Morales proceeds to reclaim the word and the idea as deserving of celebration (preferably in a medley of samba, salsa, tango, hip-hop, mambo, ska, merengue, tejano, reggae, cumbia and boogaloo). He makes Spanglish a metaphor for inclusiveness, for joy. "I am my language," he writes, "and it is continually in the process of being born."

His language is not, it should be said, a creole. For creole languages are created by children, who pour their linguistic creativity into a previously existing pidgin. Creoles are more stable than an improvised, happenstance mix like Spanglish. Regardless of where their vocabulary comes from, creoles have a structural and grammatical cohesion. Anybody who speaks one employs a syntax independent of either parent language, and uses words that have undergone substantial change. Spanglish isn't like that. Its verbs can be Hispanicized — or not. The Lord's Prayer in Spanish opens with the words *Padre nuestro que estás en los cielos*. In Spanglish it might go *Our father que estás in heaven;* or, alternatively, *Padre nuestro who art en los cielos*. But in a true Spanish-based creole — the Palenquero language of northern Colombia — it sounds like this: *Tatá suto lo ke ta riba sielo.*

In its first incarnation, Spanglish involved not the Spanish absorption of English words but an English swallowing of Spanish terms: rodeo, bronco, ranch, patio, adobe, canyon and dozens more. Morales slyly observes that "every John Wayne movie you've ever seen is in Spanglish." Flash forward to the twenty-first century: a refusal to abide by the grammatical rules and separate lexicon of either language can look like permanent indecision, a neurosis of competing words. That's seen from the outside. From the inside, according to Morales, "when we speak in Spanglish we are expressing not ambivalence, but a new region of discourse that has the possibility of redefining ourselves and the mainstream." That region is one of continual movement — a dance of tongues, perhaps scary, more likely exhilarating. Where both Spanish and English are unavoidable, do they have any choice except to join forces? "The metaphoric language of the future," Morales declares, "is Spanglish."

One afternoon I walked into a small everything shop in LA, hoping to find a few T-shirts to take home to my family. Behind the racks of clothes that paid homage to bands like Green Day and My Chemical Romance, or that announced I ♥ GAY COWBOYS, I noticed a shelf of black T-shirts with white capital lettering. CHINGA TU MADRE, said one, followed by words in smaller print: HAVE A NICE DAY. Another declared TU ERES UN PENDEJO, with the afterthought YOU ARE MY FRIEND. Children, don't repeat these Spanish phrases. They rely on the ability of a viewer to grasp the profound discrepancy between the Spanish and English meanings. Only after a society has reached a significant threshold of bilingualism does the mass-market sale of such items become profitable.

By 2006 it was eminently profitable for the LA Memorial Coliseum to host a concert by a young Mexican pop group called RBD. Their show drew more than sixty thousand fans. Tickets on eBay sold for $200. The group jived and warbled in front of a giant Mexican flag. The *Los Angeles Times* review — it was headlined "*¡Viva la revolución!,*" complete with accent and

upside-down exclamation mark — gave a description of the group's cos-
tume: knee-high black boots, red tie, "*gorra* saucily perched on their heads."
I'm not sure what a *gorra* is. But then I don't live in LA, a city founded under the name El Pueblo de Nuestra Señora de Los Angeles de Porciúncula.
In a feature article about Spanglish published in the same newspaper, a
twenty-six-year-old Chicano bluntly declared: "No puedes describir la vida
aquí without speaking both." As the años speed by and the frijolero population surges, it's muy likely that Angelenos — gringos and nongringos alike
— will celebrate a shared lengua in which English is caliente and Spanish is
cool.

Think I'm exaggerating? Then consider "Qué Onda Guero," a 2005
song by the überhip musician Beck. His ethnic origins are a mixture of
Scottish, Canadian, Jewish, Norwegian and Swedish. But his language is
something else again. Lines like "Dirty borracho says 'qué putas!'" are written in perfect — that is to say, imperfect — Spanglish. The song is pure —
that is to say, impure — LA. Tomorrow está aquí.

It's a big story. Yet it's not the whole story.

૭

"In my own family I have a cousin," Cindy Mosqueda was saying. "She's like
ten. She doesn't speak too much." Too much Spanish, that is. Cindy, a graduate student in education at UCLA, is also a prolific blogger who incorporates Spanish words, phrases and sentences in many of her postings. "It's
the way I speak," she explained. "But as a child you're kind of embarrassed
to let people know you speak Spanish — like you're a recent immigrant or
something. My cousin went down to Mexico with us a couple of years ago.
But she still wouldn't speak Spanish. I don't know if she's embarrassed or if
she's forgotten. Like I'd say, 'Go to the kitchen' in Spanish, and she'd say,
'Huh?'"

When people complain about the growing language problem in southern California, they're usually referring to an imagined threat against English. Will its grammar decay? Will its standards erode? Will it eventually be
supplanted by Spanish? Amid all the anxiety, a couple of things are missing.
The first is any awareness of Spanish as an asset, a richness, a force for creativity, a link to other nations and cultures. The second is the perspective of
Latinos, the people who are causing the supposed menace. Judging by the
ones I met in Los Angeles, the threat is wildly overblown.

Cindy grew up in the city, the daughter of parents who immigrated as children in the 1960s. Her closest friends are other bilingual Chicanas. When I asked for a second time why she likes to sprinkle Spanish through her online journals and conversations, she used the word "comfortability. Trying to be able to say what I want to say. A few nights ago I was talking to a friend and I wanted to say someone's 'already committed to an event.' But I didn't say 'committed' — I used *comprometido* instead. Sometimes you're recounting a story and the Spanish goes better."

None of which means that Cindy is content with her second-language skills. "I majored in Spanish," she said. "I listen to a lot of music in Spanish, and I talk only Spanish with my grandparents." Yet her comprehension, as she knows, is far from perfect. "It's actually difficult for me to read *Cien Años de Soledad* — I have to look a lot of words up. Sometimes I feel I'm losing my Spanish. And I don't want to." Her two younger brothers don't speak Spanish well, so she always uses English with them. Hers is a classic story of an immigrant family, the same story that Americans who struggle to hold on to their Farsi or their Yiddish, their Armenian or their Vietnamese, could tell. Perhaps the only surprising thing about Cindy's version is how familiar it sounds.

It's important to realize that the majority of Chicanos in LA were born in California and speak English, not Spanish, as a mother tongue. In her excellent book *Chicano English in Context,* the linguist Carmen Fought describes how Chicanos tend to speak with a characteristic rhythm and melody — putting the verbal stress, for example, on the second syllable of "Thanksgiving Day" and the third of "morning sickness." (Their merger of high back vowels, making "pool" and "pull" into homonyms, has begun to spread to other groups in the Southwest.) A few items in their lexicon are also distinctive: when a boy is "talking to" a girl, he's dating her. Most of the young people in Fought's study could speak some Spanish, but when they did so, they often code-switched to English because of a lack of fluency. And if their parents were unable to say much in English, the young people felt embarrassed or frustrated.

When you dig below the surface of LA's Chicano expansion, then, you find a contradictory pattern, one that highlights the challenges still facing Spanish-speakers and the limits that continue to govern that language's use. Latin music, reggaeton in particular, is the mainstay of an enormously popular radio station that calls itself "Latino 96.3, Loud and Proud" (it also flaunted the slogan "The station that puts the LA in Latino"). But the patter and publicity that follow each song happen in a hip, street-smart English. If a caller speaks Spanish on the air, the DJs quickly steer the conversation over to English, translating if necessary. In Los Angeles, English has lately been forced to share some of its space. Yet its power remains unrivaled.

The same holds true on the East Coast, where Chicanos are outnumbered by Cubans (in Florida) and Puerto Ricans (in New York). In her 1997 book *Growing Up Bilingual: Puerto Rican Children in New York*, Ana Celia Zentella describes how the impoverished kids of Spanish Harlem used a mixture of languages to assert their dual identity as "Nuyoricans": "Because they had a foot in both worlds, they never spoke in one for very long without acknowledging and incorporating the other." Code-switching was an act of solidarity. At least, that's how the first generation behaved. Second-generation Nuyoricans were less keen to talk Spanish: "In every setting, including home, school-age children usually spoke English to each other, thus weakening the connection between Spanish and Puerto Rican culture, and threatening to edge out Spanish altogether."

That kind of erosion explains why some experts think of Spanglish as merely a transitional dialect. Most immigrant groups go through a three-generation pattern of language use: the newcomers speak little English, their children can function easily in two languages, and their grandchildren are fluent only in English. Spanglish, says the linguist Brian D. Joseph, could be seen as "either the middle generation's probably limited mixing of the languages, or the more extreme mixing seen in the third generation. I suspect that the third-generation sort of Spanglish is not likely to persist, but I could imagine that an English-influenced middle-generation variety could take on a life of its own." Yet do the nearly fifty million Americans of Latino origin behave like a typical immigrant group? Or, in their numbers, their diversity and their continuing high rate of arrival, will their pattern of language use and language loss differ from that of Swedes, Italians, Koreans and so many other newcomers?

What has kept Spanish vibrant in Manhattan is a constant back-and-forth movement between two very different islands. Because Puerto Ricans are migrants to the continental United States without being immigrants, they never have to bid their homeland a permanent goodbye. The particular form that Spanglish takes in New York is different from the form it has adopted in LA — or, for that matter, in the wealthy suburbs of Miami or the border country of south Texas. In all these places the blend of languages can act as a catalyst. Spanglish inspired the birth and growth of the Nuyorican Poets Café in Manhattan's *Loisaida,* or Lower East Side — a venue at the heart of the spoken word revival, a movement that made poetry once again a vibrant force beyond the printed page.

The mixing of English and Spanish is generally seen as a phenomenon unique to the United States and the frontier cities of northern Mexico. People farther south have no great need of it. "For Mexicans living in the USA," the Mexican novelist and critic Alberto Ruy-Sánchez told me, "Spanglish is an answer to a very specific problem: how to communicate and live in the USA. So, the people living in Mexico and not having that problem do not use it." Besides, as Ruy-Sánchez admits, English is taught poorly in most Mexican schools. Despite Mexico's vexed location — "so far from God," one of its presidents wryly observed, "and so close to the United States" — English has made fewer inroads in the country than in many parts of Europe, Asia and Africa. "Why should Mexicans speak Spanglish," asks the poet and translator Hugh Hazelton, "when they've been speaking Spanish for 500 years — even a highly original form of Spanish, with all sorts of expressions from Indian languages such as Náhuatl? At over 100 million, they're by far the largest Spanish-speaking country in the world, with an extremely solid vision of their own cultural uniqueness."

Yet the Mexican resistance to Spanglish may be about to change. "As a vehicle of communication of global proportions," Ilan Stavans wrote in his essay "Spanglish: A User's Manifesto," "Spanglish is present across the hemisphere, from Buenos Aires to Santo Domingo, where, thanks to American fashion and sports and obviously Hollywood movies, it has become de rigueur for people of all backgrounds." Stavans is the unofficial laureate of Spanglish — a man who performed the quixotic task of translating part of *Don Quixote* from Spanish to Spanglish. He sees Spanglish as a highly creative idiom that is fast retracing the footsteps of Yiddish: a previous example of an informal fusion tongue that had no fixed address and that came under vicious criticism in its heyday. Only the language's near-death experience under Hitler and Stalin turned scorn into the loving nostalgia that now washes over what is left of Yiddish.

Not all of Stavans's peers delight in the power of American fashion, sports and movies. "Every Latin-American intellectual I speak to these days," says the novelist and critic Stephen Henighan, "complains about the level of Spanish emanating from TV shows. More and more of them are produced in Miami and incorporate Spanglish, beaming it into places like Peru and Argentina where Spanglish otherwise would not penetrate." Los Angeles, for better or worse, may be just a beginning.

ᗌ

"Mixing languages here is done with great gusto," Otto Santa Ana remarked. "It's a marvelous thing to listen to — like having two pocketfuls of change." Trained as a sociolinguist, Otto is now a professor of Chicano Studies at UCLA. He's also a miner's son from a small town in Arizona; growing up in Aztlán, he learned to swear in Spanish, English, Serb and Apache. Otto now spends much of his time on discourse analysis — his 2002 book *Brown Tide Rising* examines how the U.S. media use metaphors that characterize immigrants in terms of flood, crime, burden and disease. He declines to speak of language fusion as any of the above: "The greatest fun with language always comes at recess in a high school, where kids with all that energy to create language have been freed to do what they want to do." Language as fun: in the academy, that's a radical concept.

Not that Otto is blind to the difficulties Spanish-speakers face in the heartland of the world's most powerful language. "I counsel lots of young parents who want to raise their children bilingually," he said, glancing out his office window at the monolingual campus below. "And it's not easy. I tell them to find meaningful experiences that would justify using Spanish, not trying to just slip it in. Things like a visit to a soccer game with immigrants, or spending time with the grandparents. Best of all, get the kid to spend two or three weeks in Mexico so that the passive bilingual becomes active again. It's like sprouting the little, withered, Spanish-speaking plant by putting it in good soil."

We walked from his office over to his car, and Otto drove to a Mexican restaurant he wanted to try out. The rush-hour traffic having reached its usual impasse, he whipped out his cellphone, switched languages and reserved a table. Once we'd found the restaurant — a soccer game from Guadalajara lit up a small TV set in the corner — the staff didn't know whether to address us in Spanish or English. A waiter asked, in Spanish, if we wanted a *mesa* or a booth. Aptly for a linguist, Otto decided to try *lengua en mole.* But the result disappointed him. And the longer we chatted, the more his optimism appeared to fade.

"All of us suffer an atrophying of Spanish," he said. "I don't think most Chicano kids court in Spanish — Chicano English is spoken by great numbers of people here. A lot of my students are angry that they don't speak better Spanish." In the daily lives of most Chicanos, the Spanish language is far outweighed. Children are generally hungry to use English, even if their parents try to maintain Spanish at home. Nor do the city's Spanish TV and radio stations provide much of an incentive for young people to speak the language, because, in Otto's words, "the experience of mass media is passive. It blares at you." Admittedly, the website of Latino 96.3 contains a "Shoutout Box" where listeners can blare back in either language or both; but most days the English messages easily outnumber the Spanish. A typical entry: "wanna shout out to all my salvadorenas from l.a. what up with the song from randy and jowell ya no te veo."

Full bilingualism, Otto suggested, is now less prevalent among Chicano kids than it was in the 1940s — although, of course, a lot more Chicano kids are around today, many thousands of them "undocumented." Like their identity, their use of language is unofficial; often their verbs and prepositions follow a Spanish model. But that doesn't mean they're unable to communicate. "Why," asked Carmen Fought, "have we sociolinguists failed to make it understood by the general public that Chicano English is not a deficiency and bilingualism is not a threat?" Across most of the world, bilingualism is looked on as an asset, an opportunity. And the world is growing ever smaller. In *English Next*, David Graddol goes so far as to suggest that "monolingual English speakers face a bleak economic future."

⌇

One day I braved the threatening freeways and drove east for a couple of hours to Pomona, a long-downtrodden town near the border of Los Angeles County. This is where the singer Tom Waits grew up. I passed a mall where Sunshine Donuts had a special on burritos, the unfortunately named Hūng Dịch Vu was offering tax services, and Medical Weight Control peered across the asphalt at DriveThru Wienerschnitzel, with its "Big Dawgs (New! ⅓ lb.)." No thanks. Leaving Pomona behind, I headed up the road to Claremont, the improbably snowcapped mountains growing taller with each passing block. A bumper sticker on a passing car said REPUBLICANS FOR VOLDEMORT. This small and elegant city, self-consciously reminiscent of New England, is the home of the exclusive Claremont colleges. Its downtown, where people were actually walking around, boasts a Thoreau Bookshop and a Verbal Building — no, really. The Verbal Building, a former bank, contains a pizza joint. But Susana Chávez-Silverman preferred to meet me at her favorite table in a bar called The Press. The waiter knew exactly how she likes a martini.

Susana, an ebullient redhead of a certain age, teaches Romance languages at Pomona College in Claremont and is the author of a 2004 memoir, *Killer Crónicas: Bilingual Memories.* If a few of the critics are right, the book points the way to a new literary language for America. A random example: "No la puedo creer and oh god, qué horror, get over yourself, girl, I'm like an Annie Lennox song on constant replay, here come those tears again y no puede ser que padezca estas *daily* sob sessions: qué carajo me pasa?" Hers is code-switching of heroic, even manic proportions. Every paragraph, almost every sentence, jumps between languages like a rabbit on speed. You can't say the book is in either English or Spanish; it's written in a breathless, elusive, allusive, punning blend of the two. Spanglish is the only word for it.

The origins of *Killer Crónicas* lie in e-mails that Susana sent to her far-flung friends while she was living in Buenos Aires — "I'm like baroque in e-mail anyway," she told me, "very long and formal." Praise for the memoir has not been unanimous — in Puerto Rico, for example, the intellectual elite sees it as important to hold on to "proper" Spanish. (An echo, no doubt, of the great Mexican poet Octavio Paz, who once declared that Spanglish was neither good nor bad, but abominable.) "But this is not a capitulation to English," Susana told me, removing her fat and funky glasses and fixing me with a look. "It's part of me!" A part that divided her own family: "For my grandmother, code-switching está fine. But my mother was like, 'You need to speak good English and good Spanish, and nothing in between.'" The literary predecessors of *Killer Crónicas* were mostly barrio narratives, in which Spanglish emanates from lives of poverty and humiliation, the mixed-up language embodying a worn-down existence. By contrast, Susana is the daughter of an eminent scholar, Joseph Silverman, and in her world the only gangs are intellectual ones.

I asked if, when she reshaped her e-mails into book form, she found herself adding or deleting the Spanish phrases more than the English. "No," she replied without missing a beat, "it's bisexual." Such verbal bravado enables her, in *Killer Crónicas,* to set American Latinos the subversive challenge of asserting their own linguistic duality — of losing their shame about who they are. For some, the merging of languages provokes fear and annoyance. It gives Susana immense pleasure: "Y siempre, signs de mi daily Latinidad, mi Chicana, code-switching life, right here en la cuenca de Los Angeles. Simón, mano. Califas. Orale vato. Carnal, you know?"

Admittedly, few other Chicanos choose to code-switch with such zest or intensity. "Chicano life in the U.S.," Susana remarked with evident regret, "happens primarily in English, with a few words in Spanish used like a salsa to prove ethnic authenticity." (So much for Spanish as a growing menace.) With a Jewish father, a Chicana mother and a Cajun partner — "He looks like a cross between Jesu Christo and Johnny Depp" — Susana takes no interest in ethnic authenticity. In *Killer Crónicas* she celebrates hybrid cultures in an ecstatically hybrid language: "I think it's fun, and life is short. It's a privilege, that language can be a game." Of course most people don't have that privilege, or they choose not to make use of it. Pero for those who are so inclined, southern California — excuse me, SoCal — offers el máximo opportunity.

I drove back to my hotel in West LA and a freeway shone in the sun. *Radiante.* Dumb fine.

7

Every Single Trend

Black English and Hip-Hop

I T'S FORTUNATE THAT Edith Folb was good at pool. The skill allowed her to spend long hours hanging out with young black males in South Central Los Angeles, listening to them speak. Not many female, white linguists have that kind of opportunity. Folb seized it at intervals between 1967 and 1976, gaining insights for a volume that Harvard University Press would publish under the title *Runnin' Down Some Lines: The Language and Culture of Black Teenagers.* The attention she paid to their everyday language "moved teenagers to 'high sign' (show off) their knowledge . . . [prompting] not only verbal display, but a sense of pride in the user. Too many young blacks were burdened with a negative and self-deprecating image of their speech. Here was a situation in which their vocabulary use was being positively valued." Folb's book is a landmark study of an obscure inner-city culture about to become world famous.

She watched young men "shooting the dozens": playing a game of insults, with most of the abuse being tossed at their opponent's mother. "Your momma's so fat, she needs wheels to turn the corner" is among the few G-rated specimens. Sometimes the insults took the form of rhyming couplets. The dozens was usually played among friends; to attempt it with strangers was too risky, too likely to spiral up into physical combat. A similar game, "cracking on" somebody, involved hurling jokes back and forth at high speed. Amid the squalor of Watts and Compton, young men could win prestige by their command of words. An element of head-to-head competition — of battle, even — was essential to their view of life. Along with their witty or brutal dismissal of others, they would boast about their own prowess: sexual, of course, but also verbal.

Indeed, Folb explained, "Good talk — whether in the form of public performance like shooting the dozens or running down a toast (an epiclike vernacular poem in narrative form) or in private or semiprivate raps like getting over to a young lady or capping on some pootbutt — is highly valued among teenagers." A pootbutt, then and now, is a stupid or lazy person who deserved nothing better than to be lied to (capped on). A lame talker could also be badmouthed with ease. He would lose and lose again at the wordsport that brought his peers so much esteem. You needed to be adroit with language if you hoped to be a pimp. And South Central LA was, probably still is, a 'hood where lots of teenage boys shared that particular dream. For them, Folb noted, "the pimp's game is the ultimate one."

"Hey bro', what 'tis?" she recorded one young man asking another. "Playin' the game from A to Z," he replied. "Fiendin' and leanin', wheelin' and dealin', cappin' and blowin', restin' and dressin'. I'm driving in a Cad with four doors and four whores, one pimp in the trunk, sniffin' cocaine and smokin' dope and drinkin' champagne." Words of a material boy, dreaming in the material world. In the wildest and happiest of his dreams, he was already a player. Deftness at rhyming — the speech above could be printed as lines of verse — might help him attain that goal.

To read *Runnin' Down Some Lines* decades later is to experience a weird sense of déjà vu — of eavesdropping on history about to unfold. Folb was describing a bunch of youths who felt vulnerable, marginal, impoverished. In the face of white-run society — "the Man," they would have said — they seemed powerless. They expected little from the future. And yet in some important ways the future belonged to them. The future was manifest in their gangs — Brims, for example, who were not yet known as Bloods — already advertising their claim to public space by spray-painting graffiti that were not yet known as tags. The future was also manifest in their lexicon: "wannabe," "get-go," "booty," "trash talk," "homeboy" and other terms that were destined to enter the American mainstream, little though Folb or her publisher knew it (the book comes with an extensive glossary, some of which is now unnecessary). Above all, the future was manifest in their rap.

Except that hip-hop hadn't been invented back then. In the early 1970s "rap" did not mean to rhyme above a beat; it was a common word for talk itself. And in an oral culture like South Central LA, rap mattered. "See yo' rap is your thing," Folb recorded a young pool hustler as saying. "I's like your personality. Like you kin style on some dude by rappin' better 'n he do. Show 'im up. Outdo him conversation-wise. Or you can rap to a young lady, you tryin' to impress her, catch her action — you know — get wid her sex-wise. Like, 'Hey baby, you one fine lookin' woman. Let's you and me get better acquainted.' You can school the brother wi' cho rap. Run down some heavy lines, tell 'im what's happenin'." Rap could serve as a weapon, an invitation, a reproof, an education; it could be a competition or a useful service. But always it came invested with the speaker's character. Excluded from the hustler's list of meanings was the kind of formal talk required in school. Standard English, the language of report cards and government documents, failed to qualify as rap.

Put together the rap, the toasting, the boasting, the dozens and the graffiti, and you have the foundations of global youth culture stretching ahead into the twenty-first century. Without knowing it, Forb's informants were hip-hop's precursors. What's missing, of course, are what young black men in the Bronx were starting to provide at almost the exact moment when Folb stopped shooting pool in South Central: the beat and the dance; DJs and B-boys. (In the initial-rich realm of hip-hop, DJs are the ones who organize the rhythm to which B-boys dance and MCs — masters of ceremonies, or microphone controllers — rap and sing.) The pioneers of hip-hop took all this, the verbal and the nonverbal, and fused it into a movement, a "nation" whose citizens needed no passports and respected no borders. Their genius was to blend protest and pleasure, fury and joy.

When I visited that small-town high school near Montreal and listened to those white sixteen-year-olds, many of the new words I heard had started off in hip-hop. I could have had a similar experience in high schools across much of the planet. If we want to grasp the music, the dress, the behavior, the moves, the very language of the young, we need to learn about American black culture. And Black English.

❧

It goes by several names, all of them problematic: Black English, Black Vernacular, African American English (AAE) and African American Vernacular English (AAVE), to mention a few. In the mid-1990s the term Ebonics (a blend of "ebony" and "phonics") lurched to sudden fame after the Oakland Unified School Board passed a well-meaning but misguided resolution declaring Ebonics to be the "predominantly primary" language of black children. Many of those children floundered in school, where teachers scorned their accent and their speaking habits. But instead of focusing on practical ways to improve the teaching or to boost inner-city kids' chances in the classroom, the creators of the Oakland resolution announced that Ebonics was no kind of English — not even, they said, any kind of Indo-European language — but rather a "genetically based" member of the "West and Niger-Congo African Language Systems." If they wanted to make their cause look intellectually ridiculous, they could hardly have made a better job of it.

In fact, the informal English spoken on occasion by most black Americans is closely related to the dialect of southern whites. The lengthening of short vowels, a reliance on double negatives, some systematic changes in verb forms — all these are qualities of white speech in states like Alabama and South Carolina and of black speech across the United States. Given the cruelties of history, the resemblance may appear ironic. But it should not be surprising, given that both dialects emerged from the same principal source: the nonstandard English that belonged to the Scots, Welsh, Irish and emigrants from rural England in the seventeenth and eighteenth centuries. These were the colonists who had the greatest contact with newly arrived African slaves, sometimes overseeing their labor, sometimes working beside them in fields and plantations. These were the people whose voices most strongly influenced the slaves as they embarked on the painful task of becoming English-speakers.

It may be consoling to imagine that Ebonics is an African tongue, totally different from the language of the Ku Klux Klan, but it's not true. The linguist John McWhorter demonstrated this in his 1998 book *Word on the Street*. Being black himself, McWhorter was better placed than most linguists to call the myth a myth. Other authors have shied away from plain speaking, in case the truth might cause offense. The Wikipedia entry for "African American Vernacular English," as of April 2007, said this: "AAVE shares many characteristics with various Creole English dialects spoken by black people in much of the world. AAVE also has pronunciation, grammatical structures, and vocabulary in common with various West African languages."

Pronunciation, granted. But if you look at grammar, vocabulary and Creole "dialects" (a better word is "languages"), you'll find that most of the supposed similarities come down to wishful thinking. Pivotal differences exist between Black English and Gullah, a remarkable idiom that emerged centuries ago on the Sea Islands off Georgia and the Carolina coast. Those islands were populated by former slaves from the Caribbean who spoke a form of Creole. Gullah itself is a creole. Black English is not. It recalls the ancestral continent of its speakers less in its linguistic structure than in the habits of community use: a fondness for "call and response," a valuing of indirect statements, a willingness to interject and so on. Socially, rather than structurally, Black English echoes Africa.

It has just as much intellectual rigor, just as much precision as any other form of English. The year after the Ebonics controversy blew up in Oakland, the Linguistic Society of America stated: "The systematic and expressive nature of the grammar and pronunciation patterns of the African American vernacular has been established by numerous scientific studies over the past thirty years. Characterizations of Ebonics as 'slang,' 'mutant,' 'lazy,' 'defective,' 'ungrammatical,' or 'broken English' are incorrect and demeaning." Unfortunately, talk-show hosts have more power to affect how Americans think about language issues than all the linguists in the land, and there are talk-show hosts who find Black English an agreeable target. Countless dialects have suffered ridicule over the years. Few, if any, have endured so much of it as Black English.

From its birthplace amid cotton and tobacco, the dialect expanded with the northward and westward migration of African Americans that began in the late nineteenth century. Given the enormous contributions that black people have made to language and culture in America, it's dismaying to realize what meager attention most of the supposed experts on the subject used to pay them. H. L. Mencken, in the fourth edition (1936) of his seven-hundred-page book *The American Language,* referred more often to the *Baltimore Evening Sun* than to black people and their ways of speech. "The Negro dialect," he wrote, "as we know it today, seems to have been formulated by the songwriters for minstrel shows; it did not appear in literature until the time of the Civil War."

Minstrel shows? In truth, it's worth reiterating, Black English is an idiom whose speakers developed their own systematic rules of pronunciation and grammar. Yet it's not a dialect African Americans speak all, or even most, of the time. They code-switch with ease and fluency between Black and Standard English, depending on the needs of the moment. Spike Lee's first feature-length movie, *She's Gotta Have It,* is set in Brooklyn in the 1980s and has an entirely black cast. Most of the characters talk in Standard

English, but at critical moments they switch (not "lapse") into the vernacular. Lee himself plays the role of Mars, a wayward young bicycle courier.
Late one night Mars phones his girlfriend, Nola, and finds her in bed with
one of her other lovers. In his annoyance he calls another woman and says,
"Yo, Roxanne, wassup? I bin thinkin' about ya." At a tense Thanksgiving
dinner that Nola cooks for all three of her men, Mars says: "Ya ain't down,
so chill." (One of his rivals stiffly replies: "How much longer must I tolerate
these low-down ghetto Negroes?") Black talk serves much the same purpose for Lee that Indian expressions do for novelists like Anita Rau Badami:
the colloquial keeps the language real. In *She's Gotta Have It*, the formal job
descriptions of the closing credits are followed by the words

A Spike Lee Joint
Ya Dig Sho-Nuff
By Any Means Necessary

ᔐ

Working with young black men in the early 1970s, Edith Folb found them
suffering from "a negative and self-deprecating image of their speech."
Spike Lee, the most prominent black director in the history of American
movies, may have removed a small part of that burden. Much more of it
has been lifted by hip-hop, a cultural movement whose verbal style springs
from the inner city. Because the wealthiest and most famous MCs of every
background work in Black English, their rhymes give the dialect a trium-
phant, brash validation. In the words of Claire Levy, the author of a recent
essay on rapping in Bulgaria, "Hip-hop and rap music . . . constitute a
global urban subculture that has entered people's lives and become a universal practice among youth the world over. Listening to contemporary urban soundscapes, whether in shops, in discos, or from the open windows of
passing cars, the throw of low-frequency beats under rapping voices is
ubiquitous."

New York — hip-hop's birthplace, Lee's home turf — continues to
produce dominant MCs. One of the current kings of the hill, Jay-Z, is a
Brooklyn boy who grew up in a housing project in the Bedford-Stuyvesant
neighborhood. A high school dropout from a single-parent household, he
now runs a multimillion-dollar corporate empire that draws its profits not
just from music but also from jewelry, footwear, lines of clothing, a night-

club and part of a National Basketball Association basketball franchise. Jay-Z's humble background, though, remains essential to his image; it gives him the street cred that many of his enterprises need. Let's take a look at his song "So Ghetto." It showcases both his wealth and his roots — and it displays Black English in action.

The song is set in his hometown. "Nobody rap Brooklyn like me," Jay-Z brags, omitting the *s* from the third-person-singular verb. That dropped *s* is typical of Black English, as is the nonstandard pronoun in the phrase "them boys shot him." By boasting about Bentley coupes, the Grammy Awards and the White House lawn, he evokes a tremendous feeling of distance between his present way of life and the violence of his former 'hood. Yet he does so in the language of the inner city, using both its grammar (a reliance on double negatives; the loss of the verb "to be" in most of its forms) and its pronunciation (the dropping of the final *g* from verbs that end in *ing;* the replacement of a *th* sound by *d*). If you come to hip-hop as an outsider, the first time you hear the song you'll probably be lost for words, lost among words. But like any other mode of speech, Black English grows easier to follow the more you listen to it. Thanks to performers like Jay-Z — one of his albums has sold eight million copies — it's a dialect the world has learned.

Black English has been a fertile inventor of words for well over a century. In his 1994 book *Juba to Jive: A Dictionary of African-American English,* Clarence Major listed dozens of terms that were specific to the 'hoods of LA long before the advent of gangsta rap. They include old expressions such as "dinosaur" (penis), "thousand-eyes" (shoes with toe perforations), and "buy a woof ticket" (intimidate). "Homey" started off in the 1930s referring to a southerner newly arrived in a northern city; half a century later, it meant someone from your own neighborhood. By the new century, "homey" (or "homie") had become a common term on the UCLA campus in the affluent realms of West LA. It now evokes a friend, regardless of race. Introducing the 2005 edition of *u.c.l.a. slang,* Pamela Munro noted that "the most important source of slang words in current use at UCLA is African-American English" — not thanks to an abrupt influx of black students, but "due to the increasing popularity of rap music and African-American-themed television." "Homeboy" is an obvious noun. Less obvious are verbs like "front" (to pretend or lie) and "be fiending for" (to desire intensely). But the linguistic wellspring is the same.

Words that students keep hearing on their iPods become words those students speak.

To feed America's hunger for fresh vocablulary, hip-hop demands novelty. The past is good for sampling, not echoing. "African Americas are on the cutting edge of the sociolinguistic situation in the USA," proclaims the hip-hop scholar H. Samy Alim. He sees Hip-Hop Nation Language, or HHNL, as "the cutting edge of the cutting edge." "We can glimpse this inventiveness in "So Ghetto" as the song nears its end and Jay-Z, having rapped for a few minutes, says "yeah, beyotch." Urban Dictionary defiines "beyotch" as "a friendly use of the word bitch. Usually used in greeting one's friend, or when one has succeeded over someone." What started as a change in pronunciation sometimes ends up as a change in meaning. "Beyotch" and its variant "beatch" may be encroaching on "bitch"; in July 2006, a few years after "So Ghetto" appeared, an MTV announcer called the white pop singer Ashlee Simpson "one sore beyotch." Another word that began life in the inner city is "doo-rag," a covering for the head. And in a later song called "All I Need," Jay-Z enumerates his desires and finds they include "a doo-rag and a pocket full of loot."

The man with the money and the lavish habits — "I burn cheddar," he boasts — identifies himself there as "Jigga-Man." Doesn't he call himself Jay-Z? Well, yes, but at other times he has gone by Jigga Slim, Big Homie, Jay-Hova, Young Hov, Hovito and Hovi Baby — the list could go on. His government name is Shawn Carter (the man has also referred to himself as S-Dot, not to mention President Carter), and the album on which "So Ghetto" appears is entitled *Vol. 3: Life and Times of S. Carter.*

One of the first practices in the hip-hop movement was tagging: graffiti that entails decorating a surface with an artist's invented name, curlicued and distorted so as to twist language into a visual statement. Not all the early taggers were black; many were white or Latino. But most of the prominent MCs and DJs were and are black. And MCs and DJs seldom go by their original names. This is more than accidental. Name invention among black performers is a powerful device, one with deep and painful roots. "The simple English word *name*," declared the critic Houston A. Baker, Jr., in *Long Black Song*, "has an awesome significance for black American culture that it can never possess for another culture; the quest for being and identity that begins in a nameless and uncertain void exerts a pressure on the word *name* that can be understood only when one understands black American culture." During the Middle Passage from Africa to the Western Hemisphere, the identities of black people were erased. In America, slaves could not keep their African names. Many European immigrants landing on Ellis Island also experienced a slight or not so slight change of name — but they never had to take on the identity of an owner. Slaves in the New World were, literally, un-named.

After the Civil War, freedom gave blacks the chance to rename themselves. Novels by Toni Morrison, James Baldwin, Richard Wright and other black writers attest to the power of naming and misnaming; and the process carries on. In 2004 a young Jamaican-Canadian playwright and actor born as Debbie Young gave herself the name D'bi.young.anitafrika. As a white man, I can't imagine doing anything this radical. My surname goes back more than a thousand years to a village in west-central England; it grounds me in a landscape, a history. It gives me a kind of ancestral belonging. The vast majority of African Americans have been denied that sense. They owe English no reverence. It's a language they were shackled into.

Consequently they have, in genealogical terms, a deeply problematic relationship with English. In *The American Language,* H. L. Mencken's only substantial reference to black people involved "Negroes . . . reaching out for striking and unprecedented names. They have, rather curiously, inherited no given-names from their African ancestors." (It's rather more curious that Mencken didn't realize why.) He listed some remarkable names, assuming his readers would find them hilarious, and added: "The young brethren who deliver colored mothers in the vicinity of the Johns Hopkins Hospital in Baltimore sometimes induce the mothers to give their babies grandiose physiological and pathological names, but these are commonly expunged later on by watchful social workers and colored pastors. *Placenta, Granuloma* and *Gonadia,* however, seem to have survived in a few cases." Malcolm Little and Cassius Clay were not cursed by grandiose physiological names. Yet they chose new identities — Malcolm X and Muhammad Ali — and gained enormous strength. Whoopi Goldberg, Maya Angelou and bell hooks have done the same.

Many of America's black musicians have also defined themselves anew. The rapper born as O'Shea Jackson had an Irish first name and an English surname; the world listens to him as Ice Cube. Christopher Wallace shared his surname with the politician who declared, "Segregation now, segregation tomorrow, segregation forever"; he took the names Biggie Smalls, Big

Poppa and The Notorious B.I.G. Of course, the freedom to make such transformations is not always used wisely. In the 1990s Prince Nelson, better known as Prince, changed his name to an unpronounceable symbol for love, and for some years had to be called The Artist Formerly Known as Prince; eventually he reverted or dechanged.

Before hip-hop, there was rhythm and blues. Before R & B, there was jazz (originally not a style of music but a word on the lips of black Americans, meaning sex). Most of the major jazz musicians, like the major rappers, were black; and they had to earn their titles. Duke Ellington was not always a duke; he was Edward at birth. King Oliver wasn't a monarch; he was an ordinary Joe. Charlie Parker kept his own name, but many of his compositions play on his nickname: "Bird of Paradise," "Bird's Nest," "Ornithology" and the like. Likewise, John Coltrane wrote numbers he called "Blue Train" and "Chasing the 'Trane." Naming became for black jazz musicians an act of resistance to an unjust system in which their compositions were often stolen, their creativity betrayed.

Hip-hop has carried on the naming tradition to the point where up-and-coming white rappers feel impelled to create a linguistically acceptable identity. "White kids invited to the hip hop party," the great rapper Chuck D wrote on his blog in 2006, "had to walk gingerly on the black paper rug of afrocentricity. It was a entrance fee of respect beyond the registers of retail." And so Robert Van Winkle became Vanilla Ice (as part of his entrance fee, he claimed to have been enrolled at an all-black high school and to have filled his youthful days with crime; both claims were false). Robert Ritchie chose the name Kid Rock. Marshall Mathers became Eminem.

To prove he could make it as an elite MC — to prove he could "keep it real" — Eminem took key elements of Black English and expressed them in his nasal, high-pitched voice. In "Never 2 Far," a cut from his first album, he raps: "If you disagree, you missin' the key." To say "you're missing" might not stand him in good stead in inner-city Detroit ("the D"). Later in the song, Eminem uses vocabulary ("fronted"), pronouns ("them's") and verb forms ("ain't") that are familiar in Black English. Just as Paul Robeson had to master Shakespearean English before he could play Othello on the London stage, so Eminem had to make Black English his own before he could win a fat recording contract. In "Never 2 Far" he doesn't say "hey"; he says "yo."

As do countless other Americans. A friend of mine — a pediatrician in his thirties named Shuvo Ghosh — rapped in his college days at Johns Hopkins, where he was in a band named BB and the Monkey. Shuvo was BB, short for "brown boy"; he and his roommate, the Monkey, were both of Indian descent. "That name wouldn't have flown," Shuvo admits, "if there'd been an African-American guy in the group." Other members were Filipino, Korean and white. "But a few of our songs," he recalls, "really were in Black English. We were consciously writing in an old-school hip-hop style." To give the group a semblance of legitimacy, both the Monkey and BB had to assume a more aggressive posture in performance than was natural to them: "We came at it hard, as they say." Fifteen years later, Shuvo lives in Montreal; when he can find the time, he and a couple of friends perform a very different style of music. "Yet I find, because of our experience, there's hip-hop influence underlying what we do. It's the language we use."

༺༻

The language they use. Another of the songs on *Vol. 3: Life and Times of S. Carter* is called "Jigga My Nigga," and its chorus includes the line "Niggaz better get it right, bitches better get it right." On the Internet, some versions of this song spell the n-word as "niggaz," others as "niggas"; but none would use the term with an *er* ending. The distinction was brilliantly summed up by the LA rapper Tupac Shakur in an interview on MTV: "Niggers was the ones on the rope hanging out on the field. Niggas is the ones with gold ropes hanging out at clubs." The second album of his short career was called *Strictly 4 My N.I.G.G.A.Z.* It's a word that still has enough shock value for some hip-hop performers to brandish it whenever possible — DMX, a hardcore, gratuitously offensive MC, shouts about "niggas" eighteen times in "Get At Me Dog."

However violent and unpleasant his lyrics, few people would deny that DMX (a black ex-con) has a right to speak about niggas. No rapper has ever set out to please well-meaning liberals — that would be the kiss of death. But what if a white-trash boy grabs hold of the most famous element of Black English grammar, the "habitual be," and tosses the n-word into the same line? Is Eminem within his rights to claim that his "down bitches" "be like 'That's my nigga fo real'"? Is he engaging in sophisticated parody or self-parody — and even if so, does that make it any more acceptable for him to use the long-forbidden word? The question involves authenticity. In the multibillion-dollar industry that hip-hop has become, it involves money too.

Thoughtful hip-hop performers often struggle with themselves over "nigga." One of them is a black rapper from Seattle, Rob Willard, who goes by the name Life the Guardian. "It's so sad that the word is now used in common conversation," he told me. "It is even worse that blacks choose to use that word to define themselves at all. Now we have people in all races using it as a vivid description of what they like to be." I pressed him further on the point, and he responded: "The word 'nigga' is such an ill subject. I mean when I was lost in this world that's how I was and how we spoke to each other. Then I stopped using the word altogether in my songs and in life. I started asking people why they used it, and I got so many weak responses that it blew me away. It seemed like all they had were excuses and no real concrete reasons at all. There is no way you can take a word with such a bad history and suddenly make it positive."

Hip-hop is a style of dance music, but it's one (I'm tempted to say *the* one) in which language and its history matter. "Word," "word is bond," "word is born" and "word to the mother" have all been hip-hop catchphrases. Along with its offshoot, the spoken word movement, hip-hop has succeeded in restoring poetry to its ancient role as an oral medium after decades of marginalization in textbooks and graduate seminars. Of course, brilliant poetry surfaced from time to time in other genres of music — back in the day, the Beat poet Allen Ginsberg waxed ecstatic over a Bob Dylan couplet: "Idiot wind, blowing like a circle around my skull, / From the Grand Coulee Dam to the Capitol." But in rap, the rhythms are less relaxed and the rhymes tend to be more visceral. The insistent beat gives them an elemental charge that most songs, let alone poems, had lost.

Rapping is an art of language, and "nigga" and "nigger" are not the only pair of words where a subtle change in sound brings about a major change in meaning. As Life the Guardian observes, "'Sista' usually means a woman of ethnicity, while 'sister' means the opposite." Attention must be paid. Until I began to listen hard, I never grasped the audacity of hip-hop's rhymes and fresh-coined words — "cruffatin," for instance, invented by the British rapper Roots Manuva to mean a vagabond or scruffy person. "No one is quite as deliriously and unapologetically in love with the way words sound as are rappers," writes the New York journalist Adam Sternbergh. "At a time when the language of advertising and marketing has turned much of the culture into a linguistic landfill — is there any phrase more meaningless than 'Please hold the line, your call is important to us'? — rappers keep the English language exciting." To stay afloat in the music, you have to keep abreast of the words.

That's not always easy. An influential MC who emerged from LA's post-gangsta scene goes by the name Murs (sometimes spelled more loudly: MURS). In "L.A.," a secular hymn to his hometown on the 2006 album *Murray's Revenge,* he asserts that we can thank Los Angeles for "every single trend." He goes on to mention ten. The first four — bandanas, facelifts, white T-shirts and fast trips to Las Vegas — are straightforward enough. But what of the final six: Chuck Taylors, K-Swiss, poplockin', cripwalkin', chronic blunts and G-funk? When in doubt, turn to Urban Dictionary.

I could hazard a guess at cripwalkin' (a stylized walk or dance associated with the Crips gang) and chronic blunts (hollowed-out cigars filled with the finest marijuana — the street meaning of chronic is somewhat different on the East Coast). But the other terms eluded me. K-Swiss and Chuck Taylors, it turns out, both refer to shoes. G-funk is not, as I'd imagined, short only for gangsta funk; it also means ghetto funk and has a "laidback, funky, highly synthesized and heavily sample-driven sound." Poplockin' may signify a particular way of rolling joints, may be a type of dance, or (a slightly older meaning) may refer to a handgun. Who knows? My point is this: in less than two lines, Murs coolly introduces several expressions that would puzzle large numbers of English-speakers.

If you don't understand him, that's your problem. He's not going to oblige you with a glossary. Not only do rappers introduce new words, they also alter the connotations of old ones — "sick," "ill" and "bad," to name but three. Hip-hop grabs the language by the muffin top and shakes it up. "What is a hip-hop song?" the *Village Voice* journalist Greg Tate asked in 1996. He went on to answer his own rhetorical question: "One where all the words matter, compelling us to memorize every noun, verb, preposition, and gerund. Nothing about the craft of hip-hop is more amazing than that the writing — the words themselves — is as smart and stimulating as the beats, the samples, and the attitude."

Nine years later, Tate had lost his faith: "What we call hiphop is now inseparable from what we call the hiphop industry, in which the nouveau riche and the super-rich employers get richer." Once, he lamented, hip-hop was a people's culture. It has turned, or been turned, into a lucrative sideshow.

◡〜

Anyone who thinks about hip-hop needs to decide how seriously to take its lyrics. Verbal aggression, as we've seen, has been a part of the movement since it began. But in the 1990s some rappers and music producers, finding their audience weary of the usual product, began to ratchet up the invective to an ever greater level of intensity. Their decision has a parallel in the porn industry, where customer boredom is also an issue and where teenage boys and young men provide much of the revenue. The effect of gangsta rap, like that of hardcore porn, depends on transgression and repetition. The mirror it holds up to the inner city is a wildly distorting piece of funhouse glass. I won't demean myself, or you, by quoting gangsta rap at its most hate-filled — if you're desperate to find the words, the Internet will give you all you desire. Neither will I savage hip-hop by pretending that gangsta rap embodies the whole genre.

Rap has been praised as an act of political revolt, as quickfire literature, as an incarnation of black pride. It has come under attack, too, and not only from white mothers like Tipper Gore. Within the past few years, sales of hip-hop music have fallen sharply in the United States, and blacks themselves have spoken out against it. In the summer of 2006, thanks to YouTube and similar websites, a hip-hop song and dance called Chicken Noodle Soup became a short-lived hit. The music critic Rashod B. Ollison was so unamused that he compared the result to minstrelsy: "The music, dances and images in the video are clearly reminiscent of the era when pop culture reduced blacks to caricatures." (He didn't mention that the lyrics are equally ridiculous.) Others have aimed their fire at hip-hop's continuing attacks on women and its glorification of crime.

"The attitude and style expressed in the hip-hop 'identity' keeps blacks down," John McWhorter wrote in 2003. "Almost all hip-hop, gangsta or not, is delivered with a cocky, confrontational cadence that is fast becoming . . . a common speech style among young black males. Similarly, the arm-slinging, hand-hurling gestures of rap performers have made their way into many young blacks' casual gesticulations, becoming integral to their self-expression." The music has altered the visual as well as the spoken language of its adherents.

McWhorter, a political conservative, refuses to accept what some rappers argue: that hip-hop talk reveals what happens when an oppressed people seizes the language of the overlord and throws it back in his face. In a subversive cut called "Crack Music," Kanye West suggests that just as whites quashed political resistance by getting blacks addicted to crack cocaine —

"God," he asks, "how could you let this happen?" — blacks have taken their revenge by getting whites addicted to hip-hop. "Real black music," he calls it. West both celebrates and denounces the medium that has made him a star. "People, people, we are the same," Chuck D rapped in Public Enemy's brilliant song "Fight the Power." In the next breath he corrected himself: we can never be the same if "we don't know the game."

Nowhere has the music's power been proven more starkly than in hip-hop's other home, Jamaica. (The earliest of all DJs, Kool Herc, was a Jamaican immigrant named Clive Campbell, who brought to the Bronx of the mid-1970s a knowledge of the massive sound systems already being used in his homeland.) Black Americans sometimes scorn the hip-hop produced in other countries as inauthentic, not "real"; it's a charge they seldom level at Jamaican music. Dancehall, now the island's most popular genre, fuses hip-hop and reggae. Yet some dancehall lyrics are just as vicious as gangsta rap. The chorus of "That's Right," a 2002 hit by the nationally famous Beenie Man, involves burning "chi-chi man" and burning "sodomite" — "An' everybody bawl out, say, 'That's right!'" Other dancehall songs have titles like "Shot a Faggot," "Shot a Batty Boy," "Pure Sodom" and "Faggot Connection." Amid a society drenched in machismo and hellfire religion, Jamaica's gays and lesbians endure a siege of words and, on occasion, weapons. In 2004 their leading spokesman, Brian Williamson, was bludgeoned to death in his home.

Bob Marley, Jamaica's most influential musician of the last century, performed in a Rasta-spiced English. Today's singers are more likely to rhyme in a shifting mixture of English and Jamaican Creole. "Gwaan ya me gal you know a you," to quote a typical line by the dancehall singer Sean Paul, flummoxes audiences off the island. In Jamaica as in many other countries, hip-hop and its offshoots embrace an unofficial language of the streets. The reason, I suspect, has to do with hip-hop's adversarial posture, its desire not to convert but to assert. If you mean to fight the power — or even just to suggest that you could, if you chose, fight the power — you're wise to avoid a language with authority's odor.

Which is why, in Greenland, young Inuit men rap in Inuktitut as a way of resisting the colonial force of Danish. And it's why, in Montreal, Haitian Creole is now a language of prestige among young people — nowhere else in the world, perhaps, does it enjoy so high a status. Haitian-inspired music is hot in the city. One of its current rappers, Sans Pression, was born

Kamenga Mbikay to Congolese parents in Buffalo, and joined forces with a Haitian immigrant (Ti-Kid) at a high school outside Montreal. Sans Pression's songs are mostly, though not entirely, in French: "guess qui est enceinte / That's right ta petite princesse . . ." These hybrid phrases come from a song called "Ti Moun," the Creole word for children. To mix French, English and Creole words, song after song, is to build a verbal embodiment of the multilingual, multicultural city that Montreal has become.

"What you find with Montreal rappers," says Mela Sarkar, an education professor at McGill University, "is a process of forging new identities through new language." Her teenage son joined a French-language hip-hop crew — "and when he picks up the phone and talks to a friend, I'll hear him say, 'Yo, ou est-ce qu'on chill ce soir?'" Sarkar once asked her son why he wrote rap lyrics. He replied, "Pour connecter avec le peeps."

In France, many rappers are of North African and Middle Eastern origin. Their "peeps" live in the sterile high-rise blocks that infest the distant suburbs of Paris. Hip-hop allows the musicians to connect both with disaffected immigrant youths and with white French rebels (or wannabes). With its inflected endings, so rich in rhyming possibilities, French is a natural language for rapping. In 2005, a few months before riots consumed parts of outer Paris in flames, a rapper of Senegalese origin who calls himself Alpha 5.20 mentioned some of the bleakest suburbs by name: "Clichy-sous-Bois ça c'est gangsta gangsta / Et Aulnay-sous-Bois ça c'est gangsta gangsta / Word up Montfermeil ça c'est gangsta gangsta . . ." The riots made his music seem prophetic. Earlier in the song Alpha 5.20 cited Afrika Bambaataa, one of the creators of hip-hop in the Bronx, adding the rhyme "je flow historique original bombattack." The Académie Française would be horrified; this mongrel tongue is a far cry from "good French." But it's living French.

Today hip-hop flourishes across Africa. You wouldn't know it from his crew's name, but the continent's most celebrated rapper, DJ Awadi of Positive Black Soul, works mainly in the Wolof language of Senegal — a Wolof that he stretches to include terms like "journaliste politique" and "job." In the new South Africa, hip-hop is a prime source of kwaito, an edgy genre of townships music that fuses several languages into a single beat. Or the languages themselves are fused into Iscamtho, the street slang of Soweto that adds words from various tongues to a Zulu base. The borders of language and music alike are blurring, even dissolving.

"Hip-hop is more revolutionary as adopted in the Third World than in the heartland," DJ Static told me one afternoon in downtown Montreal. The blue inner walls of his apartment building were drenched with graffiti. "In the heartland hip-hop went down a really strange path and took on a really degenerate form. People in struggle around the world haven't always lived with hip-hop, but they look to it now and cling to it." Offstage, his name is Mike Lai — his English name, that is. I don't know his Chinese name. DJ Static arrived in Canada in 1988 as an eleven-year-old boy from Hong Kong. "Kids in my first school in Vancouver started passing me cassette tapes — that's how I learned English. I was repeating hip-hop lyrics before I knew what any of it meant."

Years later, hip-hop would bring him the world. DJ Static has performed in Cuba, Switzerland and the Hong Kong he left as a child; in a Montreal crew called Nomadic Massive, he spins the turntables beside performers from Chile, Argentina, Haiti and Iraq. They rap in five languages. Music is their common home. "Hip-hop is like a river," he said, a thin smile on his lips. "You're carried along. It's way bigger than you. And it takes you to a new place. For better or worse it's going to keep growing. It's going to eclipse most other things. It's going to become ever more dominant."

The music is growing fast in China. It has already made it big in India — although I'm chagrined to say that the first hip-hop song to become an Indian hit was "Thanda Thanda Pani" ("Cold Cold Water"), a Hindi adaptation of "Ice Ice Baby" by Vanilla Ice. Yet perhaps nothing suggests the global charisma of hip-hop better than the work of DJ Besho, a Kabul rapper who sports with the Dari language, infusing it with fragments of English and German. He rhymes about love and patriotism. Afghans aren't allowed to hear about "booty," and they don't need to hear about guns.

The trouble with global charisma is that it can blind you to local desire. A now defunct Basque band called Negu Gorriak were huge fans of Public Enemy, one of the most politically engaged and militant of U.S. hip-hop groups. As a gesture of political defiance toward Spain, Negu Gorriak insisted on performing in the Basque language. But they also sampled American hip-hop music and used snatches of Spanish, Arabic and English ("Power to the people!" "Do the right thing!") in their songs, videos and zines. "We admire black culture," they said. "And we identify with black nationalism." In 1992 Public Enemy gave a concert in Bilbao, the largest city in the Basque country. Negu Gorriak were overjoyed — until members of

Public Enemy greeted the audience by saying "Hello, Spain!" They also told the press they preferred playing at a U.S. Army base near Madrid, because the large number of black troops changed the feel of the crowd. To Public Enemy, Basques were not a beleaguered minority; they were European whites. To Negu Gorriak, Public Enemy were no longer role models; they were mercenaries.

✍

Part of hip-hop's power derives from its willful assertiveness — its refusal to explain or make allowances. Follow the beat, or sit down. Learn the language, or shut up. But whose version of the language? Let's put aside the spread of hip-hop into Basque, Dari, Hindi, Iscamtho, Wolof, French, Haitian Creole, Inuktitut and countless other languages, and think about its sprawl across English.

The music's popularity has given Black English an unprecedented worldwide cachet. It's evident in a city that could hardly be more remote from New York and LA: Perth, the capital of Western Australia. There, a recent study of e-mails sent by teenage Aboriginal girls shows them asking "wass up?" and writing lines like this: "so who are you going out with these days i hope it's not justin he is such a lil dogg!!!" Hip-hop terms like "dogg" mingle with elements of Aboriginal English (the girls call a desirable boy a "big feed"). Ellen Grote, the linguist who carried out the research, told me that older Aboriginals tend to identify with indigenous people in North America rather than with the African Americans whose skin color they share. Not so for the teenage girls she studied: "They all exhibited strong affiliations with African-American hip-hop culture."

Little children in Montreal also pick up elements of hip-hop language, says the pediatrician Shuvo Ghosh. The main reason, he believes, is the influence of "dubbed Japanese anime, broadcast on weekday after-school programs in the U.S. The characters make use of many phrases from the hip-hop lexicon in a totally natural fashion. I find that many of my patients — some as young as seven or eight — are using hip-hop phraseology and style on a regular basis."

Yet no matter how far the music's influence now stretches, DJ Static insists that the lived experience of black Americans is still "the engine that drives hip-hop. The shock waves come out of there. A lot of pent-up anger and aggression in hip-hop comes from the black experience. And the urgency." Like Kanye West in "Crack Music," DJ Static sees hip-hop as primarily an African-American art. The old-school New York rapper Kurtis Blow once described hip-hop as "a way for the people of the ghetto to make themselves heard. They invented it and they will keep it going. Everyone else can bite [i.e., steal] our rhymes, our dress, our steps, our style, but they still have to come uptown to find out what's really happening." By uptown, he meant Harlem. At first it wasn't clear that hip-hop would take Manhattan, let alone Berlin. On the eve of the twenty-first century, the New York writer and broadcaster Touré described hip-hop as a "nation," one that made "brothers of men black, brown, yellow and white." But, he went on, "this world was built to worship urban black maleness: the way we speak, walk, dance, dress, think. We are revered by others, but our leadership is and will remain black. As it should."

Those are fighting words. Touré claims that in their words, their movements, their clothing, even their ideas, the brothers — no mention of sisters — must emulate black men in American cities. The irony is that although hip-hop's lyrics pose a challenge to the power of Standard English, hip-hop and the English language have grown so huge as to raise very similar questions of belonging and authenticity. Can a speaker's skin color or place of residence affect our acceptance of the speaker's voice? Can a single group claim a moral right of ownership? Or can any claimant know what's happening? If we agree that English belongs to a Trinidadian woman just as much as a Liverpudlian man, must we also accept that a homeboy in the Bronx has no more say over hip-hop than a white girl in Wellington? One of the major books on hip-hop, written by an American, was entitled *Black Noise.* Hard on its heels came an equally impressive study, edited by an Australian: *Global Noise.* I want to focus briefly on a few performers whose work raises hard questions about the language that keeps rap real.

"Y'all talkin' about 'Watch where you goin'!'" the Toronto rapper Kardinal Offishall says in "BaKardi Slang." He prefers "Mind where you step!" The entire song is a catalogue of differences between Black English in the USA and the dialect he proudly speaks. Toronto is the home of hundreds of thousands of black people, most of whose families moved there from the Caribbean; their lexicon, accent and cultural history differ from those of black Americans. In "BaKardi Slang," Kardinal does everything he can to get under the skin of American rappers. They brag, for instance, about gulping Moët, a brand-name champagne and a shorthand symbol of conspicuous wealth. He favors Guinness. Like so many hip-hop songs, "BaKardi Slang" overflows with personal swagger. But Kardinal also boasts on behalf of his city: no matter where his listeners may live, "T-dot comin' much hotta."

Kardinal adopts the attitude but questions the language; another Toronto rapper, K'naan, embraces the language but spurns the attitude. Having fled Somalia as a boy, he is Canadian, African, African Canadian; but he's not African American. In his 2005 song "What's Hardcore?" he mocks the pretensions of gangsta rappers who glamorize the miseries of the ghetto. The riot-torn, mob-ridden city of Mogadishu, he insists, is "harder than Harlem and Compton intertwined." K'naan is an articulate prose writer in Standard English. Yet to give "What's Hardcore?" the potential to be heard outside Canada and Somalia, he raps in the language of Harlem and Compton. He uses "front" as a verb; he talks about criminals "fiendin' to fight"; he mentions rappers like 50 Cent. To demolish the fantasies of gangsta rap, K'naan co-opts its voice.

There's nothing gangsta about the London musician Roots Manuva. "His is the voice of urban Britain," according to *The Times* at least, "encompassing dub, ragga, funk and hip hop as it sweeps from crumbling street corners to ganja-filled dancehalls, setting gritty narratives against all manner of warped beats." Before immigrating to England, his father was a lay preacher in a Jamaican village, and a few of Roots Manuva's lyrics carry biblical allusions. His song "Bashment Boogie" has a Jamaican word in its title — a "bashment" is a party or dance — and contains lines that are pure UK: "The coach is gonna leave about quarter past 8" (not, as in the U.S., "The bus is gonna leave about 8:15"). Listeners outside Britain may have no idea what he means by "my council-flat castle," but that's a chance Roots is willing to take.

"From the beginning," write the media scholars David Hesmondhalgh and Caspar Melville, "there was a lively debate within UK hip-hop regarding the extent to which U.S. rap should serve as a model . . . Should a British rapper adopt the U.S. drawl of the Brooklyn badboys (an enterprise doomed to failure) or stick to an English accent that might sound strange?" His Jamaican heritage perhaps allows Roots to sidestep the issue. But Hesmondhalgh and Melville also ask: "Should a UK rapper adopt the Uzi-packing, carjacking, bitch-smacking lexicon of U.S. rap or develop a 'vocab' more in step with the British context, where guns are rare, few youths can afford cars, misogyny is perhaps slightly less acceptable, and the prevailing British diffidence renders public boasting (or 'bigging yourself up') relatively uncommon and frowned upon?" By mentioning coaches and council flats, and by asking God for forgiveness, Roots gives a clear answer.

Hip-hop has always been valued or disparaged as a black, male, American form. Kardinal Offishall, K'naan and Roots Manuva challenge the tradition in different ways — yet they're all black men, working in a form that has seen more than its share of violent misogyny. A more personal, more intimate challenge comes from Lady Sovereign, a young MC who happens to be white, female and English (not to mention short and scrawny). Admittedly she works in the harsh, fast-paced genre known as grime, rather than in "classical" hip-hop. But hip-hop, along with Jamaican dancehall and UK garage music, is one of the sources of grime, a current soundtrack of working-class London. In its short life grime has also gone by the names sublow, r & g, dubstep and eskibeat. The naming of musical styles can be almost as rich a source of new words as the songs themselves.

In December 2006 a video of Lady Sovereign's "Love Me or Hate Me" appeared on YouTube. Six months later, it had been viewed more than one and a half million times. The clip shows a young woman rapping about shepherd's pie, corgis, her "nonexistent bum" (not "ass" or "booty") and how, instead of drinking "fancy champy, I'll stick wit Heineken beers." These very English preoccupations attracted thousands of warring comments, some of them unprintable. "i hate british people and all of this grime shit they put out," wrote a man who identified himself as a thirty-year-old American. "Don't worry, they hate you just as much," replied a nineteen-year-old Englishman. A twenty-three-year-old using an African-American alias said, "Jay-Z is responsible for signing this chick????"

The title predicted the split response the song would elicit. But that response is not based solely on the merits or flaws of Lady Sovereign. It reflects a growing uncertainty about where the music is heading, and whose power needs to be fought.

ౚ

Nearly thirty years have elapsed since hip-hop burst into the mainstream. Its first fans are well into middle age. Many of them have gone on to discover other kinds of music, more melodic, less confrontational. That doesn't mean they've forgotten the beats and the raps they loved — who will ever forget the songs that lit our hearts and ignited our bodies when we were fifteen years old? Besides, hip-hop's use in innumerable movies and TV shows has made it familiar to people who would need to down a few Valiums before they set foot in Compton or parts of the Bronx. The emergence of a black middle class across much of the United States continues to be a painfully slow process. Yet black culture, as exemplified by hip-hop, has swept through the whitest of suburbs — even onto golf courses. In the 1990s, years before Tiger Woods became a household name, fans shouted "You da man!" when a professional golfer whipped a long drive down the middle of a fairway. Today some elements of hip-hop language are as ensconced in the overculture as in the subculture where it began.

"It's like I've blossomed into a hip-hop queen," an Iowa mother named Tana Goertz burbled in a 2005 episode of Donald Trump's TV show *The Apprentice*. "Like I wasn't a white girl. We rocked the house. I was down wit dem." Farewell, diffidence. The episode was entitled "Bling It On." The following year, a transcript emerged of a private conversation between British prime minister Tony Blair and U.S. president George W. Bush. The dialogue was recorded at a G8 summit meeting in St. Petersburg, Russia, when the microphone on Blair's lapel mistakenly remained on. Noticing the British leader some distance away, Bush called out: "Yo, Blair!" The prime minister obediently trotted over.

If you had to name the most unlikely place in America for hip-hop language to flourish, Salt Lake City — even more than Midland, Texas — might be a leading candidate. Less than 2 percent of its residents are black. Yet when the city's Downtown Alliance sponsored a New Year's Eve celebration in 2006, it did so in the words "Enjoy tasty festival foods or buy some glow-y bling to light up the party." Likewise, Dov Charney, the founder and CEO of American Apparel, is not a graduate of an inner city's meanest streets; he grew up in Jewish Montreal. In 2006 Charney was interviewed about his rapidly growing company, and his terse comments only confirm the power of hip-hop: "People say, 'Everywhere I go I see your store. I go to Paris, I go to London, I go to Mexico City.' But I tell them, 'I'm following you, bitch.'"

In the past, a sense of propriety would have prevented businessmen from making that kind of remark. People understood what was, and what was not, acceptable. Now, as many schoolteachers wearily report, this sense of propriety is being lost. Hip-hop is only part of the reason — you can, if you want, blame the whole entertainment industry — but it's a key part. The spread of terms like "yo," "bitch," "bling" and "down wit dem" doesn't mean that everyone who uses such words loves the music of Jay-Z or Chuck D. But it suggests they admire the attitude: That in-your-face pride. That hatred of submission. That refusal to apologize.

8

words@future.now

Language in Cyberspace

F RIDAY AFTERNOON in a tall-treed suburb of Montreal. Julian Krajewski had just come home after a hard day in grade eight. He climbed the stairs to his bedroom, slumped down in a blue swivel chair by his desk, turned his computer on, and clicked on the icon that would open up World of Warcraft — the most popular online game, as of March 2007, on the planet. A slim, dark-haired boy wearing track pants and a sleeveless Toronto Raptors jersey, he waited impatiently for the website to load. "I took my firewall down," he remarked in a voice not yet fully broken. "You can like host a channel. I downloaded Flash and it came with a virus."

Julian was about to enter the Frozen Throne, one element of the Warcraft universe. At that moment, about seventy-six thousand people were playing a game on the site, a small fraction of the eight million paying subscribers World of Warcraft enjoys. Julian did many things with his mouse, far too quick for me to follow, explaining, "This is where I AT." As happens so often when thirteen-year-olds try to talk to older people, his explanation needed further explanation: AT means "arrange a team." Julian would be part of a five-on-five game; he had no idea who the other players were or where they lived. Messages from all of them, friends or enemies, could show up on his screen where some statistics about the players' computers came and quickly went. Julian tried to help me out: "You want as low a ping as possible. That's like your lag. You do know what lag is, right?"

The game got under way. In the Warcraft world, Julian's identity is ACDCfreak — the wall opposite his bed flaunts a poster of the hard-rock band. For this particular game, he assumed the character Abaddon, the Lord of Avernus ("I'm LA," he said with pride). Bright, small explosions began to fill the screen. "You're all out to kill each other," he remarked. The figures were cartoonish, the action immediate — either you're gathering gold for your forces or else you're engaged in battle. Julian was far too busy to explain the messages that popped up on the left side of his screen: *mrknowitall has randomed Silencer,* or *IXL.Inseno has chosen Faceless Void.* After a scuffle, a notice briefly appeared: *mrknowitall has pawned ACDCfreak's head for 225 gold.* "What happened?" I asked. "Well, he killed me," Julian said. He didn't seem too concerned. "What happens now?" "You respawn."

When I wasn't asking dumb questions, Julian talked — either to me or to himself. "He knows I'm coming for him. But he's also scared of me. So it's a weird situation. Go go go, me." He broke a short silence by saying, "You want to fight me, little punkass?" When the game took a bad turn for his team, he typed *im coming,* quickly followed by *brt* ("Be right there") and *everyone stay bot.* But soon after that, he died again, and saw his head ransomed for 245 gold. "I was kind of foolish," he admitted. "I should have ran away." *how do you die with ulti like that,* someone asked him. He did not respond. But a couple of minutes later he was typing *heal man,* and *u better not die,* and *omfg.*

After half an hour the game finished in triumph for Julian's team. "We had ultimate creeps coming down the middle," he said happily, and went looking for another game. Within a couple of minutes he found somebody willing to play a one-on-one. "If he's like 'hi,'" Julian said, turning for a moment to face me, "then he's probably just a noob." Which is a bad thing to be in World of Warcraft; experienced players are quick to ridicule the frailties of a novice. In his second game of the day, Julian played the role of Lord Nightsorrow — "the names always change," he observed. Names are not what matter. The attack he promptly came under left him unruffled: "I've got health bars, you can't just kill me in one shot." He drew up his legs in front of him, feet on the chair's edge, right hand always on the mouse, eyes always on the screen. His gray-furred cat entered the room and left; his gray-haired father did the same. Julian paid no attention to either of them.

Through the window behind his back, the late-winter sun began to set. *Summon more Ziggurats to continue unit production,* the screen inexplicably said. To me the command sounded like a cross between ancient Sumer and the Soviet Union. Julian's opponent, who had been on the defensive, rallied. "OK, I'm screwed," Julian said. "Just 'cause he's not smart doesn't mean he can't amass orcs." A few minutes later, the danger averted, I inquired how the game would end. "When one guy destroys another guy's village." His opponent could have been a girl, but in cyberspace male language is the default option. "He'll probably leave unless he's stupid, 'cause I got way more units." A smile flickered across his face.

g g noob, he typed. (The initials are short for "good game.") "Was that an insult?" I asked. "Yeah," said Julian, gloating. He typed another message: *this is were u leave dumass.* The other player took the hint. Julian reached for a scrap of chocolate from a half-eaten bar near his schoolbooks and munched it while he searched for a two-on-two game. His patience would long outlast mine. I got up to leave the room. "Die!" Julian called after me. A friendly joke on his part. "I mean, bye!"

⌇

Let's think a little about that scene. It reflects a particular subculture; and over the centuries many subcultures have been fertile generators of words, even cream-tea devotionals in Devon. But MMORPGs — massively multiplayer online role-playing games, that is — rely on a global community that has set itself apart by means of written language. Without a shared lexicon that excludes outsiders, the pleasure of MMORPGs would be much depleted. Their copious vocabulary came to life on fingertips, not lips. In the gaming realm, words like "guild" and "owned" have taken on new meanings; acronyms like PVP and LFM have become instantly familiar; and vivid expressions like "corpse camping" and "gold farmer" have joined the parlance of millions of subscribers, not all of whom are teenage boys. As if to emphasize the priority of script over mouth, many gamers and text messagers now write "owned" (beaten, humiliated) as "pwned" or even "pwn3d" — originally, like "womlu," a spelling mistake, but now a badge of insider status. "Pwn3d" is a familiar expression in Leetspeak (also known as "L337 5p34k"), the code of hackers and gamers: a playful dialect of a self-appointed elite.

"People who are in the game call it a society," Julia Struthers-Jobin told me over coffee in a Montreal bookshop a few days after I'd watched Julian Krajewski in action. "We know what we're saying when we talk to each other. Walk into any big city in Warcraft, and someone will say, 'WTB rapier of the monkey 5G?'" Struthers-Jobin, a market researcher in her twenties, and her boyfriend are both gamers. In World of Warcraft she has reached the highest skill level, and admits to some ennui because she can go no further. "There's a term going around called wife aggro," she said. "The wife is annoyed that the husband is playing too much. I got some boyfriend aggro the other day for not playing enough."

Before we met, Struthers-Jobin e-mailed me a photo of herself — "not the best pic, but yeah" — so that we would recognize each other in the bookstore's crowded café. She also sent links to pictures showing five of her online avatars. In her e-mails, Struthers-Jobin used emoticons — the typed symbols that express a feeling linked to a facial expression — forcing me to figure out, with head canted sideways, the difference between :D and :P. (Those who are particularly adept with emoticons can use the symbols to generate images of Elvis Presley and Homer Simpson.) "I like science fiction and fantasy," she said. "I'd rather play a troll than watch some guy fixing up a home on TV. But each person has their own escape, right?" World of Warcraft is hers. Millions of other people prefer the "Metaverse" of Second Life, a virtual world where social life, commerce, artistic creation, cruising and much else flourish on the Internet. Like Warcraft, Second Life has its own rituals — and its own vocabulary.

Sometimes Struthers-Jobin finds that gaming terms like "griefed" and "cry more" cross over into real life. (To "grief" other players is to sabotage their enjoyment of the game; "cry more" is a sarcastic retort to somebody's complaint.) "When you're driving down the road and there's a police car, you might say, 'I hope I didn't catch aggro.' But if you *say* 'lol,' that's definitely a sign your nerdiness has gone too far." Slang has always been a facet of spoken language; it has the potential to cause discomfort among readers. The *English Dialect Dictionary,* published at the turn of the twentieth century, defines slang as "impertinence, abusive language." Yet many of today's impertinent words are born on a keyboard. They provoke discomfort when heard.

Even so, Struthers-Jobin and her boyfriend recently switched from typed to spoken chat. They now use a VoIP (voice over Internet protocol) program that allows up to forty people to talk while together they play World of Warcraft or any other MMORPG. The main advantage is speed. In Struthers-Jobin's words, "It's a lot faster than typing 'Hey, turn around, there's a guy killing you.'" It infuses the oral with fresh life in a medium that pulses with the written. But it also favors those who are fluent in spoken English over those who speak it hesitantly or who have a foreign accent.

As a teenager, I spent long hours talking to friends on the phone (most girls spent even longer). My younger daughter seldom does that. But she takes it for granted that she'll be able to communicate instantly with friends and cousins and friends of friends and friends of friends' cousins by sitting at a computer and typing out a conversation — typing out several conversations at once, I mean, while also listening to online music or watching a downloaded TV show or movie and, from time to time, attending to her homework. The expression of heartfelt feelings involves her fingers and eyes, bypassing her mouth and ears. Many of her friendships are a function of the written word.

So much for Otto Jespersen. A Danish linguist and a cofounder of the International Phonetic Association, he wrote an influential book called *The Philosophy of Grammar* (1924) in which he declared: "We shall never be able to understand what language is and how it develops if we do not continually take into consideration first and foremost the activity of speaking and hearing . . . Writing is only a substitute for speaking." That's not how it looks in the era of the Internet, a force so revolutionary that many people, especially in wealthy countries, can hardly imagine life without it. "Because it amplifies our potential in so many ways," Microsoft chairman Bill Gates declared in December 2000, "it's possible that the long-term impact of the Internet could equal that of electricity, the automobile and the telephone all rolled together." The suggestion might smack of dot-com hubris. Except that already the Internet has collapsed time; it has democratized knowledge; it has transformed work; and it has weakened national boundaries. Less noticed is its capacity to overturn the old relationship between written and spoken language. Admittedly, the growth of webcams and speech recognition technology has begun to reduce our dependence on keyboards, and it's possible that, decades from now, voice-in/voice-out computers will permit all electronic information to be accessible by speech alone. ("Our great-grandchildren won't know how to write or read text," a California futurist named William Crossman recently said, "and it won't matter.") Until now, though, the Internet's power to amplify our potential has flowed from our own ability to type.

Yet what kind of language flows from our keyboards? "i do my utmost not to typ lyk dis coz u no it makes me look like a doofus," Julia Struthers-Jobin told me in one of her e-mails. She's no longer a teenager, however. And in the idiom of chatrooms and text messages — a favored idiom also on youth-oriented websites like Facebook, MySpace and YouTube — capital letters, traditional spelling, regular punctuation and correct grammar have little place. Older people aren't supposed to know the meaning of codewords like PIR (parent in room), PAW (parents are watching) or IWSN (I want sex now). When older people lament the decline of language, text messaging — also known as texting, txting, text speak, txt spk and SMS (short message service) — often ranks high among the reasons.

Parents, stay calm. Just because a boy types "this is were u leave" in his private life, it doesn't mean he's unaware of the proper spellings or incapable of using them in school. If recent British research holds true, children's use of text-messaging abbreviations may actually enhance their literacy skills. (It does nothing, of course, for their handwriting; cursive writing may well become a casualty of the Internet.) Beverly Plester and Clare Wood, two psychologists at Coventry University, found that among the eleven-year-olds they studied, "there is no evidence to link a poor ability in standard English to those children who send text messages. In fact, the children who were the best at using 'textisms' were also found to be the better spellers and writers." Likewise, a study by University of Toronto linguists concluded that instant messaging by young people was not a "ruinous devastation of English grammar" so much as "an expansive new linguistic renaissance." It's only fair to add that in 2007, the chief examiner for Ireland's Department of Education came to the opposite conclusion: the examiner noted that "the emergence of the mobile phone and the rise of text messaging . . . would appear to have impacted on standards of writing," and suggested that text messaging "seems to pose a threat to traditional conventions in writing."

On a per capita basis, teenagers in Britain probably send more textisms than teenagers in any other country — in 2006, 91 percent of British twelve-year-olds owned a cellphone (a "mobile," that is), and adolescents used the device for sending text messages nearly three times more often than for making or receiving a phone call. Long messages are awkward to write; they also cost more to send. Dot Mobile, a phone company for British students, has even launched a series of classics in texting format, so as to help young subscribers choose which works to study and to assist them in revision before exams. The beginning of Hamlet's best-known soliloquy is rendered as "2b?Ntb?=?" And a drastically compressed version of Jane Austen's *Pride and Prejudice* reads like this:

5SistrsWntngHsbnds. NwMenInTwn-Bingly&Darcy-Fit&Loadd.
BigSisJaneFals4B,2ndSisLizH8sDCozHesProud.

SlimySoljrWikamSysDHsShadyPast.
TrnsOutHesActulyARlyNysGuy&RlyFancysLiz.
SheDecydsSheLyksHim. Evry1GtsMaryd.

Not quite everyone, in fact. And doesn't it consume premium space to toss an "actually" and two "really"s into the same sentence? But those are mere cavils. John Sutherland, an emeritus professor of English literature at University College London, was widely quoted as approving of the project: "Whilst some may argue that Dickens is really too big a morsel to be swallowed by text, the Great Inimitable himself began working life as a shorthand writer. He would, I suspect, have approved of the brevity if nothing else." (Those last three words offer Sutherland an escape route.) In 2006 the New Zealand government announced that if high school students used text speak on their final exams, they would suffer no penalty as long as the ideas behind the words were correct.

Txt spk allows people not just to abbreviate language but also to play with it — to revel in its charms and idiosyncrasies. In cyberspace, that desire found a fresh mode of expression in 2006 with the sudden emergence of the lolcat: a cute photograph of a cat or other animal, over which a big caption tweaks and twists conventional spelling and grammar. Animal lovers soon posted tens of thousands of lolcats online. A ginger kitten almost completely wrapped up in a towel says: *i is a burito.* A long-haired cat nose to nose with a domestic rabbit says: *im in yur gardn luvn yur bunniez.* This particular construction is what linguists call a "snowclone": a formulaic expression (like "X is the new Y" or "Have X, will travel") that allows anyone to fill in the blanks. The favorite snowclone among lolcats originated in World of Warcraft, where a player posted the laconic exultation *im in ur base killin ur doodz.* Within weeks, that locution was all over the Net.

Lolcat language has implicit, still evolving rules. On one of the best-known sites, a photograph of a dog with its head poking out of a brown paper bag came with the caption *OH HI, I'm just bagging your groceries.* Among the many comments that visitors left was this: "What odd grammar. Isn't it spelled 'hai' and 'ur'?" Another was more direct: "Ur doin it rong!" It's not enough for the pictured animal to look surprising; the animal has to speak in a surprising way. Lolcats give a linguistic pleasure that depends on their subversion of language's usual rules.

While terms like "bobfoc" are unique to English ("body off *Baywatch,* face off *Crimewatch*"), texting also brings change to many other languages. As the writer and scholar Timothy Garton Ash has noted, memories of Nazi occupation among young Poles now "weigh so lightly that the slang phrase for requesting an SMS text message on your cell phone is 'Send me an SS man.'" Texting is highly evolved in French, some of the results being even terser than the English equivalent. "See you tomorrow" (in txt spk, "CU2moro") is *À demain* in French — or, as of now, "@2m1." *Cinéma* is shortened to "6né"; *merci* becomes "mr6"; and the important question *T'es occupé?* ("RUBZ" in txt spk) turns into "TOQP." The rules and patterns behind all this are the same rules and patterns as in English: spell out as few words as possible; invent abbreviations; use a single letter or number when it sounds roughly like a word or syllable made up of several letters. And never look back.

The abbreviations can lead to confusion. One day the linguist Nick Ukiah texted his mother: "see you tom." "She thought I had sent the message to the wrong person — 'And who is Tom?' — rather than understanding 'tomorrow.'" Despite the mix-up, Ukiah reports that his mother, a schoolteacher, now spells the word "tomorow," to save space and time. Always hungry to save time, global businesses have taken the power of texting to heart. The emergence of BlackBerrys and similar devices made text messaging a normal part of many workplaces. Within a year of the devices' appearance, they were widely being referred to as "crackberries"; such is the technology's addictive power. The Chinese were particularly fast to adapt to texting — in 2003 they sent more than half of all the text messages in the world — and the writer Qian Fuchang responded to the demand by slicing his novel *Outside the Besieged Fortress* into sixty chapters of seventy characters each. It's hard for me to imagine how a "steamy tale of illicit love among already married people" could be made so brief.

Many of the people who read Qian's fiction on their phones are doubtless among the young Chinese who dismay their elders by finishing text messages and e-mails with the number 88. The Mandarin word for "eight" is *ba*, so 88 can be seen as *ba-ba* — close enough to "bye-bye" to start a trend. Other blossoms of Chinese text slang have also emerged from English roots. PK means an opponent, thanks to the English words "player killer," and if you FT, you're amazed — courtesy of "faint." 520, on the other hand, means "I love you" — spoken aloud in Mandarin, the number sounds a bit like *wo ai ni,* the three most crucial words in Mandarin or any language. In China, as in so many other places, the rise of txt spk has led to a clash of generations. Some local governments have tried to limit its use. But modest restrictions aren't enough to appease the likes of Yang Zhengde, a retired teacher who wrote a newspaper article posing the question "Just for the sake of our high-speed, fast-food lifestyle, is it worth sacrificing our language with its history of several thousand years?"

To which a fifteen-year-old student, Wu Dong, replied: "How out-of-date you are if you don't know how to use Net words. It's like someone who doesn't know McDonald's and KFC."

⌇

All of the previous chapters in this book have been a prelude or preamble to this one. The YouTube reactions to Lady Sovereign, the electronic dictionaries of Singlish and American slang, websites that promote simplified forms of English, the fan fiction of Finnish teens, the language of Microsoft employees in India, Coldplay's global online forum, the blogs and messages where Spanglish rules, the birth of "rofl," "womlu" and "keyboard nipple," software that understands the context of Japanese characters, the English-riddled e-mails of Slovakia, the virtual casino that named a monkey: all these attest to the unparalleled power of computers in our verbal lives.

That power goes far beyond online gaming and text messaging. As Sven Birkerts predicted in *The Gutenberg Elegies* (1994), a fierce and subtle book of warning, "The transition from the culture of the book to the culture of electronic communication will radically alter the ways in which we use language on every societal level." Already computers have brought enormous novelty to the lexicon. Consider a baffling article I recently found in an online encyclopedia: "Preferred peers are a subset of peers in a swarm who are known to offer the most bandwidth. Optimistic unchoking allows BitTorrent to determine which peers should be preferred by periodically testing peers." If you don't stay abreast of the terminology, even the headlines will baffle you. I was once bemused by a BBC site that proclaimed: "Nude worm tempts World Cup fans." In the opening two paragraphs of this chapter, the following words appeared: icon, website, firewall, download, channel, virus, mouse, ping, lag . . . With a few of these terms, "firewall" and "icon" in particular, the meaning belonging to the computer realm risks overshadowing if not obliterating the original sense.

More generally, the power of computer technology extends to the metaphors we use — the imagery that gives flesh to our thoughts. In 2006, when *Time* ran a cover story asking "Are Kids Too Wired for Their Own Good?," one of the people interviewed was Claudia Koonz, a professor of history at Duke University. She suggested that her students' aversion to complexity and ambiguity — their desire for simple answers — is related to their constant habit of multitasking. But Koonz expressed this notion in the following terms: "It's as if they have too many windows open on their hard drive. In order to have a taste for sifting through different layers of truth, you have to stay with a topic and pursue it deeply, rather than go across the surface with your toolbar." Two years earlier, the discovery of hobbit-sized humanoid bones on the Indonesian island of Flores provoked the *Boston Globe* to interview Bernard Wood, a professor of human origins at George Washington University. Wood declared: "These [little people] are sort of like WordPerfect 1.2 and then you don't bother to find out if there are any upgrades." We have jumped, it appears, from the evolution of software to the software of evolution.

In 1999 the president of Amazon.com happily predicted that the Internet was about to "pour gasoline on the human imagination." Because poets often work with language at combustion point, many of them now fuel their lines with terms from cyberspace and technospeak. "Last year I upgraded Boyfriend 5.0 to Husband 1.0," writes a frustrated woman in "Dear Tech Support," a poem by the Indian writer Shanta Acharya, "and noticed a distinct slowdown in the performance / of the flower, jewellery and other network applications / that had operated flawlessly in the Boyfriend system." The poem is stuffed full of computer terminology, from font color to infected files, and includes the odd pun: ". . . weekly live-updates no longer excel / in their power and are never to the point." On the following page, in "Dear Customer," Acharya provides an answer to the speaker's complaint: "Be realistic . . . bear in mind / that Boyfriend 5.0 was an entertainment package / but Husband 1.0 is an operating system."

As well as providing a rich source of metaphors, the Internet can serve as a shortcut to inspiration. Maxianne Berger, a writer in Montreal, recently composed a poem with the title "These Are the Particles." She Googled that phrase, visited dozens of the websites that came up, shaped and reordered words she found on those sites, and emerged with a twenty-seven-line poem that veers from auroras and integral spin to "the bottom of the human mind." For more than a decade Berger has belonged to an electronic creative-writing list, and she dispatched the poem to the group (she prefers the word "community") for their comments. Soon "a member backchanneled me from New York," and the work was published "in an on-line zine." Another of her poems imagines T. S. Eliot's "The Love Song of J. Alfred Prufrock" as a blog. "In a minute there is time," Eliot wrote, "For decisions and revisions which a minute will reverse." Berger's version: "On-line it can take a while / for neuroses and disclosures to show up on the screen."

The market for poetry in book form is tiny. In cyberspace, though, po-ems can find a surprisingly large audience. Gregory K. Pincus was a strug-gling author in Los Angeles when, in April 2006, he posted a message on his website (gottabook.blogspot.com) describing what he termed "Fibs" — six-line poems in which the number of syllables in each line depends on a mathematical series called the Fibonacci sequence: 1, 1, 2, 3, 5, 8 . . . Pincus decided that each Fib should stop there rather than continue on with 13- and 21-syllable lines. His first attempt reads: "One / Small, / Precise, / Po-etic, / Spiraling mixture: / Math plus poetry yields the Fib." Composers such as Béla Bartók had made use of the sequence, but poets had largely ig-nored it. Within a few days Pincus received about thirty replies, many of them Fibs. But when Slashdot — a website much admired by nerds, geeks, hackers and techies — set up a link to the original post, Fibs rapidly grew into the thousands. Two weeks after that first fateful Fib, the *New York Times* ran a feature on Pincus and his invention; by June he had a deal to publish a pair of books, the first of them all about Fibs.

The brevity, surprise and constraint of the form make it ideal for Internet circulation. Fibs are an egalitarian mode — it's fairly easy to write one with modest success — and many readers did exactly that. Yet what's striking about the story, I think, is not just the quality of responses, nor even their quantity, so much as the speed at which a new literary form bur-geoned across cyberspace. Between the moment a hopeful poet first mails out a manuscript and the moment a finished book lands on the doorstep, several years normally elapse. Further years may slip by before the re-views (if any) have trickled in. With Pincus and his Fibs, the original idea, the publication, the reader response, the media attention and the happy follow-up all occurred within two months.

Poets may decide not to keep up with change; "Ode to the West Wind" would be none the better if Shelley had instead composed "Elevated Lyric to a Consequence of Global Circulation Patterns." Lyricists, however, need to be ready to update their rhymes. "Dance with You," a 2003 crossover hit by London's Rishi Rich Project, mixes English and Punjabi lyrics. The English words rhyme "next to me" and "ecstasy" with "you'll be texting me." More subtly, the Arctic Monkeys — a young English band that shot to fame in 2005 thanks to the Internet — evoke a relationship in terms of texting: ". . . she won't be shocked / When she presses 'star' after she's pressed 'unlock.'"

Now that online speech enjoys such depth and influence, spoken language has inevitably begun to reflect its power. Not long ago I heard a woman being interviewed on the radio: "If you Google my name," she told the host, "you may get the webumentary." What are older listeners, who may not be computer literate, supposed to make of that? On October 11, 2006, a light plane piloted by New York Yankees pitcher Cory Lidle crashed into a Manhattan apartment building, briefly kindling fears of a terrorist assault. Interviewed live on TV, a NORAD spokesman described the readiness of the air defense system by saying, "We do that 24/7, 365" (pronounced "twenty-four seven, three sixty-five"). His sentence is fast and efficient to type. But its twelve syllables actually take longer to say than a nine-syllable equivalent in Standard English: "We do that every hour, every day."

Using numbers instead of words makes spoken language sound more exact, more technological, more up-to-the-minute, more fit for cyberspace. Computer-bred language, it appears, is becoming a normal part of oral communication. By the same token, the spontaneity of the oral has a profound impact on the words we write online (the term "chatroom" hints at this effect). The Internet, writes the linguist David Crystal, has given us "a mode of communication more dynamic than traditional writing and more permanent than traditional speech. In fact, electronic communication is neither writing nor speech per se. Rather, it allows us to take features from each medium and adapt them to suit a new form of expression." You might say that the improvisational brio of e-mails puts them in the same relationship to traditional letters that jazz bears to classical music — keeping in mind that composers and performers can be masters of both genres.

Looked at with colder eyes, cyberjargon is infecting how we write and speak. And the jargon changes so fast that few people outside the industry have much chance of keeping up. A survey conducted by AOL UK in 2005 found that 84 percent of home computer users did not know the meaning of "phishing." Other terms relating to online fraud — "pharming," "Trojan" and "rogue dialer" — proved equally perplexing. But cyberspace can be a treacherous realm, and without some knowledge of its lexicon, people easily fall victim to malice. Likewise, explanations of technical jargon and insider code need to be written by someone who understands the human mind, not just technology. In a twelve-page newspaper supplement about VoIP, I found a glossary that defined "transmission control protocol" in these words: "The transport layer protocol developed for the ARPAnet which comprises layers 4 and 5 of the OSI model. TCP controls sequential data exchange in TCP/IP for remotely hosts in a peer-to-peer network." (Yes, "remotely hosts.") Can anyone other than a specialist understand such arcane rhetoric?

Those who spend their working lives among computers are sometimes less gung-ho about the medium than outsiders. I talked to Rob Chapman, a veteran troubleshooter for IBM (his e-card identifies him as an "Advisory Availability Systems Specialist") who resolutely avoids speaking of people as "programmed" or "hard-wired." "We do not adequately understand ourselves," he said, "and most of the folks using these expressions do not really understand the world of technology. Hard-wired means predetermination and no free will. That's a pretty good description of most technology. Not so good as a description of us." The machinery we have created, Chapman warns, should not be used as a metaphor for our selves.

This is, however, exactly the direction in which the language is heading. Consider how "plugged in" functions as a synonym for "well informed." "Ever since computers became so important in our lives," wrote the novelist Russell Smith in 2007, "the words nerd, geek and dweeb have undergone an almost complete reversal of connotation, from negative to positive. The nerd is the expert, the millionaire, the guy with the insider's blog. A geek no longer means someone with no social skills, but someone with specialized knowledge." Instead of saying "I happen to know a good deal about investing, and I made a fair amount on the stock market last year" — or even "I'm quite rich" — someone will announce, "I'm a finance geek." Nerdiness is so fashionable that, Smith claims, "electro-punk-hip-hop hipsters" — three hyphens must signify the ultimate in cool — have begun to dress like science teachers.

⌒

Cecily Cardew was born a century too soon. In Oscar Wilde's play *The Importance of Being Earnest,* her governess chides the young woman for writing a diary. Cecily is unmoved: "I keep a diary in order to enter the wonderful secrets of my life. If I didn't write them down, I should probably forget all about them." She informs her future husband that the diary "is simply a very young girl's record of her own thoughts and impressions, and consequently meant for publication. When it appears in volume form I hope you will order a copy." A present-day Cecily wouldn't need to worry about publication. Algernon could read her thoughts and impressions on his laptop, for Cecily would be writing a blog.

Tens of millions of people do. The explosion of blogs in the past few years tempts me to use the word "incredible," a bombastic term I normally avoid. But consider: the word "blog" — a shortened form of "web log" — didn't exist until 1997. Blogs enjoyed a steady increase over the next few years; in 2003, the tracking firm Technorati found about a million worldwide. Then their growth became spectacular. By June 2007 the total number of blogs had surpassed 86 million, with about 175,000 new ones emerging every day. Small wonder that on Technorati's homepage, a question appeared: "Is the blogosphere crushing you?" English accounts for the largest number of blogs, Japanese is not far behind, and together Japanese and Chinese make up more than 40 percent of the total.

"A blog is just a medium," Ed Hawco told me. "It's not a form in itself, it's a publishing platform. It comes with a set of technologies, but then so does print journalism." Hawco works as a technical writer in downtown Montreal, where I met him one winter's day. He has blogged, in a fashion, since before the beginning: in the mid-1990s he was one of the hosts of Café Utne, a community forum on the *Utne Reader* website. "I've always liked to write," he said, "but also to be read. What's the point of a journal if it's going to be kept under your bed?" (Cecily Cardew would have agreed wholeheartedly.) Hawco created his blog in 2000, comparing it to both "my own personal Google" and "having my own magazine." At first the readers of Blork.org were few. But Hawco sensed their number would grow. "Now I'm aware I'm opening up a topic," he said. "Sometimes I get twenty to thirty comments, which is nice."

His blog concentrates on food, his city and himself; readers know petty details of his character, such as his fondness for lemon-pepper linguine with scampi. (Even if some bloggers are shy in person, they benefit from a degree of exhibitionism.) "When I started the blog," he remarked, "one of my goals was to improve my practice. I wanted to become a better writer — I mean, I'll edit a post I wrote three years ago. But a lot of people who blog aren't good writers; they aren't mindful of the fact that they're not good writers; and they don't care that they're not good writers."

As a good blog writer, Hawco is fully aware of the need to keep on feeding his audience, and willing to do just that. His conversation was full of vivid jargon: "meatspace," "eyeballs," "RSS feeds." "When you write online," he said, "what you gain is hypertext: the ability to link. I wrote an entry about the TV show *24*, which I both love and hate. And when I talked about it not yet 'jumping the shark,' I didn't have to explain — I just had to link to Wikipedia." He paused for a moment. "What you lose when you write online is the physical page: the pause for reflection." Maybe it was my presence — a meatspace arrival from the world of print, scribbling in an old-fashioned notebook — but Hawco went on to sound an alarm about the impact of blogs. He is, I belatedly realized, a man who not only watches mainstream TV but also reads literary novels, and comments on them shrewdly.

When people criticize the blogging genre, he noted, they usually focus on weaknesses in the writing. "Few people actually edit and scope their blogs to the quality you'd expect in a print publication — that's just the reality of the thing. But what of the quality of *reading?* My posts tend to be a little longer than most — a thousand words, maybe — and someone will come in with a comment that makes you realize they didn't read the whole blog; they just picked up on a single point. I think blogs are dumbing down reading more than writing. Reading online has been shown to lower comprehension by about 30 percent. Start with that; then you get fanatics who read two or three hundred blogs a day; and I worry that we're creating a generation of skimmers, people who read with no depth at all." Indeed Sarah Horton, one of the gurus of online "usability," advises web designers to break all text into short segments for easy skimming. "Web readers are goal-oriented," she writes. Paragraphs as long as this one bog them down.

A reflective blog like Hawco's may soon appear archaic, for by the summer of 2007 microblogging from cellphones had become the rage. "It's all about staying in touch with your digital tribe on a moment-by-moment basis," explained one proponent, or "twitterer." The ability of microblogging to link frequent short messages with social networking sites meant that "tweets" into the "twitosphere" appeared likely to catch fire. As Marshall McLuhan often noted, to understand media also means to understand the effects of media. And if brevity is now the soul of written communication, the consequences for book publishing can only be dire — although some companies are finding the market hungry for "blooks," or blogs that have been turned into books. "The book as we know it," Robert McCrum recently warned in the London *Observer*, "may be going the way of the codex and the illuminated manuscript." That depends on how thoroughly the printed word will be displaced by digital code.

Don't get me wrong: I'm not speaking as a Luddite, and I'm as guilty, or innocent, as anyone else. I know I read fewer books than I did fifteen years ago, when the Internet was still in its infancy. When I'm working on my computer and I need to check a word or a fact, I instinctively click on Dictionary.com or Wikipedia, even though I own several printed dictionaries and two encyclopedias. The habit of seeking information online has quickly become ingrained in me. (And I have no illusions about the reliability of Wikipedia, whose article on Kazakhstan once stated that the president was Borat and the national anthem began: "Kazakhstan greatest country in the world, / All other countries are run by little girls.") The Internet provides us with instant information, most of it true. What it cannot give is instant wisdom — for wisdom, by definition, grows over time. Wisdom relies on understanding, not merely on facts.

The most starstruck devotees of blogging would find that irrelevant. To them, a book, a newspaper and a magazine are all "old media." "What is really going on," the American commentator Hugh Hewitt declared in his 2005 book *Blog*, "is an information revolution similar in consequence to the Reformation that split Christianity in the sixteenth century. The key to that Reformation was the wide dissemination of Scripture among an increasingly literate laity. Today we do not have a canon, but we do have an appetite for information, the arrival of a new technology of distribution, and a million willing content providers." Hewitt, who makes use of both a blog and a talk-radio show to promote an ideology of the far right, credits bloggers with ruining the chances of John Kerry being elected president in 2004. He admitted that the creative force of blogs is "only dimly understood." But in its speed and intensity, "the destructive energy of the blogosphere is fierce indeed when focused."

That destructive energy has become depressingly clear in the attacks that women now endure in cyberspace. "On some online forums," Jessica Valenti wrote in 2007, "anonymity combined with misogyny can make for an almost gang rape–like mentality." Of course, men can also suffer abuse in blogs, chatrooms, newsgroups and the like. But, Valenti says, "the sheer vitriol directed at women has become impossible to ignore." One study suggested that someone with a female username is twenty-five times more likely to be harassed than someone with a male username. "Most disturbing is how accepted this is. When women are harassed on the street, it is considered inappropriate. Online, though, sexual harassment is not only tolerated — it's often lauded. Blog threads or forums where women are attacked attract hundreds of comments, and their traffic rates rocket."

The edgy rebelliousness that bloggers often claim may, in English-speaking countries, be largely an illusion. Voices of dissent are marginalized here without being silenced. Yet in some parts of the world a blog, even a text message, can be a truly radical use of words. For nearly three years, Abdel Karim Suleiman — a law student in Alexandria — wrote an Arabic-language blog in which criticisms of Egypt's government, attacks on radical Islam and pledges to defend the rights of women were mixed with song lyrics and personal notes. Such writing was unacceptable to the regime and, in 2007, a judge sentenced Suleiman to four years in prison (his trial is said to have lasted five minutes). In the United Arab Emirates, which combine enormous wealth and extreme social conservatism, the use of text messaging and Web-based telephones has given young people a taste of freedom in spite of the taboos against informal contact between the sexes. And from Ukraine to the Philippines, text messages have played a role in toppling unjust regimes.

In Iraq, some websites try to help citizens avoid the torture and murder perpetrated by militias and death squads. But the Web has also become a weapon for jihadists. "The Internet is the key issue," Gilles Kepel, a leading professor at the Institut d'Études Politiques in Paris, recently said. "In the old days, one sought a fatwa from the sheikh who had the best knowledge. Now it is sought from the one with the best website." Jihadists maintain their own blogs and online magazines. Kepel has described Osama bin Laden as "the supreme hacker."

The potential inherent in these technologies became a little clearer when a terrifying tsunami hit Southeast Asia in December 2004. Sanjaya Senanayake, a young TV producer in Sri Lanka, sent out text messages from a remote, devastated coastline at a time when phone signals were weak and unreliable. His blogging friends in India captured the messages and immediately posted them on a website. In so doing, they made Senanayake's firsthand assessment of conditions in Sri Lanka freely available to aid agencies and governments everywhere. By contrast, Charles McCreery, director of the U.S. National Oceanic and Atmospheric Administration center in Hawaii, responded to the disaster by telling a reporter, "We don't have contacts in our address book for anybody in that part of the world." A *USA Today* columnist, Kevin Maney, jumped on the remark: "Phone calls! Address books! How sad is that? Even if somebody answers, telephones are one-to-one communication — a terrible waste of time in an emergency. The Net has brought one-to-many communication to everyday life: blogs, Web pages, bulletin boards like Slashdot, even e-mail lists. Any Net user can post so millions of others can see it." The Net, among its other attributes, acts as a giant mouth.

Millions of people watched Michael Wesch's four-and-a-half-minute video essay, "Web. 2.0 . . . The Machine Is Us/ing Us," in the first few weeks after he posted it on YouTube in January 2007. Wesch teaches cultural anthropology at Kansas State University, and most of his video is a quick survey of HTML formatting, blogs, Google, Flickr and the like. Jaunty electronic music accompanies the ever-changing text, which ends in a burst of triumphalism when the screen announces, "We'll need to rethink a few things." What things? Here is Wesch's list: copyright, ownership, identity, ethics, aesthetics, rhetoric, governance, privacy, commerce, love, family, ourselves.

Is that all? The music stops. The screen goes blank.

༄

"Because of the ease of creation and dissemination," Kevin Kelly claimed in 2005 in his famous essay "We Are the Web," "online culture is *the culture.*" There is no other; or, at least, any others scrape a living only in dark corners and insignificant margins. What the Web's builders have achieved in little more than a decade, Kelly said, is stupendous — "spookily godlike. You can switch your gaze of a spot in the world from map to satellite to 3-D just by clicking. Recall the past? It's there. Or listen to the daily complaints and travails of almost anyone who blogs (and doesn't everyone?). I doubt angels have a better view of humanity. Why aren't we more amazed by this fullness? Kings of old would have gone to war to win such abilities."

Something about the Web seems to encourage overblown rhetoric. No, the past is not encoded in digital information; the past is gone, the past is no more, the past is dead, just as it always was. And no, not everyone blogs. But somehow computers — even before the Web was born — have tended to foster grandiose claims. "The nature of knowledge cannot survive unchanged," wrote the French philosopher Jean-François Lyotard in his 1979 book *The Postmodern Condition*. "It can fit into the new channels, and become operational, only if learning is translated into quantities of information. We can predict that anything in the constituted body of knowledge that is not translatable in this way will be abandoned, and that the direction of new research will be dictated by the possibility of its eventual results being translatable into computer language." If such predictions lead to *qualitative* research being starved of money and attention, they can easily turn into self-fulfilling prophecies.

"Quantities of information," mind you, is exactly right. By now we are surrounded, enveloped, dwarfed, overwhelmed by data. The total amount of digital information generated around the world in 2006 was enough, according to the technology consulting firm IDC, to fill a dozen stacks of books stretching from Earth to the sun. In its report *The Expanding Digital Universe: A Forecast of Worldwide Information Growth Through 2010*, IDC estimated the total amount of data created in 2006 to be 161 billion gigabytes. The projected total for 2010 was more than six times larger. Those numbers may mean more to you than they do to me. What does carry a freight of significance is a second image from IDC: if all human language spoken since the dawn of time could somehow have been stored in digital form, it would occupy less space than the total e-mail traffic in 2006 alone.

Research on translation machines, Lyotard noted, was already well advanced in the 1970s. But the nuances, subtleties and pitfalls of ordinary speech have proven more complicated for machines to grasp than most of the experts believed. After my trip to Japan, I wanted to check that I hadn't erred in jotting down the name of the eighth-floor restaurant in Kyoto's railway station as "Honey Bee." When I Googled "honey bee Kyoto station," more than seventy-nine thousand results came up. A Japanese site looked promising, and I clicked on a link for automatic translation. What emerged was this: "Furthermore when already the single step it climbs, view spot of the オススメ where the wind blows through from south side. Dispersing the sock, if it sits down in the bench and starts to approach to enormous object, tired of traveling and insufficient sleep with the inn which is not accustomed blow offs, probably will be." I still wonder about that sock.

One day in February 2007, I typed a few casual lines into a well-known translation site, babelfish.altavista.com: "My top bands? Pink Floyd, The Who and the Rolling Stones. Or, not so far back, The Clash." Curious to see how the site would cope, I asked for a translation into Spanish, then from Spanish to French, on into German and finally back to English. The result was this: "My bandages of the cover? Floyd responding, that and the stones of the equilibrium. Or not to today posteriora part, the shock." I tried the same procedure with an informal line you might hear in Newfoundland or Ireland: "Buddy turned tail and headed for the pond." Four translations later, the website came up with "Adhesive in view of the stake, which turned, and which was steered toward the grouping." It seems clear that colloquial idioms remain a thorn in the side of automatic translation. I take an odd comfort in knowing that the boasts of any loquacious drunk at a bar may be harder for software programs to comprehend than the gambits of a chess grandmaster.

The potential immortality of words on the Web leads to a different type of problem. A hilarious book by Douglas Adams and John Lloyd, *The Meaning of Liff*, consists of hundreds of made-up words from real-life place names, mostly in Britain — words that should exist, but don't. ("Fulking" is a good example: "pretending not to be in when the carol-singers come round.") Many of these definitions have acquired a new life on the Internet. Yet errors creep in. Adams and Lloyd defined "glossop" as "a rogue blob of food," especially the kind that lurches off your spoon onto your host's table. The original phrase thrived online. But so did "huge blob of food," "large blob of food," "rough blob of food" and (now more common than the original) "rouge blob of food." More seriously, Wikipedia's brief entry on a Toronto professor, Paul Axelrod, mistitled one of his books and wrongly credited him with founding a school of educational thought. When Axelrod discovered the errors, he fixed them. "But," in his words, "the original gaffes have since found their way onto other websites and may float in cyberspace forever." From rogue blogs to rouge blobs, the Internet is a paradise for amateurs. At times it brings to mind oral tradition gone berserk.

I have little idea what marvels its ruthlessly upgraded future will hold. They may be priceless. But they won't be cost-free. Google's stated mission is "to organize the world's information and make it universally accessible and useful." If it were to succeed, or even come reasonably close, then most of our body of knowledge would belong to a single company, a company

with the power to decide on the exact meaning of "useful." British researchers are now developing "virtual Post-it notes" that attach text messages,
photographs and video footage to physical locations. The result, one researcher claimed, will be "a completely different virtual world superim-
posed on the real world." No place will be immune from language. And the
digital divide between the plugged in and the left out will grow ever vaster.

In the corner of the real world occupied by the Massachusetts Institute
of Technology, scientists at a huge venture named Project Oxygen are
working on "pervasive human-centered computing." That means the creation of a world in which the ability to process information would be built
into objects around us, on an "eternal" (MIT's word) basis. The environment itself would be computerized. One step further than that lies what
the techno-futurist Ray Kurzweil calls "the Singularity": a point where "information technologies will encompass all human knowledge and proficiency," and where no distinction can any longer be made "between human and machine, nor between physical and virtual reality." Any use of any
language will be digital information. The World Wide Web will become a
World Wide Mind. Kurzweil looks forward to this.

Whether or not all this is desirable, it may, who knows, be unstoppable. The one thing I find certain is that it will be achieved, if that's the word,
at a huge psychological cost. Already we're paying a heavy price for our advances into cyberspace. Linda Stone, a former vice president of Microsoft,
has called our age one of "continuous partial attention," saying: "We're so
accessible, we're inaccessible. We can't find the off switch on our devices or
on ourselves . . . We are everywhere — except where we actually are physi-
cally." This continuous partial attention is doing nothing for our intelligence levels. A study commissioned by Hewlett-Packard in 2005 found that
the constant checking of e-mail and text messages temporarily lowers a
person's IQ by up to ten points — more than twice as much as smoking
marijuana. It was very clever, and very misleading, for the makers of the
BlackBerry to choose as a marketing slogan "More time for life." In fact,
our love of immediacy — or our addiction to it — leaves us less time for
anything other than work: 24/7, 365.

The widespread use of iPods, MP3 players and mobile phones has
given many of us a beloved personal soundtrack. It has also cut us off from
the audible, tangible world all around. "We trade so much to know the virtual," writes the Scottish poet John Burnside, "we scarcely register the drift

188 THE PRODIGAL TONGUE

and tug / of other bodies." Technology frees us to tailor our reading and viewing habits, as well as our listening ones, to our own taste. And the result? "Atomization by little white boxes and cell phones," says the author and commentator Andrew Sullivan. "Society without the social . . . Human beings have never lived like this before. Yes, we have always had homes, retreats or places where we went to relax, unwind or shut out the world. But we didn't walk around the world like hermit crabs with our isolation surgically attached." Today we can close ourselves off from harsh words and contrary beliefs. Masters of our own convictions, we keep other people at a safe distance. And, Sullivan suggests, we thereby narrow our lives.

Even if we have more and more trouble dealing with strangers, coping with stress, tolerating solitude, accepting silence and listening to voices that speak from a different perspective than our own, aren't we better informed? That depends on what you mean by informed. In 2005 a professor of journalism at Iowa State University asked his first-year students what they thought about John Roberts's recent nomination to the Supreme Court. None of them had an opinion; none of them understood the question. But when the professor inquired about Ashlee Simpson lip-syncing on *Saturday Night Live,* every student in the class knew the story. These were, remember, aspiring journalists, most of whom came to class brandishing a few electronic gadgets. The students were well equipped, but they were not well prepared, let alone well read.

"There's such a glut of information," Will Hochman told me, "today's student is just used to getting it and downloading it." A poet who has taught writing since 1976, Hochman now plies his trade at Southern Connecticut State University. He admires some of the writing that appears in online communities, and has called for computers to be integrated more actively into university teaching. Yet he admits that most students need help in evaluating the information they so effortlessly gather: "There's less need for paraphrasing when you can just copy and paste. Even the word 'grab' is no longer as negative as it was, because in cyberspace we're taught to grab things quickly. It's a culture of immediacy." I'm reminded of a line from T. S. Eliot's poem "The Dry Salvages": "We had the experience but missed the meaning." Today anyone with a laptop can look up that poem, and countless other works of art, on the Internet, gaining a superficial knowledge of their thematic gist, their history, their narrative, their symbolism, their cultural significance. What happens, I wonder, if we have the meaning but miss the experience?

Some years ago Hochman helped to produce a volume of *Letters to J. D. Salinger,* and as part of the task, he and his coeditor created a website on which people could post their own messages to the reclusive author. Thanks to their work, cyberspace contains epistles that begin "Hey J. D. Salinger, How are the writtings coming along," and "Dear J. D. Salinger, Holden Caulfield is sooo hot!" I find them strangely poignant, these letters that will never have an answer, these casual cries from the adolescent heart. "Dear J. D. Salinger, Hey what's up!" Maybe, by now, most of us feel stranded in a random, perplexing world, watching images of other people riding painted horses on a virtual carousel in the park. What's left to us is our technology: the cursor, that shadow self. It allows us, if we want, to tell everybody everything. But in etymological terms, and perhaps in spiritual ones too, "cursor" and "cursory" are intimately related.

Good grief, I haven't checked my e-mail for nearly ten minutes.

ﭼ

Theirs was a twenty-first-century romance. It filtered infatuation and desire, promise and commitment, friendship and passion, through new technologies and several countries. It unfolded according to the interlocking demands of computers and the heart. It united two people who, prior to the Internet, would probably not have met, let alone fallen in love. Their love blossomed through the written word. (How traditional can you get?) Their relationship depended on microchips. (How untraditional can you get?) The story of Lee Ann and Denis — they have asked me to use only their first names — suggests the enormous impact of cyberspace on the way we now cope with language. Not to mention the way we live.

She was the mother of a toddler in Boston, an unhappily married writer and editor who had converted, following her husband, to Orthodox Judaism. He was a software engineer, a Frenchman who had followed his Peruvian girlfriend to Montreal. Lee Ann and Denis met because of music. More precisely, they met thanks to a woman in Barcelona who had started a Yahoo! forum devoted to Noa, a multilingual Israeli singer. In his spare time, Denis served as the forum's moderator. In 2001 Lee Ann's e-mails to Barcelona led to an invitation to join the forum — "and I found they didn't just talk about Noa," she recalls. "My musical horizons were blown apart — it opened up my world. When you're talking to someone about music, you get straight to very personal topics, stuff you wouldn't normally say." Denis agrees: "This mailing list is very special, *sentimentalement* — the level of personal involvement is very high. You don't talk about love on World of Warcraft!" That November, Noa gave a concert in Framingham, a short drive west of Boston. Denis and his girlfriend came down from Montreal; by chance he and Lee Ann were seated next to each other at the concert. She felt an immediate physical attraction. But she didn't know who the Roman-nosed, curly-haired man beside her was, and he didn't recognize the short blonde dressed in black.

Back home, thanks to e-mail, they discovered where they had sat. "He was in shock," Lee Ann says. "He was like, 'Do you realize I spent the entire time trying not to look at you?'" They began writing to each other outside the confines of the Yahoo! group. "I had an idea of his personality, though not of his sense of humor. And when he started e-mailing me personally, he just cracked me up. We could send twenty e-mails a day and still not have enough time to talk." Lee Ann's first e-mail was the longest Denis had ever received; her messages, he says, were on average ten times longer than his. After a month or so, they began to talk about their disintegrating partner-ships. Looking back, she says: "I feel we both sold each other a new and im-proved version of ourselves."

Denis flew to Australia alone to visit his father. During a stopover at Singapore Airport, he e-mailed Lee Ann to say "I've been on a plane for 16 hours, I feel like shit, but I'm thinking about you." Then he went on a camping trip in the outback. Lee Ann had a nightmare that he was caught in an explosion. The next day, she learned that a propane tank had blown up on his father's truck. "He was in tears, and we spent a couple of hours e-mailing as if it was a chat program." In writing, intimacy was easy. "But the first time we talked on the phone," she recalls, "we thought maybe we'd better stick to e-mail. It was so bizarre, hearing his voice. It made what we were doing real." After a momentary pause, she adds: "Also I couldn't un-derstand his accent."

They decided to meet offline. By now Lee Ann and her husband were living on opposite sides of the house. On a Sunday morning in February 2002, she drove up to Montreal, surviving a minor accident in a blizzard near the U.S. border. She called Denis on her cellphone to tell him she'd be late. It was three o'clock in the afternoon before she limped into town. "And I still remember the feeling of my stomach and heart in my mouth when I saw Denis walk down Saint-Hubert. I fell apart. I went into tears — it was very odd emotionally for both of us. He hadn't planned on this being more than a friendship." They hung out in the Calvin and Hobbes section of a bookstore and visited the planetarium. Then they and Denis's girlfriend ate a sushi dinner. He ordered Lee Ann a sea urchin with a raw quail's egg: "It's quite a special flavor. You either hate it or you think you've died and gone to heaven." Five years later, her eyes have a faraway look in them. "I thought I'd gone to heaven."

His girlfriend was not so ecstatic. She spent much of the meal talking on a cellphone to her sister in Spanish. After dinner Denis took Lee Ann to a nearby hotel, "and decided not to sleep with me." But the following morning he found a garage for her injured car, and while it was being fixed they talked, not just face to face, but heart to heart. "When I dropped him off at work, we were in tears. We both felt we were being ripped apart from the person who mattered most to us in life." Once Lee Ann was back in Boston, they e-mailed each other as many as thirty times a day. Soon they began to use a chat program called ICQ, allowing for instant, private conversations.

In April 2002 Lee Ann made another trip to Montreal, ostensibly to attend a literary festival where a poet friend would be reading. She and Denis met again, and slept together for the first time. The following day he broke up with his girlfriend. "After that it rapidly progressed to 'I don't just want to date you.' In May he sent me a webcam for my birthday — what a shock to see him on my computer screen every day! We were still using ICQ, because the voice mechanism on the webcam didn't work very well, and also my daughter was around. One day he put up a sign saying 'Will you marry me?' I put up a sign that said 'Yes.' He said to me, 'I have turned my life upside down to be with you. I expect no less from you.'"

Lee Ann fulfilled her part of the bargain, although more than a year would elapse after their postmodern engagement before she received a divorce and obtained her Canadian immigration papers. As a way of communicating, they shot MP3 music files back and forth online. "At a certain key point, he sent me *Opening* by Philip Glass. It's a piece for solo piano, a killer! I can't listen to it now without crying." On another occasion they began listening to Mike Oldfield's *Amarok* at the same moment, typing together on keyboards in different countries while the hourlong piece unfolded.

In September 2003 Lee Ann moved with her daughter to Montreal and married Denis. By virtue of language and technology, they had become a couple. Thousands of hours on a Yahoo! forum, e-mails, an ICQ program, phone calls, shared MP3 files and a webcam had led to this. "But our first year together," she admits, "we found very difficult." The couple were used to adoring each other at a distance. Differences in their e-mailing habits were "nothing compared to the misunderstandings of face-to-face talk. We've had knock-'em-down, drag-'em-out arguments based on complete misunderstandings of pronunciation and phrasing." Old-fashioned communication of the meatspace kind threatened to shatter the relationship. Still, it survived.

And now? "I send messages to Denis throughout the day," Lee Ann says. "If he hasn't heard from me, he worries." Cyberspace still nourishes their use of language, keeping them constantly in touch with each other's words. She spends long hours on e-mail and writes a blog; he creates software programs for IBM and maintains an avatar in Second Life. When they go on holiday, they take along a laptop. Theirs is a twenty-first-century marriage. Sometimes at home they each play World of Warcraft, sitting side by side, clicking a mouse in front of different screens.

9
Whoa, How Very
Words and the Fictional Future

THIS IS HOW novelists used to imagine the future would sound:

> Nowadays, on the contrary, society is so constituted that there is abso-
> lutely no way in which an official, however ill-disposed, could possibly
> make any profit for himself or any one else by a misuse of his power.
> Let him be as bad an official as you please, he cannot be a corrupt one.

This is how novelists in our time imagine the future will sound:

> I blinked my Soul on Hae-Joo's handsony to learn about my own alias,
> Yun-Ah Yoo. I was a student genomicist, born Secondmonth 30th in
> Naju . . . The data onscrolled for tens of pages, hundreds. The cur-
> few faded away. Hae-Joo woke, massaging his temples. "Ok-Kyun Pyo
> would love a strong cup of starbuck."
>
> I decided the time had come to ask the question that had seized me
> in the disneyarium. Why had Union paid such a crippling price to pro-
> tect one xperimental fabricant?

By now we've examined a host of changes affecting English and other
languages. Let's shift our attention to writers, starting in the 1880s and carrying on into the twenty-first century, who have imagined the fate of words
in times unborn. Speculative fiction used to ignore questions of language
whenever possible. But today new expressions, just as much as new machines, have become essential to the genre. The science-fiction writer J. G.
Ballard caused a small storm in 1962 when he declared: "It is *inner* space,
not outer, that needs to be explored." Time has vindicated his argument.
Contemporary works of science fiction and (especially) cyberpunk serve as
a rich breeding ground of words and ideas; their authors are adept at notic-

ing current trends in language and taking them to a logical conclusion. Literary novelists also seek to interpret the future, and ask how it will enable or allow us to communicate. For in the same way that any reconnaissance of outer space is dependent on technology, any exploration of inner space must rely on language.

All this writerly activity reflects an awareness of the pace and importance of language change. The light of any society shines through the words it uses, and speculative fiction, by definition, is all about novelty. If you're working on a book set a century from now, only in exceptional circumstances would you want your characters to sound like your grandfather. But the persistent focus of today's writers on altered grammar and vocabulary suggests something more: a desire among many writers to make language a means of probing the troubles that afflict us. Mutated, distorted words are not merely a byproduct of change and turmoil; they're its embodiment.

When an imagined culture or planet falls into disarray, that disorder needs to be reflected in its language. Some science-fiction authors still transfer their own and their readers' anxieties to alien cultures living on inconceivably distant globes. But more and more often, the fictional planet in difficulty is the real one below our feet, and the society struggling to cope with a distressing onslaught of change is an outgrowth of our own. The words that writers imagine today are also warning signs. Perhaps, as time slips by, their linguistic visions will seem prophetic.

"Science fiction now," says the American writer Bill McKibben, "isn't like the science fiction of my boyhood, which was all happy fantasies about people zipping around in rocket ships." Forget the innocent pleasures of old SF: "It's now the most dystopian and depressing aisle in the bookstore. You know, movies like *The Matrix* are absolutely indicative of the genre. They're about technology on a scale so powerful that it crushes the human, and what you're left with is some small brave band of people struggling to retain some vestige of humanity against something very large. I think that testimony is worth paying attention to."

∽

Edward Bellamy's mind was on ideas, not words. Living in Massachusetts late in the nineteenth century, he dreamed of a socialist Utopia that Americans in decades to come would construct. Bellamy poured his hopes into a novel, *Looking Backward: From 2000 to 1887,* exploring how the unjust society of his own time could be transformed. The novel gained enormous popularity and serious influence: "Bellamy clubs" were formed across the United States by way of tribute. Today their political hopes seem a mirage. But one reason *Looking Backward* feels so out-of-date, so mired in its own day and age, is that the author paid no attention to how his language might be expected to change over the next eleven decades.

The opening quote in this chapter comes from Bellamy's book. It's spoken by Dr. Leete, a man who in the year 2000 has offered welcome and sustenance to Julian West, the time-traveling narrator. Presumably it did not strain the credulity of readers in the 1880s that more than a century later, a man would declare: "How strange and wellnigh incredible does it seem that so prodigious a moral and material transformation as has taken place since then could have been accomplished in so brief an interval!" The strangeness to us is in the whalebone wording. Paradoxically, West sounds most modern when he leaves the happy future and moves back in time. In the 2000 of *Looking Backward,* nobody needs to advertise personal goods and services; buying and selling are obsolete. But in 1887, the narrator sees walls, windows and newspapers smeared with desperate appeals: "Help John Jones. Never mind the rest. They are frauds. I, John Jones, am the right one . . . Let the rest starve, but for God's sake remember John Jones!" Though it was meant to incarnate the fury of the past, this casual speech looks ahead. Its lack of dignity rings true. The twentieth century would chip away at the verbal formality that Bellamy knew from his own day and thought proper for Utopia.

Bellamy was a contemporary of Jules Verne and H. G. Wells, two of the founding fathers of science fiction. (Mary Shelley, the founding mother, lived a couple of generations earlier.) Wells was aware that language change could pose difficulties for any writer contemplating life in the future. In "A Story of the Days to Come," a short story written in 1899, he foresaw the birth of intercontinental air travel, the decline of railways, even the existence of a kind of personal computer. He also provided an explanation as to why Londoners in the twenty-second century would make remarks like "You have assaulted me, you scoundrel!" and "He is . . . a mere attendant upon the stage on which the flying-machines from Paris alight." The explanation is this:

"In spite of the intervening space of time, the English language was still almost exactly as it had been in England under Victoria the Good. The invention of the phonograph and suchlike means of recording sound, and the gradual replacement of books by such contrivances, had not only saved the human eyesight from decay, but had also by the establishment of a sure standard arrested the process of change in accent that had hitherto been so inevitable." You may not find this line of reasoning persuasive — I certainly don't — but it's significant that Wells felt a need to devise it. Unlike Bellamy, he realized that issues of language could not realistically be ignored. Later in his long career, as we have seen, he promoted Basic English as an idiom with the potential to be spoken everywhere, enhancing social harmony in the process. He glimpsed how intimate the relationship between language and politics could be.

Totalitarian regimes are apt to take language very seriously. A few years after the Bolshevik revolution had turned Russia into the Soviet Union, the Central Committee of the Communist Party formed a unit to supervise the press, oversee school texts and distribute works of Communist doctrine. The unit aimed to fuse speech, or *agitatsiya*, with propaganda. It became known as "agitprop." The word crossed over into other European languages, English included, where it was noticed by a writer with a keen interest in political speech. Though he called himself a socialist, George Orwell had no patience with socialist rhetoric: "When the ordinary person hears phrases like 'bourgeois ideology' and 'proletarian solidarity' and 'expropriation of the expropriators,' he is not inspired by them, he is merely disgusted. Even the single word 'Comrade' has done its dirty little bit towards discrediting the Socialist movement." So Orwell argued in his nonfiction book *The Road to Wigan Pier* (1937). A decade later, he placed the abuse of language at the heart of a bleak vision of Britain to come. After 1984 — or rather, after 1949 — no literary work set in the future could easily take language for granted.

The hero of 1984, Winston Smith, lives in an England known as Airstrip One, part of the vast empire of Oceania. The empire is ruled by a single party using the image of Big Brother: not a reality TV show, but a dictator whose picture, voice and slogans are inescapable. Big Brother's subtlest, most effective means of control is verbal. The official language of Oceania is Newspeak — Oldspeak being the recognizable form of English that most people on Airstrip One still use. What does Newspeak sound like? "Agitprop" served as a model for some of the words Orwell concocted: "artsem" (artificial insemination), "Miniluv" (the Ministry of Love, i.e., the home of detention and torture), "FicDep" (the fiction department of the Ministry of Truth) and so on. Words in Newspeak are short, ugly, rational and pre-dictable — "bad," "horrible" and "miserable" have all been replaced by "ungood."

The aim of Newspeak is to control what people believe and imagine, not just what they say. The language allows for "doublethink": "To know and not to know, to be conscious of complete truthfulness while telling carefully constructed lies, to hold simultaneously two opinions which can-celled out, knowing them to be contradictory and believing in both of them . . ." Oldspeak encouraged nuance and ambiguity, making double-think hard; Newspeak makes it easy. Doublethink goes along with "black-white": the "loyal willingness to say black is white when party discipline de-mands this. It also means the ability to *believe* that black is white, and more, to *know* black is white, and forget that one has ever believed the con-trary." Those who live in Newspeak can entertain no opinions that devi-ate from the party line; all doubts and independent thoughts qualify as crimethink. Winston Smith's rebellion gets under way with a classic piece of crimethink: he starts to keep a diary.

Orwell would have been dismayed, though perhaps not surprised, to find that military language in the twenty-first century often follows the truncating pattern of Newspeak. The Pentagon has a fondness for the stac-cato abbreviation of nouns: CentCom, SecDef and the like. The names of its military operations rely heavily on paired nouns — in the year after the invasion of Iraq, such operations included Bulldog Mammoth, Iron Justice, Devil Siphon and Bayonet Lightning. The Pentagon also acts as a rich source of new phrases — "blue force tracking" and "intra-theater lift," for example — in which ordinary words are militarized. More generally, just as Newspeak twists the meaning of common words beyond recognition, so does the Pentagon use a term like "rendition" in a singular way: not an interpretation, a performance or a translation, but the secret delivery of a prisoner for torture. Likewise, the accidental explosion of what it calls "friendly nuclear weapons" — a coinage as grotesque as Orwell's "joy-camp" — would lead to "nuclear collateral damage."

Orwell's achievement in 1984 was to create a form of language that embodies the most insidious type of social repression. His work became a model for any novelist who sets out to comment on contemporary life by imagining how current trends might unfold decades ahead. Reading him, other writers grasped that the vocabulary and syntax of the future would not be the same as our own, and they saw how novels set in the future could comment on language change in their own time. In *A Canticle for Leibowitz,* for instance, the American writer Walter M. Miller, Jr., imagined a novice monk in the twenty-sixth century struggling to decipher fragments of twentieth-century English that survived a nuclear apocalypse. Having mastered Latin, Brother Francis finds pre-catastrophe English lacking in clarity:

> The way nouns could sometimes modify other nouns in that tongue had always been one of his weak points. In Latin . . . a construction like *servus puer* meant about the same thing as *puer servus,* and even in English *slave boy* meant *boy slave.* But there the similarity ended. He had finally learned that *house cat* did not mean *cat house,* and that a dative of purpose or possession, as in *mihi amicus,* was somehow conveyed by *dog food* or *sentry box* even without inflection. But what of a triple appositive like *fallout survival shelter?* Brother Francis shook his head.

Miller was onto something. Nearly two decades after the 1959 publication of *A Canticle for Leibowitz,* Bruce Price wrote an essay for the language journal *Verbatim* entitled "Noun Overuse Phenomenon Article." Instead of "more people working," he observed, we read about "increased labor market participation rates." Speakers of English in the past would never have tolerated such a pileup of noun upon noun. Price's most flagrant example, discovered in a Long Island newspaper, was "U.S. Air Force aircraft fuel systems equipment mechanics course." I haven't been able to find any strings of nouns that surpass this phrase in length, though a twenty-first-century headline from the BBC's website perhaps exceeds it in ambiguity: "Cell death mark liver cancer clue."

Price believed that the phenomenon he described was not an innocent one. He quoted a description from the National Academy of Sciences of a military research project: "Work has included development of empirical and rational formulae for aerosol survival, formulae for predicting human lethal dose, and quantification of disease severity." The polysyllabic abstract nouns disguise what is really being talked about: germs and poison gas. With a nod to Orwell, Price called the phenomenon Nounspeak.

⸎

Orwell began to write *1984* soon after Hitler's death, when Stalin was still very much alive. It was natural for him to imagine that a brutal government would have the power to define and decree language change. Later authors realized that unpleasant changes in language could arise from below, instead of being imposed from above. And so, in his bitter fantasy *A Clockwork Orange* (1962), Anthony Burgess gave voice to a British culture of random adolescent violence in a future language heavily influenced by Russian. That language — a dialect or argot, more exactly — is called Nadsat, the Russian suffix for "teen." Burgess was not implying that the Red Army would soon overwhelm the United Kingdom; but, as the Cold War lingered on, his use of Russian terms gave the teenagers' boastful talk a menacing edge.

For the most part he left the grammar of English intact, lobbing in strange words like so many hand grenades: "There was me, that is Alex, and my three droogs, that is Pete, Georgie, and Dim, Dim being really dim, and we sat in the Korova Milkbar making up our rassoodocks what to do with the evening." Alex is the Beethoven-loving thug who narrates the novel, using words like droogs (friends), Korova (cow) and rassoodocks (minds) that are all derived from Russian. When he feels like praising something, Alex calls it "horrorshow" (from *khorosho,* the Russian for good). *A Clockwork Orange* features dozens of such words. Burgess also coined expressions without a Russian connection, some of them babyish ("appy polly loggy" for apology, "baddiwad" for bad), and he imagined plausible meanings for existing terms: a cigarette in the novel is a "cancer," an erection a "pan-handle." He knew that even common words can gather fresh, unexpected senses — who, as late as 1980, could imagine the destiny lying in wait for "windows," "warming," "aids" and "web"? Who, in 2005, knew that a redefinition of the solar system would make "pluto" a verb meaning to demote?

Burgess's surefooted insertion of Russian vocabulary gave his readers a powerful feel for language change in action. The irony is that he envisioned a process closer to what befell English in the distant past, when French expressions crossed the Channel thick and fast, than to any likely future for his own language. Today English absorbs new words from all over the world, no source being paramount. Yet the process Burgess evoked is now transforming the vocabulary of many other languages — with English playing the role of Russian. Remember those *oversekst, overboord statussymbools* we glimpsed in Dutch, or the *shadoh* and *hippu hangu* that girls wear in Japan? Russian cows show no sign of infiltrating English, yet English milk (*miruku*) is now part of Japanese.

Looking back on *A Clockwork Orange,* Burgess observed that "the strange new lingo would act as a kind of mist half-hiding the mayhem and protecting the reader from his own baser instincts. And there was a fine irony in the notion of a teenager race untouched by politics, using totalitarian brutality as an end in itself, equipped with a dialect which drew on the two chief political languages of the age." *A Clockwork Orange,* like *2001: A Space Odyssey,* was filmed by Stanley Kubrick. But whereas in *2001* Kubrick took few liberties with language, in the later film he adopted many of Burgess's neologisms and verbal idiosyncrasies. Admittedly, the stylized violence and the shocking use of classical music dilute the full power of Nadsat. Yet it remains essential to the movie's impact.

Burgess's searing vision of the future in *A Clockwork Orange* seems light and cheerful compared to that of William S. Burroughs in *Nova Express,* a book whose climax sees language annihilated, nothing but remnants of "word dust" being left behind. After Auschwitz and Hiroshima, leading authors of science fiction also began to show anxiety about words and their abuse. In *Fahrenheit 451,* for instance, Ray Bradbury imagined a future America in which books have been banned and a "fireman" is not someone who quenches fires but someone who sets them. Writing *The Languages of Pao,* Jack Vance conceived of a world where character flows directly from language. A usurping dictator on the planet Pao tries to install three new languages; soldiers will now talk in Valiant, a tongue "rich in effort-producing gutturals and hard vowels" whose word for shame also means relaxation. Likewise, the Valiant word for pleasure has an additional sense: overcoming resistance. And with *Babel-17,* Samuel Delany named a novel after a language — or, as it turns out, an artificial language being implanted into people's brains so as to remove their autonomy and turn them into machines. The sweet-sounding code is an invasion; the novel, a warning.

ℒ

Of course, many other writers have continued to produce the traditional kind of science fiction in which physics far outweighs linguistics. Arthur C. Clarke is a prime example. Yet as he found in his *Space Odyssey* series — *2001, 2010, 2061* and *3001* — language issues are inescapable.

The whole series began with a short story, "The Sentinel," written in 1948. It's narrated by a lunar explorer who has discovered, not a black monolith, but "a glittering, roughly pyramidal structure . . . set in the rock like a gigantic, many faceted jewel." The technology behind the tale seems amusing now — the Moon's residents live in cabins, where they cook sausages flown in from Earth, yet they have atomic energy (and use it to destroy the pyramid). The language is downright old-fashioned: "I loved the Moon, and now I knew that the creeping moss of Aristarchus and Eratosthenes was not the only life she had brought forth in her youth . . . If the pebble had vanished at that invisible barrier, I should not have been surprised." "She," "forth," "her" and "should" remind us of Clarke's origins as a middle-class Englishman born during the First World War.

Twenty years after "The Sentinel," with the Apollo missions in full swing, Clarke's novel *2001: A Space Odyssey* and Stanley Kubrick's movie appeared almost simultaneously. Much of Kubrick's brilliance lay in cutting the explanations and relying on images, not words, to tell the story — language is not among the film's special effects. A few of Clarke's expressions have a forward-looking quality: before his travelers embark for the moon, a recorded message asks for their "voice print identification." Yet languages alter when society, not just technology, abandons its previous codes. Clarke uses "men" to mean "people," and that recorded message goes on to ask lunar travelers for their "Christian name" — a phrase that, in official usage, would give way to "first name" or "given name" years before the real-life 2001.

In 1982, when the sequel *2010: Odyssey Two* came out, the author made some shrewd verbal choices to signal the growing power and sophistication of machines. New technological words are almost always nouns, and on the first page, Clarke mentions "wave-guides" and "antenna feed." Writing a decade before the advent of the World Wide Web, he appears to have foreseen something like it: a news item appeared "on *Aviation Week*'s videotext at least a month ago." By using terse compound nouns like "videotext," "comset" and "viewphone," Clarke makes his technological novelties sound linguistically plausible. Yet in other ways the style of *2010* did not keep up with the subject matter. Rather than quoting modern literature — or no literature — the characters cite Shakespeare, Cervantes, Melville and Lewis Carroll. And, in an improbable burst of metaphor, a doomed Chinese astronaut beams up a radio message to a nearby Russian-American spaceship and says, in English, "Imagine an oak tree — better yet, a banyan with its multiple trunks and roots — flattened out by gravity and trying to creep along the ground."

How different is all this from science fact? A NASA Web page updated in October 1995 — halfway between the date of Clarke's writing and the date when his novel is set — explained the work of a flight controller, or payload activity planner (PAP). To suggest a typical dialogue between the controller and a mission scientist aboard the space shuttle, the website gave the following:

> "M-Sci, this is PAP, your loop."
>
> "Go ahead, PAP."
>
> "M-Sci, the new STDCE run requested on OCR SRDCE-015 can begin at 4/10:30 MET. PS-2 can perform the crew steps."
>
> "I copy 4/10:30 MET, performed by PS-2. Thank you, PAP, I'll confirm with the experiment team."

Those are two humans speaking. Yet the passage sounds more like what we might expect a computer to say than do the words of Clarke's imaginary HAL. Fiction writers need to explore character and emotion, making it hard for any novelist to rely on this kind of unfeeling, acronym-laden language.

Clarke was seventy years old in 1987 when the next book in his series, *2061: Odyssey Three,* came out. The space travelers are still quoting Shakespeare and Tennyson, and their English sounds more and more old-fashioned — staring at a newly formed peak on a remote moon, one man remarks: "Is *that* what all the fuss was about? Looks like a perfectly ordinary mountain to me." Action and diction are seriously at odds. Readers were entitled to wonder how on earth (so to speak) Clarke would manage when, in 1997, his publishers announced a fourth volume, *3001: The Final Odyssey.* Now, instead of imagining the world and its voices a few decades in the future, he was peering ahead an entire millennium.

As it turned out, he managed pretty well. Clarke's hero is Frank Poole, the astronaut who was jettisoned by HAL in *2001* — he's rescued in the opening pages by a spacetug beyond the orbit of Neptune. Poole's body is "so far below the freezing point that there was no metabolism"; therefore he can be brought back to life. In the world of 3001, he speaks an archaic English almost no one can understand. Dramatic changes have swept over the language since his own time, with new scientific words proliferating. "More frustrating, however, were the myriads of famous and infamous personal names that had accumulated over the millennium, and which meant nothing to him. For weeks, until he had built up a data bank, most of his conversations had to be interrupted with potted biographies." Small wonder people talk to him slowly, awkwardly.

Poole's rescuer, Captain Dimitri Chandler, is formally known as M2973.04.21/93.106//Mars//SpaceAcad3005 — his "ident." People in 3001 receive an ident at birth, via a nanochip in each palm. Without one, Poole is told, "no input device would recognize your existence." His head is shaved so that he can receive a Braincap: a snug-fitting metal helmet with nanowires that worm down through his scalp to his brain. Information is stored in electro-optical tablets, somewhat like the computer diskettes from Poole's youth. With the help of data compression, one of these tablets "could store not only the memories — but the actual person." Two pages of the novel — Clarke uses them to convey ideas that would otherwise weigh down the plot — are an "extract, text only, from *Tourist's Guide to Outer Solar System, v. 219.3.*" It's not a lonely planet anymore; it's a lonely galaxy.

By 3001, traditional religion is extinct and nobody eats "corpse-food." Many terms have additional meanings — "sunscreen," for instance, now refers to "wrapping a comet's core in a sheet of reflective film." But along with the new wording, technical or otherwise, Clarke still draws on old figures of speech. In his first pages we learn that "the human race had too many eggs in one fragile basket," we hear of "a witches' brew of carbon and sulfur compounds," and we're told "This was the third wild-goose chase . . ." Egg baskets, witches and wild geese have nothing to do with the astonishing world that Frank Poole enters. But it would require a poet — something Clarke is not — to invent metaphors that light up both his own and his characters' time. He can imagine the technology of the next millennium far more easily than its language.

⌇

The old innocence about language has gone. Today's readers, unlike Bellamy's, understand that language change is inevitable. And so, for the sake of realism, most futuristic novels and films include a few unfamiliar expressions to indicate the passage of time. P. D. James was an elderly woman in 1992 when her futuristic novel *The Children of Men* appeared: a visionary book, but verbally and technologically a conservative one. Well over a decade elapsed before the story reached the screen, having undergone major changes (many of them for the worse). Somewhere along that tortuous path, one or more of the five screenwriters who adapted the book infused it with new words. So, in the 2006 film *Children of Men,* terrifying news from "BCC" flashes across TV screens; religious extremists are introduced as "Renouncers"; desperate refugees go by the name "Fugees." None of those terms appear in the novel. But without them, or others like them, its language seems redolent of the past. Invented expressions are one of the ways the *Children of Men* screenwriters tried to "keep it real."

Amid all the imagined disasters, the heartfelt calamities, few writers of speculative fiction have chosen to embody a healthy, peaceful society in a language to match. J.R.R. Tolkien's Elvish provides an obvious exception, though his Elves are doomed to leave Middle-earth in the rough hands of men. A second exception comes from the great fantasy and science-fiction writer Ursula K. Le Guin. Her alertness to questions of language has been a constant throughout her career. Let's take a quick look at one of her lesser-known books: *Always Coming Home* (1985). Le Guin is the daughter of anthropologists, and surely no other novel in the history of fiction has included kinship charts, pictorial symbols, poems, recipes, essays, folktales, a cassette of songs, descriptions of dances and musical instruments, notes on medicine and technology — and a fifteen-page glossary.

Always Coming Home focuses on the Kesh people in what we know as northern California, long after the world has suffered some kind of industrial apocalypse. The Kesh are still dealing with the aftereffects (Styrofoam is apparently eternal). Their society relies on cooperation, hard work and an intimate grasp of the natural world; they are indigenous to a beloved land, though by no means primitive scientifically. They enjoy vineyards, trains and electricity; they use condoms and diaphragms (nobody is allowed to sire or bear more than two children); they make books; and they offer successful, nonviolent resistance to a neighboring people known as the Condors, a warmaking society much closer in spirit to us than we are to the Kesh.

As part of Le Guin's invention of a world and a culture, she also creates a language. The Kesh word "ambad," for instance, means "giving, the act of giving; generosity; wealth." "Kesh grammar," the author tells us, "makes no provision for a relation of ownership between living beings. A language in which the verb 'to have' is an intransitive and in which 'to be rich' is the same word as 'to give' is likely to turn its foreign speaker, and translator, into a clown." (In fact, as Le Guin knows, many indigenous cultures of the Northwest Coast did measure wealth in terms of giving.) "Paó" — a nod to Jack Vance, I suspect — has a trio of meanings: "achievement; sowing; ejaculation, male orgasm." It's matched by "banhe": "acceptance, inclusion; insight, understanding; female orgasm." The verb "heyiya" exemplifies Le Guin's ability to evoke a grounded philosophy, a way of being, through a brief definition. It means "to be sacred, holy, significant; to connect; to move in a spiral, to gyre; to be or to be at the center; to change; to become. Praise; to praise."

The wisdom embodied in the language of the Kesh also suggests what is *not* present in our own speech. In English, sexuality is unrelated to insight, the sacred is what never changes, and "to have" demands an object. The words of the Kesh are meant to be a challenge, a reproach. The Kesh flourish, in Le Guin's archaeology of the future, only because we have died out.

ᔕ

The message from countless writers, artists and filmmakers is clear: we're in deep trouble. Our way of life is not sustainable. Read the science fiction of the past twenty-five years, and you'll become intimate with ecological disaster, social disorder, genetic mishaps, rampant plagues, private corporations run amok, religious fanaticism, diseased and mutated children, armies out of control, perpetual surveillance, random and extreme violence, economic breakdown and a black-market trade in everything from hormones to human organs. Nature is dead or on life support. Civilization survives only in some beleaguered form, usually virtual or artificial. If the earth can no longer cope with us — if we can no longer cope with ourselves — what kind of language will we utter?

"Art does not imitate life," the novelist Jeanette Winterson has said. "Art anticipates life." Here is a fragment of one anticipation, brilliantly imagined by the American writer Russell Hoban:

> Bad Tym it wuz then. Peapl din no if thay wud be alyv 1 day tu the nex. Din even no if thayd be alyv 1 min tu the nex. Sum stuk tu gether sum din. Sum tyms thay dru lots. Sum got et so uthers cud liv. Cudn be shur uv nuthing din no wut wuz sayf tu eat or drink & tryin tu keap wyd uv uther forajers & dogs it wuz nothing onle Luck if enne 1 stayd alyv.

This all happened long ago, the boy tells us. In Hoban's 1980 novel *Riddley Walker,* the title character is a twelve-year-old man-child wandering through what was once the English county of Kent, telling stories about his people: the baffled descendants of those who survived a nuclear catastrophe that destroyed London and terminated the modern world. They don't know exactly what happened and have reverted to a hunter-gatherer mode of life. Legends, names, images and artifacts from the bright age continue to haunt them. They spend enormous effort digging up ancient machines with the aim of melting them down. They keep trying to reassemble the fragments of a lost meaning.

The strange spelling is only the beginning of the linguistic changes that Hoban foresees. Words in *Riddley Walker* are drastically shortened. Names have eroded — Dover and Folkestone have become dead towns known as Do It Over and Fork Stoan. Vocabulary has shrunk: many expressions are used again and again. Syntax too has altered. Prepositions are scarce, adverbs scarcer; sentences are often long but seldom complex. Knowledge is encapsulated in rhymes and riddles, though the words they contain have grown mysterious. Riddley sings about "the sarvering galack seas and flaming nebyul eye" without realizing what those phrases once meant. Just as the boy has to struggle to explain his life, Hoban makes us struggle to understand his telling:

> The sky gone grey the stoans gone grey the dogs gone back to how they lookit befor and come down on to all 4s. It wernt a circel it wer another shape they were running like a black rivver out and a roun out and a roun it wer a big shape they were running in amongst the rubbl and a roun I begun to run it with them. It wer 2ce as wide acrost as the divvy roof at How Fents I run it 3 times roun befor I knowit jus what shape it wer.

Like so many films and novels set in the future, *Riddley Walker* can be read as a portent and a prophecy. If society explodes or implodes, language will not emerge intact from the ravages. Over and over, Riddley's people repeat the tale of Eusa, who split "the Littl Man the Addom" in his thirst to make the "1 Big 1," and who paid a terrible price for his greed. Everything Eusa knows and loves is lost in the "Master Chaynjis." Riddley sees evidence of his mistake in what we, not he, can recognize as the white shadow left on an old concrete wall by the flash of a nuclear explosion. Pondering the stories that broken words convey, his people grapple with the legacy of their ancestors' failure. The human spirit endures — Riddley is one smart boy. But the verbal realm, like the physical, is maimed.

Riddley Walker had a lasting influence on the English novelist David Mitchell, whose 2004 novel *Cloud Atlas* is one of the most complex and dazzling works of literature to appear in our young century. *Cloud Atlas* is told in eleven sections and set in six historical periods, the connections between them being subtle and slow to emerge. The first section, narrated by an American notary crossing the South Pacific in the mid-nineteenth century, stops in midsentence and resumes as the final chapter; the second section picks up again as the tenth; and so on. At the novel's heart, a long unbroken chapter is narrated by a future human called Zach'ry, who recalls the extraordinary events that took place when he was a boy.

Zach'ry grew up on the Big Island of Hawaii centuries after an apocalypse devastated the planet. As in *Riddley Walker,* the fall has led to verbal truncation and amputation. Words have reverted to a future past: "Snailysome goin' was them rockfields, yay, jus'brush that rock light an' your fingers'd bleed fast'n'wetly, so I binded my boots'n'hands in strips o' hidebark . . ." Irregular forms like "bound" have become regular; "of" and "and" are even briefer than before; "yay" and "nay" have replaced "yes" and "no." Mitchell also coins words, "snailysome" being an example. Zach'ry is fond of adverbs that end with "some," as in "Fiercesome he speaked at me." If the result brings *Huckleberry Finn* to mind, so be it. Freedom was one of Mark Twain's great themes, and freedom is the overriding concern of *Cloud Atlas.*

Its absence, the need for it, the hunger for it dominate the fifth and seventh sections of the novel: a long interview between an archivist and a prisoner facing execution in a terrifying Korea of the twenty-first century, shortly before the apocalypse. The second quotation at the start of this chapter comes from these pages. Sonmi-451, the prisoner, is a rebel fabricant, created to be a slave (for reasons too complicated to explain, a hologram of her testimony was preserved, making her a kind of goddess to Zach'ry's people). Fabricants are "perfect organic machinery," grown in wombtanks. Instead of eating, they ingest a special formula called Soap, and would die without it. After twelve years of servitude they're killed and their body parts reused. In one of many echoes of *1984,* the political system in power — Unanimity — disguises truth by a systematic distortion of language: cloned pets are "living dolls," and prostitutes are "comforters." (During the Second World War, Japanese soldiers called their Korean sex slaves "comfort women.") Mitchell's use of language in the Sonmi sections echoes *1984:* it warns of the vile uses to which words can be put, and points up the distance between liberty and power.

Take "soul," for example. In Sonmi's time, it has become an instrument of social control — a morsel of technology that allows the authorities to distinguish a pureblood human from a fabricant. When Sonmi is on the run with two malcontents, "Hae-Joo . . . sliced off the tip of his left index, gouged, and xtracted a tiny metallic egg. He threw it out of the window . . . Xi-Li also xtracted his Soul." Other religious terms suffer equal distortion: the fabricants begin their day with matins, end it with vespers, and know their catechism by heart.

Unanimity's leadership is called the Juche: the name of the current tyranny in North Korea. But in *Cloud Atlas,* the economic system that relies on fabricants' labor goes by the name "corpocracy." "A Soul's value," slaves declare in their catechism, "is the dollars therein." Waste disposal is provided by ShitCorp, oxygen by AirCorp, sex by PimpCorp. Brand names surviving from the past stand for a whole class of object: any movie is a "disney," any photograph a "kodak." Language is at the mercy of commerce. Following another pattern from our own time, many nouns do double duty as verbs. Sonmi works in a fast-food restaurant before she rebels, and must "input orders, tray food, vend drinks, upstock condiments . . ." The technical name for this is "conversion." If conversion keeps on expanding, the linguist Jean Aitchison has written, "the eventual result may be complete interchangeability of items such as nouns and verbs, which were once kept rigidly apart." (Conversion was also a key feature of Newspeak in 1984.) Rebellion lessens Sonmi's use of converted nouns, liberating her to speak with verbs.

All in all, Mitchell's imagined blend of science, religion and commerce requires a language of dizzying novelty. Yet in its emphasis on the corporate power of naming, its reliance on technology, its blend of East and West, its fondness for conversion and its willingness to coin high-sounding expressions that conceal a disagreeable truth, that language is a direct heir of our own. When Sonmi is being readied for freedom, "the amnesiacs in my Soapsac were reduced . . . and ascension catalysts instreamed." If society continues to undergo changes as great as it has witnessed over the past century, language would no doubt experience its own form of instreaming ascension. *Cloud Atlas* spells out some of the consequences.

⌇

Novelists don't face an easy task when they highlight words to come. "Try to write in what will be the language of the future," Robert J. Sawyer told me, and "you risk losing an awful lot of readers. And the sad truth is that futuristic idioms and slang can sound ridiculous." Sawyer writes speculative fiction of big ideas — one of his novels culminates in the birth of God — but he sets much of his work in the present, not the future. "We're a bit gun-shy," he admits. "A lot of hard SF has moved into being post-singularity literature, because once the technological singularity hits, we're in Clarke's world of any sufficiently advanced technology being indistinguishable from magic. The Net is changing almost yearly — from an e-mail medium to a discussion group medium to a social networking medium to a video distribution medium to . . . well, to what, who knows?"

Who indeed? Something very much like Clarke's vision of our distant future — the ident at birth, the nanowires worming through the scalp, even the electro-optical tablets that can store a person — may come to pass long before 3001. "I think the future is going to be a lot stranger than anyone imagines," says Ramez Naam, one of the creators of Microsoft Outlook and Internet Explorer — he's also the author of *More Than Human: Embracing the Promise of Biological Enhancement.* He goes on to echo J. G. Ballard: "In science fiction we imagine the future is outer space. But it looks like the future is inner space. The future is not so much about all of us leaving this planet, it's about gaining control over our genes, gaining control over our bodies, gaining control over our brains and minds, and being able to alter them." Clarke and Naam look forward to this with keen anticipation. To others their dream is a nightmare, the locus of appalled imagining.

As Bill McKibben noted, one of the most popular forms such imagining has taken is the *Matrix* trilogy (the subject of more than twenty books of criticism and analysis). The world its hero, Neo, thinks he knows is actually "a computer-generated dreamworld, built to keep us under control." Or so Neo is informed by Morpheus, his guide and mentor in revolt. That dreamworld — that "neural interactive simulation" — is the Matrix, which also appears on computer screens in the form of downward-streaming lines of code. What used to be the fertile earth is now a poisoned, inhospitable wasteland. The evil Agent Smith — both a character and a program — calls human beings a virus, a disease, a cancer: "You are a plague and we are the cure." Visually and conceptually, *The Matrix* (at least, the first of the three films) is stunning.

Linguistically, it's a huge disappointment. Even though its events take place two centuries in the future, there's almost nothing strange or different about the words that fill the actors' mouths. Some of Morpheus's remarks — "This is a war and we are soldiers," or "I believe in Providence" — might well have been lifted from a John Wayne movie. To see what the language of

The Matrix could have been, and to learn where many of its ideas come from, we need to turn back to literature.

"He'd operated on an almost permanent adrenaline high, a byproduct of youth and proficiency, jacked into a custom cyberspace deck that projected his disembodied consciousness into the consensual hallucination that was the matrix." That casual explanatory sentence appears on the third page of *Neuromancer,* the 1984 novel by William Gibson that has its seedy jumping-off point in Japan. This is one of the places where the notion of the matrix originated; it's also the source of the term "cyberspace." Gibson coins words with deadpan flair. He didn't invent "microsoft" — though Microsoft was just a modest programming firm in its pre-Windows days when Gibson used the term in *Neuromancer* to mean a silicon sliver implanted into a socket in the brain. "Simstim" was his invention: an electronic device that allows one character to suffer or delight in another's sensory experiences. Because of simstim, "I feel your pain" in *Neuromancer* is not a metaphor.

Earlier writers of science fiction had also created words that refused to stay still on the page. The Czech writer Karel Čapek invented "robot" in 1921; following in his footsteps, Isaac Asimov came up with "robotics." Computer "worms" — programs that reproduce themselves across a network — began life in *The Shockwave Rider,* a 1975 novel by the British author John Brunner. Philip K. Dick coined "kipple" in his novel *Do Androids Dream of Electric Sheep?,* the basis for the movie *Blade Runner.* Hollywood screenwriters have given us "replicant" (*Blade Runner*) and "lightsaber" (*Star Wars*). But the cyberpunk writers seem especially gifted at word creation. Bruce Sterling, the movement's first theorist, invented "spime," "buckyjunk" and "Wexelblat disaster," among other expressions.

Unlike a lot of science-fiction writers, Gibson takes care to leave some of his coinages and allusions unexplained. "They're def triff, huh?" a woman says to the hero, Case, as he inspects "five huge Cibachromes of Tally Isham." "'Mine. Shot 'em at the S/N Pyramid, last time we went down the well. She was *that* close, and she just smiled, *so* natural. And it was *bad* there, Lupus, day after these Christ the King terrs put angel in the water, you know?' 'Yeah,' Case said, suddenly uneasy, 'terrible thing.'" His unease mirrors our own, for Gibson never puts the story on pause to explain its lexicon. As a result, language in *Neuromancer* remains slightly out of reach. If all its words were readily explicable, the future wouldn't provoke so much anxiety — a foretaste of simstim, perhaps, giving Gibson's readers a jolt of the same bafflement that his off-kilter hero feels. Anxiety is oxygen to his work.

In *Neuromancer,* Gibson also plays with an old tradition about the power of language. "To call up a demon," Case learns near the climax, "you must learn its name. Men dreamed that, once, but now it is true in another way. You know that, Case. Your business is to learn the names of programs, the long formal names, names the owners seek to conceal. True names." Language, in the virtual sense, is most true when it is but a code. To fulfill his destructive mission, Case has to cut through a skein of elaborate illusions and discover one true name. He succeeds, and "the cityscape recedes: city as Chiba, city as the ranked data . . . as the roads and crossroads scribed on the face of a microchip." Revelation has come to mean comprehending the language of a machine.

By 2007, when Gibson's novel *Spook Country* was published, technology had caught up with much of his early imagining. So the author, like technology, moved on. His latest book, set in the present, features an investigative reporter looking into "spatially tagged hypermedia," or locative art — a means of attaching virtual installations to physical places by using a GPS grid. Hackers are now "geohackers." Cyberspace is "everting," or turning itself out from the computer screen into the world at large. "And once it everts," a character says, "then there isn't any cyberspace, is there? There never was, if you want to look at it that way. It was a way we had of looking where we were headed, a direction. With the grid, we're here. This is the other side of the screen." Interviewed on television in September 2007, Gibson described life in the twenty-first century as "invariably stranger than anything I or any other science-fiction writer have ever made up."

Science fiction has long posed the questions "What is human?" and "What is real?" Fantasies of monsters, robots and androids allowed writers in earlier times to play with the issue — it's the main preoccupation behind both Mary Shelley's *Frankenstein* and *Do Androids Dream of Electric Sheep?* In our time, virtual reality entails a similar exploration. Our newest machines delight and intimidate, amaze and unnerve us. As a prefix, *cyber* has taken up the role that *jet* and *astro* played in the 1960s and '70s: a sign of the ultramodern. But it's noteworthy that terms like "jetway," "jetport" and "jet age" now sound decidedly creaky; even "jet set" has acquired a few wrinkles. So much for the luminous promise of travel around the globe. Reality eventually sets in — and so the phrase "jet lag" has neither creaks nor wrinkles.

The compounds beginning with *cyber* are much younger. Many of them already express doubt and fear: "cyberbullying," "cybercrime," "cyber-squatter," "cyberstalk," "cyberterrorist," "cyberwar" and so on. "Cyberpunk" embodies them all. Language tells us that if we're hoping to escape our woes, computers are the wrong place to look.

⮑

"Yo, Y.T.," Roadkill says, "'sup?"
  "'Sup with you?"
"Surfing the Tura. 'Sup with you?"
"Maxing The Clink."
"Whoa! Who popped you?"
"MetaCops. Affixed me to the gate of White Columns with a loogie gun."
  "Whoa, how very!"

This phone conversation takes place early in Neal Stephenson's remarkable cyberpunk novel *Snow Crash* (1992), between a fifteen-year-old skateboard courier and her loser boyfriend. It's a brief exchange, less than forty words, yet it delivers a series of linguistic punches. Names have been replaced by initials ("Y.T.") or abbreviated ("Tura" is short for Ventura Boulevard in Los Angeles). Brand names have been invented ("White Columns") or adapted from existing slang ("MetaCops," "The Clink"). Nicknames or aliases ("Roadkill") are prevalent. Current slang ("yo," "'sup," "whoa," "maxing") is joined by invented slang ("how very!"). Current verbs are used in a rare sense ("popped" for caught) or a new one ("surfing" refers to couriers who attach their skateboards to cars or trucks, then ride along in the slipstream). Finally, Stephenson coins a new phrase to denote an invented object: "loogie gun," meaning a weapon that shoots out a fibrous, snotty wad of matter to immobilize a target. Like many other *Snow Crash* terms, "loogie gun" now enjoys an independent life on the Internet.

At the end of their short conversation, Roadkill asks where his girlfriend is:

"Buy'n'Fly number 501,762."
  "I'm on my way to Bernie with a super-ultra."
  As in San Bernardino. As in super-ultra-high-priority delivery. As in, you're out of luck.

Buy'n'Fly is one of the countless "franchulates" in *Snow Crash* — others include Mr. Lee's Greater Hong Kong, Reverend Wayne's Pearly Gates, Nova Sicilia (i.e., the Mafia) and New South Africa (for white supremacists). Power has fractured into corporate globules, all of them sinister. Stephenson's verbal inventiveness is constantly at the service of his eye for social and political trends. So, when an area has been abandoned to its toxic fate, it becomes a National Sacrifice Zone. And the heavily guarded, autonomous zones that rich families inhabit go by the name of Burbclaves. Like *Neuromancer*, *Snow Crash* succeeds as both a harbinger and an engine of language change: the word "burbclave" has now entered the lexicon of people who may never have read a word of cyberpunk fiction. A California member of an urban-planning newsgroup posted a message in 2005 asking: "Have you ever known any technologist, engineer (outside the civil or planning side of things), or computer programmer who has any interest at all in culture or the built environment outside the 'burbclave or the office park?"

As well as imagining the language of the wired young, Stephenson also parodies several types of current discourse. When the MetaCops arrest Y.T., one of them tells her: "We are equipped with devices, including but not limited to projectile weapons, which, if used, may pose an extreme and immediate threat to your health and well-being." His partner translates: "Make one funny move and we'll blow your head off." Y.T.'s mother — a programmer in Fedland, the sorry remnant of the United States government — is assigned 15.62 minutes to read "a new subchapter of the EBGOC Procedure Manual" concerning BTDUs — bathroom tissue distribution units, formerly known as toilet rolls: "The problem of distributing bathroom tissue to workers presents inherent challenges for any office management system due to the inherent unpredictability of usage." Then there's the Nipponese singer Sushi K, who raps like this:

Sarariman on subway listen
For Sushi K like nuclear fission

Fire-breathing lizard Gojiro
He my always big-time hero

His mutant rap burn down whole block
Start investing now Sushi K stock . . .

The central character in *Snow Crash* is a half-black, half-Asian computer genius with the apt name of Hiro Protagonist. As in *Neuromancer*, *The Matrix* and many other works in the cyberpunk genre, a solitary hacker is the young hero — accompanied by a gorgeous girl, of course. (In some ways, cyberpunk is deeply traditional.) A software designer and pizza delivery boy, Hiro freelances for the Central Intelligence Corporation — an amalgam of the CIA and the Library of Congress. He was also an early programmer of what Stephenson calls the Metaverse; the novel flips back and forth between the chaotic "real world" and Hiro's no less dangerous life online. In his acknowledgments Stephenson writes: "The words 'avatar' (in the sense used here) and 'Metaverse' are my inventions, which I came up with when I decided that existing words (such as 'virtual reality') were simply too awkward to use."

An avatar was once — and, of course, still is — the incarnation of a Hindu god. But in the 1980s, it began to signify something else: the onscreen representation of a player in a video game. Stephenson took this usage and ran with it, using "avatar" to mean an intricate, 3-D simulation in the Metaverse. Some avatars are cheap and low-tech; others are grotesque. Hiro's avatar looks just like its creator, except that it always sports a black leather kimono.

This was all fiction in 1992. Today it's not. Chatrooms and instant-messaging programs use avatars. So, as we've seen, do role-playing games. But it's in 3-D fantasy worlds where self-designed avatars are most crucial. The best known of them, Second Life, has acknowledged a huge conceptual debt to Stephenson. By June 2007, Second Life claimed to have about seven million subscribers. Many of them have spent large amounts of money online to equip their avatars with the trendiest fashions, the latest vehicles, the largest houses, the most sensational body parts. That money — Linden dollars, named after the company that founded Second Life — is convertible to U.S. dollars. Not only does the fantasy world have its own economy; it also has its own vocabulary. Reuters news agency has dispatched a correspondent into Second Life to report to real-world readers on the virtual goings-on. After Honda and Toyota moved into Second Life, a Japanese politician announced plans to open an office there. Many universities, including Harvard, have made use of it for "virtual learning." In 2007 the Swedish Institute — an arm of the Swedish government — set up an embassy. And the Royal Liverpool Philharmonic performed live before an audience of avatars, in a video streamed across the Internet onto a screen in a simulated Art Deco hall.

Penguin Books is one of the many corporations now taking close interest in the economy of this and other virtual worlds. In 2006 it set up shop in Second Life. The first book its avatars offered for sale? *Snow Crash.*

10

The Soul's Ozone
Keeping Language Real

NOTHING DATES MORE QUICKLY than the new. New England, New York, New Orleans, New Mexico, New South Wales, New Guinea, New Brunswick, Newfoundland: we've grown so used to the sound of these names that we scarcely hear the "new" in them any longer. In Oxford, the novelty of New College had waned by 1400. New France was over and done with by 1760; Art Nouveau stopped being new before the end of the nineteenth century; the New Deal, the New Left, the New Wave and the *nouveau roman* have all faded into history. Most things New Age now seem old hat, and even *nouvelle cuisine* has given way to other styles of cooking. Anything I've described as new in these pages will not remain so for long.

Yet — bearing in mind how quickly the new subsides into the middle-aged — it's only fair to ask what are the most significant findings of this book. I did, after all, set out to look for the new. I did promise to explore and interpret the verbal revolution. In the first chapter I quoted David Crystal's "vision of a linguistic future which is radically different from what has existed in the past." And if we look at some of the processes and movements that nourish such a vision, we'll find that they apply not just to English but also to many other widespread languages.

In English, as we've seen, the prevalence of slang and new expressions among the young — especially in the company of electronic devices — tends to baffle older people. The same is true for Mandarin. It is, says the linguist Brian D. Joseph, "undergoing a major influx of acronyms from foreign languages, mainly English, and they are often represented by English letters rather than traditional Chinese characters." Many girls and boys who write in Mandarin now take a word in Chinese characters and add the suffix -*ing*. For many centuries Mandarin demanded the use of a complex system of honorifics — a counterpart to Japanese *keigo*. But in recent decades this system has largely dissolved. No longer do Chinese men and women identify themselves by words that mean "I, the insignificant," "I, the insignificant and female," "I, the unintelligent" or "I, who am without talent." (It's tempting, I realize, to suggest that a few of these phrases should be imported into English.) China's languages are extraordinarily rich in insults. "May your child be born with a deformed anus" is a Mandarin curse you might say to someone you regard as a bastard — a "turtle grandson," that is. But insults evolve. Just as "sick" and "ill" are now uttered as praise by young people in North America and Britain, so has one of Mandarin's many words for penis morphed from an attack into a compliment. To say that something is great in Mandarin, you may now want to call it the "cow's vagina."

Cantonese, the most widely spoken language in southern China, has long been renowned for its bluntness. In 2004, an article in the *South China Morning Post* quoted a social worker with the surprising name of Bottle Shiu Ka-Chun who explained that in Hong Kong, Cantonese slang is fast moving into the mainstream. "Before, only teenagers spoke slang," he explained, "but now even educated people use it. The life of each term is much shorter than it used to be. For the whole 1980s and '90s, we used the term *kau* [mixing] for courting; now we use *gai* [cutting open]. New terms keep coming up." Triad gangs are a common source of fresh Cantonese expressions, some of which are openly offensive. Yet they have found a home in workplaces and apartments, movies and TV shows, even the Hong Kong legislature. "Hong Kong is like a factory," one linguist said, "churning out these interesting expressions."

The old rules of language use in many countries are eroding — and the erosion may be long overdue. "If some people long for the lost feminine voice in the writings of modern Bengali women," the Bangladeshi author Taslima Nasrin has said, "they are asking for the lost world where women's language was the language of the subordinate and meek." Bengali ranks among the dozen most widely spoken languages in the world, and its literary tradition goes back well over a thousand years. For almost all that time, it was a tradition that belonged to men. Women were not expected or encouraged to master the language's cultivated register. Nasrin observes: "It used to be said of the Bengali girl that even though her heart rends, her lips never part to speak. Well, she has started to speak out now." Her outspokenness carries enormous risk — religious extremists have placed a large bounty on her head. Nasrin takes pride in using "the refined vocabulary of men" to question and subvert what most Bengali men still believe.

Elsewhere, the very idea of linguistic refinement is under siege. "Vocabulary and syntax are disastrously, ignobly degraded," wrote Maurice Druon, an elderly novelist who belongs to the Académie Française. "The French no longer respect their language because they are no longer proud of themselves or their country. They no longer love themselves, and thus no longer love what was once the instrument of their glory." His remarks betray an old-fashioned assumption that the French language and nation are indissoluble; Algerians, Canadians, Haitians, Belgians, Swiss and people from many African countries would disagree. But Druon is right to perceive French as rife with change. Often the changes begin on the margins of society. Aside from their delight in text messaging and their willingness to use Anglicisms, many young people in France speak an evolving form of slang known as *verlan* — the guiding principle involves a reversal of sounds and syllables, so that *fou* (mad) becomes *ouf,* and *bizarre* turns into *zarbi.* Those who are proficient in *verlan* sometimes re-reverse the syllables into a form even less comprehensible to outsiders.

French is one of many languages in which informality meets an ever greater level of acceptance. English is another. Little more than fifty years ago — to judge by a 1954 phrasebook called *The Traveller in Italy* — an English visitor needed to know the Italian for expressions like "This beret suits me, does it not?," "Please book me a seat in the motor-coach for this afternoon," and "I should be obliged if you would send this letter." Times have changed. The *Lonely Planet Spanish Phrasebook,* published in 2003, gives colloquial translations for "We're having a party," "It's crap," "Are you horny?" and "I've been raped." Influenced by the casualness of everyday speech — and by the still evolving conventions of e-mails — written languages are becoming less buttoned up. Fewer and fewer letters composed in French now end with distended formulas like *Je vous prie, madame, d'accepter l'expression de mes sentiments les plus sincères.* Instead they finish with *Bien à vous* or *Sincèrement.*

The street French of Montreal is so different from its Parisian counterpart that Quebec films are occasionally subtitled for French audiences. English has even greater differences among its many varieties. Here too, parallels exist in other languages, notably Spanish and Portuguese. We may have no trouble distinguishing a frijole from an enchilada, but many Chileans are unfamiliar with those Mexican words; a taco in Chile means the heel of a shoe. Even a common term like "banana" has at least four equivalents in Spanish, depending on where the fruit is being eaten. As for Portuguese, many times more people speak it in Brazil than in the small European country where the language began. But the Brazilian and Portuguese versions of the language are very different — as the scholar and novelist Stephen Henighan observes: "The Portuguese swallow their words and speak in an ashamed grumble, while Brazilians enunciate everything to an almost comical degree." In a recent memoir, the distinguished translator Gregory Rabassa confirms the point: "I have heard of Brazilians who speak English when they go to Lisbon because they would have trouble understanding their native language as it is spoken there."

Fueled by the Brazilian entertainment industry, Portuguese is now spreading fast in African countries like Angola and Mozambique. As it does so, it begins to blend with local tongues. This is one of the many edges along which languages are drawing together. The informal, contested mixture of English and Spanish in Los Angeles is echoed by the fusion of English and Asian idioms in Singapore, by the blend of French and English in Montreal, and by the mixed languages so prevalent in parts of India. Such blending can, if necessary, occur at great speed. As the Frenchman Sim Kessel wrote in his memoir *Hanged at Auschwitz:* "You had to learn every language spoken in camp — German, Russian, Polish, Yiddish; eventually a combination of these four became the special dialect of Auschwitz." Although there's nothing uniquely twenty-first century about the process, today's mixings involve a greater number of cities, countries and peoples than ever before.

In the past, mixed idioms were seldom written down. Today most of them exist in written as well as spoken form. The main reason is the Internet. A few clicks of the mouse will take you to "I do'wan to talk to him, lah. He always so bin chow chow one," and hundreds of other inimitable expressions in the online version of the *Coxford Singlish Dictionary.* On a World of Warcraft message board based in the Philippines, someone going by the name of thebong02 posted this comment in January 2007: *ok din yung avernus. i-maximize mo yung gamit ng shield. pero mas survivor sya kaysa killer kasi ulti nya pang buhay.* The message has two words of Spanish and at least five words of English. "Ulti" is a gaming term that originates in English, "avernus" a name that comes from Latin. All the other words are in Filipino — as far as I know. I don't suppose that thebongo2 set out to make a linguistic point; he (or she) simply mixes words and languages as though it were the most natural activity in the world.

Perhaps it is. In many countries, multilingualism is only natural. But traditionally, speakers would keep each of their languages in a separate realm. I traded e-mails with an Englishwoman, Anne-Marie Swift, whose "partner grew up in Sri Lanka where his family all spoke English at home, Sinhalese with their community, Arabic for the mosque, and Tamil with Tamil people. It didn't seem strange to them. Equally, in Morocco, I worked with kids who routinely spoke Berber at home and Moroccan Arabic in the street, worshipped in 'proper Arabic,' and studied in French."

Things weren't always so neat and tidy, of course. But today the barriers that once kept languages apart are crumbling. Salman Rushdie has suggested that what the people of his home city, Bombay, actually speak is "Hug-me": Rushdie's acronym for an unsettled mixture of Hindi, Urdu, Gujarati, Marathi and English. "The language of the urban Pakistani," adds Masud Alam, an Urdu-language broadcaster for the BBC, "is now a hotchpotch of Urdu, Punjabi and a few words of English spoken with an accent that can be understood only by someone who speaks the same way."

In South Africa, linguistic barriers were never as high as political and economic ones. After the downfall of the apartheid system, its new government decided the country would have eleven official languages: Afrikaans, English, Xhosa, Zulu and seven other indigenous tongues. There was method in what some people saw as madness, for none of these languages is the mother tongue of even a quarter of the nation's population (Zulu has the most speakers, with English ranking fifth). Yet no matter how unjust their political and economic system may have been, the people of South Africa have always figured out ways to address each other. Their languages contain the proof.

Xhosa, for example, drew heavily on the ancient languages of the Khoisan (occasionally referred to by the old name of Bushmen and by the derogatory term Hottentots) — clicks and all. It has also taken numerous words from two languages with European roots: Afrikaans and English. In the nineteenth century, English soldiers would call any Xhosa man "Johnny"; the Xhosa returned the favor by making their word for soldier *ijoni.* Afrikaans, too, gathered a rich harvest of words from other tongues; were it not for these words, indeed, Afrikaans would still be a dialect of its Dutch parent. The structures of power and wealth played a critical role in determining how South Africa's languages grew over time. Miners were black; their supervisors and overseers were not. In the mining areas a pidgin evolved, Fanakalo, that allowed the bossed and the bosses to communicate with each other. (Although its origins go back to the Victorian era, it rose to prominence in twentieth-century gold mines.) Its vocabulary relied largely on Zulu and English. But Fanakalo was a language of labor, not pleasure; it was nobody's mother tongue; few people chose to speak it if they had any other alternative.

Now consider the rapid, bewildering growth of two languages that have emerged in the gaping townships of South Africa in recent decades. Iscamtho is widely spoken in Soweto; it draws its lexicon mostly from languages indigenous to black South Africans, such as Zulu and Sotho. By contrast, Flaaitaal takes much of its lexicon from Afrikaans — the language of the former government. Its origins are said to lie in the jargon of thugs and thieves in the mid-twentieth century. The young men who created Flaaitaal seized hold of their rulers' tongue and bent it to their own purposes.

There's no agreed-upon spelling for either of these languages. Nor do they have a single accepted name — Flaaitaal goes by at least sixteen different names, Tsotsitaal being the best known (*taal* is the Afrikaans word for language). But they reek of life. "I wanted [the movie] to come out of the streets where it belongs and in the language in which it is most powerfully resonant," said Gavin Hood, who directed *Tsotsi,* the Academy Award winner in 2006 for best foreign language film. "Frankly, for many years I have been feeling that many films made in our country, set in our country, made in the English language, well intentioned, using some big names, many of whom are wonderful actors, have somehow lacked the smell of truth." In certain domains — food and drink, police and prison among them — Flaaitaal is what linguists call overlexicalized: it has too many words. To speak of a friend or someone who belongs to your group, you could choose to say *bra* (from the English "brother"), *bab* (from Zulu), *budi* (from Afrikaans), *brikhado* (from Portuguese), *mri* (from Sotho) — or you could resort to at least two dozen other terms, all with a smell of truth. Whatever languages you happen to know, Flaaitaal will be glad to make use of them.

"Anyone who does not keep abreast," writes K.D.P. Makhudu, "is soon left behind by the rapid turnover of vocabulary." Today that's true for almost any major language and any country you care to mention, but it's especially so for South Africa. And it can't be easy for anyone to keep abreast of Flaaitaal when, in each of the areas where it thrives, it has a slightly different lexicon. Eventually, perhaps, it will be standardized, or it will merge with Iscamtho. But not yet. A generation or two ago, Flaaitaal's speakers were men and teenage boys. Now both it and Iscamtho are being spoken within families, and children are growing up with it as a first language. Flaaitaal, unlike the pidgin Fanakalo, is used out of free choice. It's an urban tongue, redolent of a South Africa in which many languages enjoy official status, all of them act as a source of new words, and any of them can smudge at the margins.

Can fuse at the margins, I mean. What applies in food, music and fashion holds true in language as well: idioms that once existed far apart, distinct in time and place, are beginning to unite. The counterpart to a piece of worldbeat music featuring marimbas, djembes and electric guitars — the counterpart to a restaurant dish containing lamb, squash and lemongrass — is a message-board posting in Filipino, English, Spanish and Latin.

⟡

When languages approach and touch each other, their speakers have a larger vocabulary to draw on. That doesn't mean they face a greater complexity of grammar and syntax. Our technologies, our jobs and many aspects of our daily lives are getting more and more complicated, but our languages are not. The grammar of Mandarin is far simpler than that of English. Yet plenty of other languages, especially tribal and indigenous ones, employ a grammar system compared to which the intricacies of English are weightless fluff. In an essay on the joys of learning Ancient Greek, Tom Mueller pointed out that a verb in that language could have as many as 350 forms. "They might yodel (in the past) for themselves" — Mueller calls it "the first aorist middle optative third-person plural" — shows English struggling to convey at length what Ancient Greek captured in a word. So does the equally cumbrous sentence "You are about to be having been yodeled."

The trend in many languages is toward a simplification of the standard grammar. Countless fluent speakers of French would be unable to conjugate its verbs in the pluperfect subjunctive. No matter. If you're thinking about learning Modern Greek, rest assured: you won't have to master hundreds of forms of any verb. What you will need to learn, of course, are the words for thousands of objects and concepts that were unimaginable to Sophocles and Plato. Languages are enlarging — the healthy ones, that is. If the speakers of a minority language cease to invent new words, that language is almost certainly on its way out.

"When I took the first survey of my undertaking," Samuel Johnson wrote in 1755, in the preface to his landmark dictionary, "I found our speech copious without order, and energetic without rules: wherever I turned my view, there was perplexity to be disentangled, and confusion to be regulated; choice was to be made out of boundless variety, without any established principle of selection; adulterations were to be detected, without a settled test of purity." And so on. Decades later, as an old man, Johnson had every right to look back with pleasure on the impact of his work. Though impurities still remained, he could declare with satisfaction that rules, principles, regulations — in a word, order — had been established. He had hacked through the perplexities of English with rational glee.

If Johnson saw and heard the language today, he would be mortified. Wherever you look, you find more choices, more entanglements, more adulterations. It's absurd to suppose that anyone, even with the industry and bullheadedness of a Samuel Johnson, could possibly define all of the language's words — could possibly *know* all of its words. Boundless variety reigns supreme. The voracious spread of English at its blurring edges — in Singapore, in India, in South Africa and so on — is one of the reasons. Another is the endless growth of scientific and technological language. But there's a third factor, too: the way we now conceive of language as embracing, not rejecting, words that come from the margins and subcultures of society.

As we have seen, early lexicographers wanted their dictionaries to serve as a moral force. Johnson hoped his work would edify. That meant keeping slang words out. Eric Partridge, who packed tens of thousands of them into his great *Dictionary of Slang and Unconventional English*, defined slang as "the special vocabulary . . . of low, illiterate, or disreputable persons; low, illiterate language." It's an interesting definition, because it relies on a hierarchy of both people and language: if some forms of language are low, then others must be high. Today we've lost that faith. Just as English lords are invariably mocked in popular culture, so is pompous speech regarded with general disdain. To make any TV character seem like a buffoon, all a scriptwriter needs to do is have him say "exiguous" or "hortatory." In the wealthy countries of the world, the vast majority of people are literate. But, contrary to what a reader of Partridge's definition might expect, slang has not fallen away. It frolics in the mainstream. Consider: in 2007 the Canadian brewers of Bud Light put up billboards describing that insipid liquid as "1970s pimp smooth."

Two years earlier, faced with slumping car sales, Chrysler aired a TV commercial that paired its former chairman Lee Iacocca with the rap star Snoop Dogg — on a golf course, of all places. "Now everybody gets a great deal," Iacocca says. Snoop Dogg replies, "Foshizzle, I kazizzle." Adapting Iacocca's famous line "If you can find a better car, buy it," Snoop Dogg ends the ad by rhyming: "If the ride is more fly, then you must buy." Like the Bud Light billboard, the commercial attests to the marketing power of hip-hop — and to the desire of big business to co-opt the lexicon of the young. But it also speaks volumes about our willingness to keep on stretching and breaking the bounds of acceptable speech. If you think back a few generations, it's hard to imagine Henry Ford teaming up with Muddy Waters — not just for reasons of race, but for reasons of language.

The remorseless expansion of the overculture goes hand in hand with the birth and growth of subcultures. We all need to find our niche. And when we've found it — yesca-smoking, warbler-watching, MMORPG-playing, embroidery-making, whatever — we protect and cherish it in words that only people within the chosen group will be able to understand. "Subcultures and specialized linguistic phenomena seem to arise spontaneously and simultaneously," wrote David Maurer in his fascinating book *Language of the Underworld;* "language seems to lie at the heart of their cultural genesis." Why? Because a specialized vocabulary (sometimes accompanied by minor changes in grammar and pronunciation) builds and sustains group identity, "providing a strongly affective identification for its speakers." Today there are more and more of these specialized vocabularies. Whether because of the Internet, consumer advertising or social mobility — or, perhaps, our desire to make language as inclusive as possible — special lexicons keep spilling over into conventional society, often producing surprise and puzzlement along the way.

Informal language keeps it real. Or so we think. By contrast, official language smacks of rules. "The language of airports has become the language of our private lives," Pico Iyer writes in *The Global Soul*, "as we speak of holding patterns and living on autopilot, fly-by-night operations and getting bumped. Yet the language we meet in airports is rigorously impersonal, all passive tense and 'congestion-related flight delay.'" (Airports are places, he added, "where Henry James dramas are played out to an MTV beat.") Sometimes the rigorously impersonal is hard to distinguish from the intolerably pedantic. I made a will not long ago, and — despite two degrees in English literature — I have trouble understanding much of what it says. "All the property bequeathed to me or that which may subsequently represent it and the fruits and revenues arising therefrom are bequeathed as alimentary support and shall be exempt from seizure for the debts of my legatees except as a result of express hypothecation or pledge and the bequest hereunder . . ." The will uses words like "dispositions," "compromise," "servitude" and "minute" in ways I don't recognize. My "liquidator," I now discover, will have the power to "alienate" all my property, "real and personal." What on earth have I agreed to?

Lawyers and judges have a vested interest in language stability. Verdicts depend on an agreed-upon sense of what documents say and what witnesses mean. But the language of law may be becoming so arcane as to appear beyond all common understanding. The language of academic discourse, too, has grown more and more opaque in recent decades. I happened to come across a report submitted in 2006 to Britain's Economic and Social Research Council on the topic of everyday speech. A typical exchange quoted in the report goes like this: "I er-mean they they don't know him" / "m-hm" / "they don't know" / "they said — it just came overnight practically" / "wow" / "um and uhh we'd been up in Berlin." It could be a raw draft of a Harold Pinter play.

But stumbles, missteps, pauses and repetitions are part of how people talk — and, I strongly suspect, how they talked a century ago. There's no good reason to believe that our ancestors always spoke in perfect sentences, or that our descendants will be any more or less articulate than we are. Scrutinizing such talk, twenty-first-century scholars couch their findings in polysyllabic abstractions that are almost laughably far from the words being discussed: "The phonetic analysis employed both qualitative parametric auditory and quantitative acoustic techniques to examine clusters of general phonetic parameters in order to structure their contributions to interaction . . ." The words have Latin's bulk without its clarity. And this is a mild example — academic writing in the humanities and social sciences often appears designed to obfuscate, not to inform. No wonder the unofficial register of language thrives.

It has a subversive strength, an ability to grab hold of official phrases and turn them to its own ends. When he interviewed members of the Hindu nationalist party Shiv Sena in Bombay, the Indian-American author Suketu Mehta kept hearing the word *powertoni:* "He will even beat up his brother for me. I hire him for powertoni." At first Mehta was baffled. Then, as he explains in *Maximum City: Bombay Lost and Found,* he understood: the word was "a contraction of *power of attorney,* the awesome ability to act on someone else's behalf or have others do your bidding, to sign documents, release wanted criminals, cure illnesses, get people killed." The success of Shiv Sena at the polls, Mehta realized, depends on powertoni. Its origins are formal and foreign, but in Bombay the word has become both casual and indigenous.

$\backsim$

"Any technology," wrote Marshall McLuhan, "gradually creates a totally new human environment." Admittedly, the electric toothbrush has so far failed to do so. But computers have transformed the way we live and work beyond the wildest imagining of scientists and engineers just half a century ago. Here, surely, is the core of what Crystal described as a "revolution." For the effect computers have had on language is not just a question of function but of imagination. In 2007, a Chinese couple were so starry-eyed about cyberspace that they tried to give their newborn baby the name @. Open a book of ethics by a twenty-first-century philosopher, and you're liable to find sentences like the following: "Whether sending mp3 files to my friends by e-mail or sitting around at home running Unreal Tournament, ICQ, and Battlechat simultaneously, I am using up a huge chunk of bandwidth."

Joseph Heath's arguments don't depend on a knowledge of computers, but some of his examples and illustrations do. Any sustained metaphor reflects a larger culture. When the culture changes, the metaphors need to change as well, or else they become obsolete. This is a natural process. It doesn't occur to me to "follow a train of thought" as often as it once did, for now that words and images flow all around us in cyberspace, the image of mental life as a ride along a metal track in a single, predetermined direction has less and less allure. The phrase "information superhighway," so popular a few years ago, has also fallen out of favor. Traveling through cyberspace bears a closer kinship to steering a flimsy vessel across a wild sea. Which is why we often say we "navigate." Or else the vessel has no engine, no tiller and no braking device — in which case, we "surf."

But the technology races ahead at such a pace that innumerable metaphors drop behind, red-faced and panting. "Our programs were written when the human race was young," the Russian author Victor Pelevin wrote in a preface to his 2005 novel *The Helmet of Horror,* "at a stage so remote and obscure that we don't understand the programming language any more." Myths are the "shell programs" of the mind, Pelevin suggests: "mental matrices we project onto complex events to endow them with meaning." His novel retells the story of Ariadne in a chatroom, where the labyrinth is the endless maze of the Internet, the heroine likes to gossip about manga, and the Minotaur hacks into strangers' minds.

Now that language has plunged into cyberspace, marketers are in hot pursuit. The Sweethearts Conversation Hearts that children bought for Valentine's Day in 2007 included messages like U-R GR-8 and I'M 4-U in pastel sugar. Aiming at a slightly older crowd, Calvin Klein introduced a pair of perfumes for the "technosexual generation" — the company's phrase, not mine — named CK in2U. The ad campaign featured the lines "She likes how he blogs, her texts turn him on. It's intense. For right now." The perfume fills a small curved bottle made of glass and white plastic, much like an iPod. Calvin Klein's description of the in2U fragrances, each fewer than forty words long, could hardly be less subtle: the one for boys has "penetrates . . . rushes . . . delicious journey . . . climax . . . finish," while the girls' equivalent has "opens . . . surge . . . rushes . . . flush . . . afterglow." (ROFL.)

One thing computers allow us to do — anybody who uses them, I mean — is take an active part in the evolution of language. Like it or not, boys who play World of Warcraft, typing throwaway phrases like *this is were u leave dumass* — even boys who try to persuade Urban Dictionary that BLUUUUUUGGHBTHLTH is a word — are staking a legitimate claim to the prodigal future of English. Because of computers, language has been democratized. Knowledge has been democratized. Meaning itself has been democratized. We're at liberty to wonder, of course, whether so much democracy is a good thing.

The printing press was crucial in the long, slow process by which spelling became standardized — during the Middle Ages, through Shakespeare's time and beyond, common words could be spelled in a variety of ways. Order finally emerged, with Samuel Johnson and Noah Webster instructing their readers as to the proper spelling of every word in their dictionaries. Cyberspace is doing the opposite: reversing history, if you will. Urban Dictionary can provide me with a (barely acceptable) white person's term for a black person, but it can't tell me if this term ought to be spelled *nukka, nukkah, nukga, nucca, nuccuh, nucha, nucker* or *nucka*. "The word belongs in oral speech," you say, "so it doesn't matter how it's spelled." That's true, up to a point. But in the past few decades the barricade between oral and written language — like so many other barricades — has fallen away. The style of newspapers, magazines and books has grown more offhand and flexible. Besides, anything you say can be typed online, free of copyeditors.

It wasn't like this in the elder days. No, I don't mean what J.R.R. Tolkien did when he coined that phrase: the first three ages of Middle-earth; a long-vanished epoch. I mean the time of PDP-10 and the ARPANET. The "elder days," according to the Free Online Dictionary of Computing, refer to "the heroic age of hackerdom." Before 1980, that is.

⌇

Subscribe to the business website 50lessons.com, and you'll be able to watch a stern-faced banker from JPMorgan Chase announce: "You must adapt to change." Go to an aviation training site, and you'll be instructed: "You have to enthusiastically embrace change . . . In life and in your career, you have to 'Adapt or Die.'" If you read an online magazine aimed at men, a "stress management specialist" will insist: "You need to learn to embrace change . . . Once you've reevaluated your relationship with change, you can lay out a battle plan for your life with changes as your main artillery." But what if you don't conceive of life as a battlefield? And what if all these blunt imperatives leave you sick of being told what to do?

Nearly forty years have passed since Alvin Toffler published his celebrated book *Future Shock*. The concept moved quickly into popular consciousness — though it did so, I think, as a mere description and not as the warning Toffler intended. We've grown inured to the notion of massive change; that concept is part of how postmodern society defines itself, with complacency and even pride. The idea of staying still makes us uneasy. Mobility is so obviously preferable to immobility, we want to keep perpetually on the go. But Toffler, having surveyed the transformation of American society in the 1960s, declared that future shock was a sickness with many victims.

"Unless intelligent steps are taken to combat it," he wrote, "millions of human beings will find themselves increasingly disoriented, progressively incompetent to deal rationally with their environments. The malaise, mass neurosis, irrationality, and free-floating violence already apparent in contemporary life are merely a foretaste of what may lie ahead unless we come to understand and treat this disease." His rhetoric was a bit alarmist, but I wouldn't argue with his analysis. Since the publication of *Future Shock* in 1970, change has kept on accelerating — change in our homes, change in our workplaces, change in our belief systems, change in the entire fabric of our societies, not all of them brought about by the microchip. Toffler barely foresaw the horrific threats now facing the planet's biodiversity, and in a book of more than 560 pages, he devoted only four of them to trends in language.

But surely unease, fear and distress about language play a significant part in what Toffler called "Future Shock: The Psychological Dimension." He diagnosed a kind of collective pathology — manifest in everything from drug culture and occult enthusiasms to a pervasive sense that the world has gone crazy — that leads people to flee reality. To his mind, the root cause of this pathology was "the uncontrolled, non-selective nature of our lunge into the future." In retrospect it sounds like a foretaste of the nightmare world of cyberpunk fiction, minus the hackers. But that uncontrolled lunge is also a verbal one. Language seems addicted to speed. Faced every day with new words we don't recognize, metaphors we can't understand, misspellings we find annoying, instructions we fail to decipher, and song lyrics that leave us perplexed, how can we be expected to "enthusiastically embrace change"? Why should we even try?

I'm not going to lay out a battle plan. I don't want to suggest that people should add to their stress levels by feeling compelled to do anything dramatic. I would say only that clear, vivid, exact, plainspoken language is the best tool we have for coping with the verbal future. Such language stands up to time. It does not easily go out of date. "To every thing there is a season, and a time to every purpose under the heaven: a time to be born, and a time to die; a time to plant, and a time to pluck up that which is planted; a time to kill, and a time to heal; a time to break down, and a time to build up." That passage comes, of course, from the King James Bible of 1611. But how much less dated it sounds, how much less old-fashioned, than this extract from F. T. Marinetti's "Futurist Manifesto" of 1909:

> We will sing of . . . the gluttonous railway stations devouring smoking serpents; factories suspended from the clouds by the thread of their smoke; bridges with the leap of gymnasts flung across the diabolic cutlery of sunny rivers; adventurous steamers sniffing the horizon; great-breasted locomotives, puffing on the rails like enormous steel horses with long tubes for bridles; and the gliding flight of aeroplanes whose propeller sounds like the flapping of a flag.

Horses, steam trains, propeller aircraft and polluting factories are likely to strike contemporary readers as emblems of the past, not the future. Aside from which, Marinetti's breathless willingness to mix his metaphors — his subordination of the external world to his own noisy emotions — makes his words likely to fade over time. His rhetoric is vivid, but neither clear nor exact.

Or perhaps we have simply lost faith in the future. It cannot be denied. But some aspects of it can be resisted. Speakers of Italian resisted Marinetti's thirst to destroy conventional syntax and eliminate the nuances of language — although in the 1930s and early '40s Italy did not, unfortunately, resist his glorification of war, "the necessary and bloody test of a people's strength." Speakers of English resisted the desire of the composer Percy Grainger to create a language purged of all words based in Latin and Greek, so that a restaurant would turn into an "eat-take-ment" and a museum a "past-hoard-house." Speakers of all languages have resisted the proponents of Interlingua, Lingua Franca Nova, Volapük and other invented idioms who claim that traditional ways of speaking can never be adequate to face the future.

The dreams and schemes of futurists often end up being of purely historical interest. Le Corbusier, thank goodness, never managed to destroy entire neighborhoods of Paris so as to build his Ville Contemporaine, which would have surrounded a central airport near the River Seine with sixty-story skyscrapers. So take courage. One way to offer a principled resistance to forms of language change you dislike is by following the advice George Orwell gave in his great essay "Politics and the English Language": Don't use an artificially inflated style. Don't let your mind be invaded by ready-made phrases. And don't let a debased type of speech corrupt your thought. Defending the language, Orwell emphasized, "has nothing to do with archaism, with the salvaging of obsolete words and turns of speech, or with the setting up of a 'standard English' which must never be departed from." Orwell was content to see the disappearance of old words and idioms that had outlived their usefulness. Words are not valuable for their own sake; clarity of meaning is more important than correctness of grammar. "What is above all needed is to let the meaning choose the word, and not the other way around. In prose, the worst thing one can do with words is surrender to them." As long as you're telling the truth, you have no need for puffed-up rhetoric. Insincerity is the enemy of clear language.

In the twenty-first century, that means resisting the use of what the German scholar and linguist Uwe Poerksen calls "plastic words." "Process," "structure," "interface," "problem": abstract nouns like this go a long way toward establishing a modular international language, deprived of anything specific or verifiable. "Information" is a prime example of a plastic word, for it can mean anything and nothing. "The insatiable craving for more and more information," Poerksen writes, "is not an indication of the riches to be had in this universally desired elixir, but rather of its impoverishment. It never satisfies." We can never get enough of it. We're so often told that we live in an information society, it's no wonder that we're nervous about not being well informed. I knew a man who, after his retirement, spent most of his waking hours watching CNN. Perpetually thirsty for information, he lived his last years in a state of constant anxiety.

Plastic words stifle clear thinking. Of them all, the bland term "development" may be among the most pernicious. All sorts of abuses have been perpetrated in its name. "With a word such as 'development,'" Poerksen observes, "one can ruin an entire nation." Many plastic words are interchangeable. What's the difference between "the development of structural process," "the process of structural development" and "the structure of developmental process"? There's no going back to the stomp and thud of a monosyllabic past. But there's also no need to assume that abstract polysyllables are an inevitable language of the future. We always have a choice. We can always say what we mean.

Not that history makes it easy. Having lived through nearly all of Israel's wars — the most recent took the life of his beloved son — the novel-ist David Grossman came to realize that "the language with which the citizens of a sustained conflict describe their predicament becomes pro-gressively shallower the longer the conflict endures. Language gradually be-comes a sequence of clichés and slogans." What begins with rhetoric from the army, the police and the government filters down to the news media, "germinating an even more cunning language that aims to tell its target au-dience the story easiest for digestion." In the end, the half-truths, general-izations and banalities seep into "the private, intimate language of the con-flict's citizens." Neither side in a war is exempt from linguistic attrition.

Against this gradual corruption, Grossman writes, "the correct and precise use of words is sometimes like a remedy to an illness." It can't alter the past. It can't bring back the dead. But it can reawaken honesty and re-store emotional depth. Only "the tenderness and intimacy I maintain with language, with its different layers, its eroticism and humor and soul, give me back the person I used to be."

☙

One snowy winter afternoon, I spoke to a professor of medicine in Ontario, P. K. Rangachari, who grew up in southern India in the 1940s and '50s. He has an informed love of poetry and a lifelong devotion to language. Indeed, language is the focus of one of his earliest memories. "Being born into a Brahmin family," he told me, "meant a submersion in rituals. One particu-lar ritual was the auspicious day a child was taught the alphabet." The fam-ily, not just the education system, had the task of making children see writ-ten language as a gift, a blessing. "An elder, in this case my grandmother, held my hand, and I was made to trace the first letter of the Tamil alphabet on a plate of rice. Grain was the symbol of plenty, and this testified to the Brahmin's inordinate faith that learning was the key to success."

With a gust of wind, that letter would have been erased. Language is a fragile vessel. It's also a very powerful one. Sixty years later, when much else has been lost to memory, Rangachari can recall the tender, intimate feel of his fingertip pressing a meaning into the tiny grains. The alphabet was the introduction to a small boy's future. No relics exist of Jesus, Mohammed, Moses or Confucius — and no certain relics of Gautama Buddha — except for their words. We remember the stories they are said to have told. What Neil Armstrong actually *did* on the surface of the moon has been largely forgotten. Yet his first words back to Earth remain alive in millions of minds.

Before long his message may seem obsolete. The phrase "one giant leap for mankind" culminates in a word that has, at various times over the centuries, referred to the male sex, to strong or shameless women, even to cruelty and ferocity. Armstrong used it to mean our whole species — women and children as well as men. Yet since his fateful stroll in 1969, the radiance of "mankind" has dimmed. Many people find it natural to speak instead of "humanity," a more obviously inclusive term. To them, "mankind" sounds sexist. It would be ironic indeed if the phrase that sums up a walk on the moon became archaic.

But that's language for you. It won't stop in its tracks, no matter how fervently you or I or anyone else may yearn for stability. "No one can really predict how we will adapt to the transformations taking place all around us," Sven Birkerts wrote in *The Gutenberg Elegies*. He feared the worst. Yet he admitted that language may be "a hardier thing than I have allowed. It may flourish among the beep and the click and the monitor as readily as it ever did on the printed page." Birkerts hoped so, and I hope so too, for, in his words, "language is the soul's ozone layer and we thin it at our peril."

g g noob. Sooner or later, language change makes noobs of us all, even the impossibly young and the perpetually plugged in. Yet however we feel about the torrent of new expressions rushing our way, we can always speak our mind. We can try to stand our ground, even as the ground shifts under us. *this is were u leave* . . . Foshizzle, homie. This is where I leave, too.

Acknowledgments

T HIS BOOK WAS commissioned by Eamon Dolan, and he edited a draft and a half with his usual mixture of sympathetic insight and merciless panache. I received enormous benefit from his work and from that of Jane Rosenman, whose calm intelligence saw me through the later stages. My gratitude also goes to Larry Cooper for a superb job of manuscript editing, and to Benjamin Steinberg, Taryn Roeder and everyone else at Houghton Mifflin.

Anne Collins is a dream publisher for nearly every writer lucky enough to know her. My thanks to her, Geoff Allen, Kylie Barker and the staff of Random House Canada, as well as to Jason Arthur and his colleagues at William Heinemann in London. Special thanks to Ravi Mirchandani and Nicole Winstanley, who arranged publication with Heinemann when the book was but a gleam in the eye. Jackie Kaiser, my agent, went the extra mile and far beyond; I'm profoundly grateful for her encouragement, her wisdom and her gentle chiding. Thanks also to Natasha Daneman and the others at Westwood Creative Artists.

My heartfelt thanks go to two friends, Charles Foran and Denis Sampson, who read most of the chapters at an early stage and offered critical encouragement. Charlie also put me in touch with Nury Vittachi and introduced me to *Cloud Atlas*. I'm indebted to several people who read and commented on particular chapters: Ray Beauchemin, Ann Beer, Stephen Gaudet, Shuvo Ghosh, Brian Miller and Denise Roig. Tetsuo Kinoshita not only provided helpful remarks on my chapter about Japan, he also made several key contacts before my visit there.

I'm grateful to those people who agreed to an interview or who responded to my e-mailed requests for help; many of them are identified in the text, and I won't repeat their names here. It has been a pleasure to listen to them all — well, almost all. For morsels of information, useful advice or both, I offer my thanks to the following people (whose names have not previously appeared in the book): Audrey Berner, Peter Boullata, Pauline Broderick, Julie Bruck, Mike Casey, Xiao Lan Curdt-Christiansen, Bryan Demchinsky, Paul Fenn, Douglas Gibson, David Gutnick, Jeffrey Haller, Ted Hodgetts, Bob Holman, Mikhail Iossel, Marcy Kahan, Adrian King-Edwards, Walter Krajewski, Bob Ladd, Bronwen Low, Janice McAlpine, Ian McGillis, Suzanne Nesbitt, Dave Pinto, Alaisdair Raynham, Howard Richler, William Scott, Tom Shippey, Eric Siblin, Jaspreet Singh, Helena Sirpa, Mary Soderstrom, Helen Stevens, Anne-Marie Swift, Philip Szporer, Salil Tripathi, Saima Varangu, Adam Williams, Clare Woodcock, Carol Zall and the late Abbott Conway.

The travel and research for this book were made possible by a grant from the Canada Council for the Arts and by a fellowship from the John Simon Guggenheim Memorial Foundation. I am honored to acknowledge their support. My thanks to those who recommended me for the Guggenheim: Charles Foran (again), Michael Ignatieff, John Kelly and Linda Leith.

Much of this book was written in the shadow of serious illness. For getting me through it, I'm grateful to Dr. Brian Gore and Dr. Armin Aprikian.

Recommended Reading

BOOKS ABOUT LANGUAGE

Adams, Michael, *Slayer Slang: A* Buffy the Vampire Slayer *Lexicon.* New York: Oxford University Press, 2003.

Aitchison, Jean, *Language Change: Progress or Decay?* Third ed. Cambridge: Cambridge University Press, 2001.

Ayto, John, *Twentieth Century Words.* Oxford and New York: Oxford University Press, 1999.

Berrey, Lester B., and Melvin Van den Bark, *The American Thesaurus of Slang: A Complete Reference Book of Colloquial Speech.* New York: Thomas Y. Crowell, 1942.

Brown, Adam, *Singapore English in a Nutshell: An Alphabetical Description of Its Features.* Singapore: Times Media, 1999.

Comrie, Bernard, Stephen Matthews and Maria Polinsky, eds., *The Atlas of Languages: The Origin and Development of Languages Throughout the World.* New York: Facts on File, 1986.

Crystal, David, *English as a Global Language.* Second ed. Cambridge: Cambridge University Press, 2003.

———, *A Glossary of Netspeak and Textspeak.* Edinburgh: Edinburgh University Press, 2004.

———, *The Language Revolution.* Cambridge: Polity Press, 2004.

———, *How Language Works.* Woodstock and New York: Overlook Press, 2006.

———, ed., *The Cambridge Encyclopedia of Language.* Second ed. Cambridge: Cambridge University Press, 2003.

Dillard, J. L., *Black English: Its History and Usage in the United States.* New York: Random House, 1972.

The English Dialect Dictionary. 6 vols. 1898–1905.

Essinger, James, *Spellbound: The Surprising Origins and Astonishing Secrets of English Spelling.* New York: Bantam Dell, 2007.

Folb, Edith A., *Runnin' Down Some Lines: The Language and Culture of Black Teenagers.* Cambridge, MA: Harvard University Press, 1980.

Fought, Carmen, *Chicano English in Context.* Basingstoke: Palgrave Macmillan, 2003.

Fowler, H. W., and F. G. Fowler, *The King's English.* Third ed. Oxford: Clarendon Press, 1930.

Goh, Colin, and Y. Y. Woo, eds., *The Coxford Singlish Dictionary.* Singapore and Gold Beach, OR: Flame of the Forest Publishing, 2002.

Görlach, Manfred, ed., *A Dictionary of European Anglicisms.* Oxford: Oxford University Press, 2001.

Graddol, David, *The Future of English?* London: British Council, 1997.

——— , *English Next.* London: British Council, 2006.

Green, Jonathon, *Chasing the Sun: Dictionary Makers and the Dictionaries They Made.* London: Jonathan Cape, 1996.

Hitchings, Henry, *Defining the World: The Extraordinary Story of Dr. Johnson's Dictionary.* New York: Farrar, Straus and Giroux, 2005.

Jespersen, Otto, *The Philosophy of Grammar.* London: Allen and Unwin, 1924.

Johnson, Samuel, *A Dictionary of the English Language: An Anthology,* ed. David Crystal. London: Penguin Books, 2006 (originally published in 1755).

Jones, Mari C., and Edith Esch, *Language Change: The Interplay of Internal, External, and Extra-Linguistic Factors.* Berlin and New York: Mouton de Gruyter, 2002.

Labov, William, *Principles of Linguistic Change,* vol. 1: *Internal Factors.* Oxford: Blackwell, 1994.

Ling, Low Ee, and Adam Brown, *English in Singapore: An Introduction.* Singapore: McGraw-Hill, 2005.

Major, Clarence, *Juba to Jive: A Dictionary of African-American Slang.* New York: Viking, 1994.

Maurer, David W., *Language of the Underworld.* Lexington: University Press of Kentucky, 1981.

McArthur, Tom, *The Oxford Guide to World English.* Oxford: Oxford University Press, 2002.

McCrum, Robert, William Cran and Robert MacNeil, *The Story of English.* London and Boston: Faber and Faber, 1986.

McFedries, Paul, *Word Spy: The Word Lover's Guide to Modern Culture.* New York: Broadway Books, 2004.

McWhorter, John, *Word on the Street: Debunking the Myth of a "Pure" Standard English.* New York: Perseus Books, 1998.

Mencken, H. L., *The American Language: An Inquiry into the Development of English in the United States.* Fourth ed. New York: Alfred A. Knopf, 1936.

Mesthrie, Rajend, ed., *Language in South Africa.* Cambridge: Cambridge University Press, 2002.

Mugglestone, Lynda, *Lost for Words: The Hidden History of the Oxford English Dictionary.* New Haven: Yale University Press, 2005.

Munro, Pamela, ed., *u.c.l.a. slang 5.* Los Angeles: UCLA Department of Linguistics, 2005.

Nadeau, Jean-Benoît, and Julie Barlow, *The Story of French.* Toronto: Alfred A. Knopf Canada, 2006.

Ogden, C. K., *Basic English: A General Introduction with Rules and Grammar.* London: Paul Treber, 1930.

Ostler, Nicholas, *Empires of the Word: A Language History of the World.* London: HarperCollins, 2005.

The Oxford English Dictionary. 1928 and 1989.

Pakir, Anne, ed., *The English Language in Singapore: Standards and Norms.* Singapore: Singapore Association for Applied Linguistics, 1993.

Partridge, Eric, *A Dictionary of Slang and Unconventional English.* New York: Macmillan, 1961.

Pinker, Steven, *The Stuff of Thought: Language as a Window into Human Nature.* New York: Viking Penguin, 2007.

Poerksen, Uwe, *Plastic Words: The Tyranny of a Modular Language,* trans. Jutta Mason and David Cayley. Philadelphia: Penn State University Press, 2004.

Poteet, Lewis J., *The South Shore Phrase Book.* Hantsport, NS: Lancelot Press, 1983.

Richler, Howard, *Global Mother Tongue: The Eight Flavours of English.* Montreal: Véhicule Press, 2006.

Shibatani, Masayoshi, *The Languages of Japan.* Cambridge: Cambridge University Press, 1990.

Smitherman, Geneva, *Black Talk: Words and Phrases from the Hood to the Amen Corner.* Boston and New York: Houghton Mifflin, 1994.

Stavans, Ilan, *Spanglish: The Making of a New American Language.* New York: HarperCollins, 2003.

Suzuki, Takao, *Reflections on Japanese Language and Culture.* Tokyo: Keio University, 1987.

Todd, Richard Watson, *Much Ado About English: Up and Down the Bizarre Byways of a Fascinating Language.* London and Boston: Nicholas Brealey Publishing, 2006.

Webster's Third International Dictionary of the English Language, Unabridged, 1961 and 2002.

Wentworth, Harold, and Stuart Berg Flexner, eds., *The Pocket Dictionary of American Slang.* New York: Pocket Books, 1968.

Winchester, Simon, *The Meaning of Everything: The Story of the Oxford English Dictionary.* Oxford: Oxford University Press, 2003.

OTHER BOOKS

Acharya, Shanta, *Looking In, Looking Out.* West Kirby, Wirral: Headland Publications, 2005.

Adams, Douglas, and John Lloyd, *The Meaning of Liff.* London: Faber and Faber, 1983.

Amis, Martin, *Visiting Mrs. Nabokov and Other Excursions.* London: Jonathan Cape, 1997.

Badami, Anita Rau, *The Hero's Walk.* Toronto: Alfred A. Knopf Canada, 2000.

Baker, Houston A., *Long Black Song: Essays in Black American Literature and Culture.* Charlottesville: University of Virginia Press, 1972.

Bellamy, Edward, *Looking Backward.* New York: Signet Classics, 2000 (originally published in 1888).

Berger, Maxianne, *Dismantled Secrets.* Toronto: Wolsak and Wynn, 2008.

Bergman, Catherine, *From the Japanese: A Journalist's Encounters.* Toronto: McClelland and Stewart, 2002.

Birkerts, Sven, *The Gutenberg Elegies: The Fate of Reading in an Electronic Age.* New York: Faber and Faber, 1994.

Bradbury, Ray, *Fahrenheit 451.* New York: Ballantine, 1953.

Burgess, Anthony, *A Clockwork Orange.* London: William Heinemann, 1962.

Burnside, John, *Selected Poems.* London: Jonathan Cape, 2006.

Burroughs, William, *Nova Express.* New York: Grove Press, 1964.

Carey, Peter, *Wrong About Japan: A Father's Journey with His Son.* New York: Alfred A. Knopf, 2005.

Cepeda, Raquel, ed., *And It Don't Stop: The Best American Hip-Hop Journalism of the Last 25 Years.* New York: Faber and Faber, 2004. (See especially the contributions by Touré and Greg Tate.)

Chang, Jeff, *Can't Stop, Won't Stop: A History of the Hip-Hop Generation.* New York: Picador, 2005.

Chávez-Silverman, Susana, *Killer Crónicas: Bilingual Memories.* Madison: University of Wisconsin Press, 2004.

Clarke, Arthur C., *2001: A Space Odyssey.* London: Hutchinson, 1968.

——— , *2010: Odyssey Two.* New York: Ballantine, 1982.

——— , *2060: Odyssey Three.* New York: Ballantine, 1987.

——— , *3001: The Final Odyssey.* New York: Ballantine, 1997.

Defoe, Daniel, *An Essay upon Projects.* New York: AMS Press, 1999 (the Stoke Newington edition of Defoe's works). Originally published in 1697.

Delany, Samuel, *Babel-17.* New York: Ace, 1966.

Didion, Joan, *Where I Was From.* New York: Alfred A. Knopf, 2003.

Dunn, Charles, *Highland Settler: A Portrait of the Scottish Gael in Cape Breton and Eastern Nova Scotia.* Wreck Cove, NS: Breton Books, 2003 (originally published in 1953).

Ezekiel, Nissim, *Collected Poems.* New Delhi: Oxford University Press, 2005.

Fitt, Matthew, *Kate o Shanter's Tale and Other Poems.* Edinburgh: Luath Press, 2003.

Franklin, Ursula M., *The Real World of Technology.* Rev. ed. Toronto: House of Anansi Press, 2004.

George, Cherian, *Singapore: The Air-Conditioned Nation. Essays on the Politics of Comfort and Control, 1990–2000.* Singapore: Landmark Books, 2000.

Gibson, William, *Neuromancer.* New York: Ace, 1984.

——— , *Idoru.* New York: Putnam, 1996.

———— , *Spook Country*. New York: Putnam, 2007.

Harrison, Stephanie, ed., *Adaptations: From Short Story to the Big Screen*. New York: Three Rivers Press, 2005. (See "The Sentinel" by Arthur C. Clarke.)

Heath, Joseph, *The Efficient Society: Why Canada Is as Close to Utopia as It Gets*. Toronto: Penguin Books, 2001.

Hewitt, Hugh, *Blog: Understanding the Information Revolution That's Changing Your World*. Nashville: Thomas Nelson, 2005.

Hoban, Russell, *Riddley Walker*. London: Jonathan Cape, 1980.

Horace, *Epistles*, trans. David Ferry. New York: Farrar, Straus and Giroux, 2001.

Iyer, Pico, *The Global Soul*. New York: Alfred A. Knopf, 2000.

James, P. D., *The Children of Men*. London: Faber and Faber, 1992.

Kajikawa, Y., *Ueno Norio, 2000–2005*. Kyoto: Kahitsukan and the Kyoto Museum of Contemporary Art, 2005.

Kepel, Gilles, *The War for Muslim Minds: Islam and the West*, trans. Pascale Ghazaleh. Cambridge, MA: Belknap Press, 2006.

Kessel, Sim, *Hanged at Auschwitz*, trans. Melville Wallace and Delight Wallace. New York: Stein and Day, 1972.

Kon, Stella, *Emily of Emerald Hill*. Singapore: Constellation Books, 2002.

Kubica, Chris, and Will Hochman, eds., *Letters to J. D. Salinger*. Madison: University of Wisconsin Press, 2002. (For a website containing a large number of other letters, many of them from young people, go to http://members .aol.com/jdsletters/guest.html.)

Le Guin, Ursula K., *Always Coming Home*. New York: Harper and Row, 1985.

Lyotard, Jean-François, *The Postmodern Condition: A Report on Knowledge*, trans. Geoffrey Bennington and Brian Massumi. Minneapolis: University of Minnesota Press, 1984 (originally published in French as *La condition postmoderne*, 1979).

Maclear, Kyo, "Race to the Future," in *Taking Risks: Literary Journalism from the Edge*, ed. Barbara Moon and Don Obe. Banff, AB: Banff Centre Press, 1998.

Manguel, Alberto, *A History of Reading*. New York: Viking Penguin, 1996.

McClain, James, *Japan: A Modern History*. New York: W. W. Norton, 2002.

McLuhan, Marshall, *The Gutenberg Galaxy: The Making of Typographic Man*. Toronto: University of Toronto Press, 1962.

———— , *The Essential McLuhan*, ed. Eric McLuhan and Frank Zingrone. Toronto: House of Anansi Press, 1995.

Mehta, Suketa, *Maximum City: Bombay Lost and Found*. New York: Alfred A. Knopf, 2004.

Miller, Walter M., Jr., *A Canticle for Leibowitz*. Philadelphia: Lippincott, 1959.

Mitchell, David, *Cloud Atlas*. London: Hodder and Stoughton, 2004.

Mitchell, Tony, ed., *Global Noise: Rap and Hip-Hop Outside the USA*. Middletown, CT: Wesleyan University Press, 2001. (See especially the contributions by Claire Levy on Bulgaria, Jacqueline Urla on the Basque country, and David Hesmondhalgh and Caspar Melville on the United Kingdom.)

Morales, Ed, *Living in Spanglish: The Search for Latino Identity in America*. New York: St. Martin's Press, 2002.

Newby, Eric, ed., *A Book of Travellers' Tales*. London: Picador, 1986. (Contains an excerpt in Indian English by V. R. Ragam.)

Orwell, George, *The Road to Wigan Pier*. London: Penguin, 2001 (originally published in 1937).

——— , *1984*. New York: Plume, 2003 (originally published in 1949).

——— , *Essays*. London: Everyman's Library, 2002.

Pelevin, Victor, *The Helmet of Horror*, trans. Andrew Bromfeld. Edinburgh and New York: Canongate Books, 2006.

Rabassa, Gregory, *If This Be Treason: Translation and Its Discontents*. New York: New Directions, 2005.

Rowland, Wade, *Spirit of the Web: The Age of Information from Telegraph to Internet*. Third ed. Toronto: Thomas Allen, 2006.

Rushdie, Salman, *Imaginary Homelands*. London: Granta Books, 1991.

Santa Ana, Otto, *Brown Tide Rising: Metaphors of Latinos in Contemporary American Public Discourse*. Austin: University of Texas Press, 2002.

——— , ed., *Tongue-Tied: The Lives of Multilingual Children in Public Education*. Lanham, MD: Rowman and Littlefield, 2004.

Selody, Kim, *Suddenly Shakespeare*. Toronto: Playwrights Co-op, 1988.

Shapiro, Peter, *The Rough Guide to Hip-Hop*. London: Rough Guides, 2005.

Shipley, David, and Will Schwalbe, *Send: The Essential Guide to Email for Office and Home*. New York: Alfred A. Knopf, 2007.

Stephenson, Neal, *Snow Crash*. New York: Bantam Books, 1992.

Swift, Jonathan, *A Proposal for Correcting, Improving and Ascertaining the English Tongue*. Oxford: Blackwell, 1957 (originally published in 1712; also available online).

Toffler, Alvin, *Future Shock*. New York: Random House, 1970.

Traub, Charles H., and Jonathan Lipkin, *In the Realm of the Circuit: Computers, Art, and Culture*. New York: Pearson Prentice Hall, 2004.

Vance, Jack, *The Languages of Pao*. London: Avalon Press, 1958.

Wells, H. G., *The Shape of Things to Come*, vol. 2. London: Hutchinson, 1933.

——— , "A Story of the Days to Come," *The Complete Short Stories*. London: Ernest Benn Ltd., 1948.

Wilberforce, William, *An Appeal to the Religion, Justice, and Humanity of the Inhabitants of the British Empire, in Behalf of the Negro Slaves in the West Indies*. Cornell University Library Digital Collections. Originally published in 1823.

Wilde, Oscar, *The Importance of Being Earnest and Other Plays*. London: Penguin, 2001 (originally produced in 1895).

Yeats, W. B., *Collected Poems*. London: Macmillan, 1961.

Zentella, Ana Celia, *Growing Up Bilingual: Puerto Rican Children in New York*. Oxford: Blackwell, 1997.

NEWSPAPER AND MAGAZINE ARTICLES

Ashton, Emily, "Learn Jafaikan in Two Minutes," *Guardian Weekly* (London), April 20, 2006.

Ayoub, Georgine, "An Odyssey of Words: Evolution of the Arabic Language in the 20th Century," *Al Jadid*, vol. 8, no. 40 (Summer 2002).

Baldauf, Scott, "A Hindi-English Jumble, Spoken by 350 Million," *Christian Science Monitor*, Nov. 23, 2004.

Brooke, James, "For Mongolians, E Is for English, F Is for Future," *New York Times*, Feb. 15, 2005.

enRoute, Oct. 2005 (numerous articles and ads).

Flynn, Seán, "Texting Damages Standards in English, Says Chief Examiner," *Irish Times*, April 25, 2007.

French, Howard, "Tokyo Journal: To Grandparents, English Word Trend Isn't 'Naisu,'" *New York Times*, Oct. 23, 2002.

————, "Uniting China to Speak Mandarin, the One Official Language, Easier Said Than Done," *New York Times*, July 10, 2005.

Gibson, Owen, and Tara Conlan, "BBC Governors to Be Scrapped," *Guardian* (London), March 2, 2005.

Gilb, Dagoberto, "Taco Bell Nation," *Los Angeles Times Magazine*, March 19, 2006.

Gleick, James, "Cyber-Neologoliferation," *New York Times Magazine*, Nov. 5, 2006.

Gorney, Cynthia, "How Do You Say 'Got Milk?' en Español?," *New York Times Magazine*, Sept. 23, 2007.

Grossman, David, "Writing in the Dark," *New York Times Magazine*, May 13, 2007.

Hedges, Chris, "A Language Divided Against Itself," *New York Times*, Jan. 29, 1995.

Heilman Brooke, Elizabeth, "Is Proper Japanese Losing Out amid a Foreign Invasion?," *International Herald Tribune*, May 30, 2006.

Hernandez, Daniel, "A Hybrid Tongue or Slanguage?," *Los Angeles Times*, Dec. 27, 2003.

Kamiyama, Masuo, "Getting 'Yuusu' Lingo 'Peki-Peki' a Real Chore for Adults," *Mainichi Daily News*, Oct. 15, 2005.

Kelly, Kevin, "We Are the Web," *Wired*, Aug. 2005.

Kiyoi, Mikie, "Dear English Speakers: Please Drop the Dialects," *International Herald Tribune*, Nov. 3, 1995.

Lee, Sherry, "Word on the Street," *South China Morning Post*, Aug. 6, 2004.

Maney, Kevin, "Cell Phones, Net Could Have Saved Thousands from Waves," *USA Today*, Jan. 5, 2005.

McCrum, Robert, "So, What's This Globish Revolution?," *Observer* (London), Dec. 3, 2006.

McWhorter, John, "Rap Only Ruins," *New York Post*, Aug. 10, 2003.

Moody, Nekesa Mumbi, "Beating the Rap on Rap," *Gazette* (Montreal), March 8, 2007.

Mueller, Tom, "Greek to Me," *Hemisphere,* Nov. 2006.

Nasrin, Taslima, "Bengali Women: Tongues Untied," *World Press Review,* June 1995.

Ollison, Rashod D., "Can Blackface Be Far Behind?," *Baltimore Sun,* Nov. 26, 2006.

Price, Bruce, "Noun Overuse Phenomenon Article," *Verbatim,* Feb. 1976.

Richie, Donald, "Way to Go Keigo: A Loaded Language of Politeness," *Japan Times,* July 25, 2004.

Smith, Russell, "Do You Speak Kitteh?," *Globe and Mail* (Toronto), May 31, 2007.

Sternbergh, Adam, "Got Bub All Up in the Hizzle, Yo!," *National Post* (Toronto), March 15, 2003.

Sullivan, Andrew, "Society Is Dead, We Have Retreated into the iWorld," *Sunday Times* (London), Feb. 20, 2005.

Tate, Greg, "Hiphop Turns 30: Whatcha Celebratin' For?," *Village Voice,* Jan. 4, 2005.

Taylor, Jerome, "Koran Provides the Ultimate Memory Test for Muslim Boys," *Independent* (London), Oct. 11, 2006.

Valenti, Jessica, "How the Web Became a Sexists' Paradise," *Guardian* (London), April 6, 2007.

Vittachi, Nury, "Crazy Talk Too Much La," *Far Eastern Economic Review,* April 24, 2003.

———, "Business English, Asian Style," *Far Eastern Economic Review,* May 15, 2003.

Wallis, Claudia, "Are Kids Too Wired for Their Own Good?," *Time,* March 27, 2006.

Watts, Jonathan, "Empire of Signs," *Guardian* (London), Feb. 16, 2006.

Yagoda, Ben, "American Idioms Have Gone Missing," *Chronicle of Higher Education,* June 18, 2004.

Useful Websites

(accurate as of November 2007)

www.abc.net.au/rn/linguafranca/ (The website of an excellent Australian radio program about language.)

www.amherst.edu/~spanglish/HistorySpanglish.html ("Spanglish: A User's Manifesto" by Ilan Stavans, 2004.)

http://babelfish.altavista.com (Perhaps the best-known site for machine translation.)

http://news.bbc.co.uk/2/hi/south_asia/6500227.stm (Masud Alam's reflections on the use of English in Pakistan.)

www.blork.org (Ed Hawco's blog.)

www.britishcouncil.org (Contains links to electronic editions of both *The Future of English?* and *English Next.*)

www.cbc.ca/andsometimesy (The website of a radio show about language from the Canadian Broadcasting Corporation.)

http://coldplay.com

www.dictionary.com

www.doubletongued.org (A lexicon of "fringe English," with many comments by lexicographer Grant Barrett.)

www.ethnologue.com/web.asp (A detailed overview of the world's languages.)

http://freenet-homepage.de/grzega/BGE.htm (Joachim Grzega's description of "Basic Global English.")

http://gottabook.blogspot.com (The source of poetic Fibs.)

www.hiphoparchive.org/lx/ (A valuable website on linguistics and hip-hop.)

http://itre.cis.upenn.edu/~myl/languagelog/ (A collaborative blog by leading linguists.)

http://itre.cis.upenn.edu/~myl/languagelog/archives/000457.html (Posting by Mark Liberman about Somali words for camels.)

http://johnhawks.net/weblog/reviews/evolution/speciation/duck_species_collapse
_hybridization_2006.html (About the onslaught of mallard genes.)

www.jpn-globish.com (In praise of Globish. The material is largely but not exclusively written in French.)

www.languagemonitor.com ("Media tracking and analysis.")

www.language-policy.org (A site on language planning and government policy, with many useful links.)

www.losangelesfilm.org/film/transcript.html (Transcript of a fascinating documentary about Los Angeles.)

http://loteriachicana.net (Cindy Mosqueda's blog.)

http://macvaysia.blogspot.com/2004/05/macvaysian-invasion-english-words-in
.html (An informative look at English words in Malay and at "Manglish.")

www.mtholyoke.edu/acad/intrel/orwell46.htm (Online text of George Orwell's great essay "Politics and the English Language.")

www.nvtc.gov/lotw/languageList.html (Includes a description of many language families.)

www.pbs.org/speak/education/curriculum/college/aae/# (On the nature and history of Black English.)

www.pbs.org/22ndcentury (See the interviews with Bill McKibben and Ramez Naam.)

www.rapdict.org (A very helpful dictionary of hip-hop slang.)

www.sljfaq.org/afaq/wasei-eigo.html (An interesting though brief list of pseudo-English words in Japanese.)

www.spellingbee.com (Official site of the Scripps National Spelling Bee.)

www.talkingcock.com (In praise of Singlish.)

www.unh.edu/linguistics/Resources/resources.html (Based at the University of New Hampshire, this site contains links and papers of keen interest to keen linguists.)

www.urbandictionary.com

www.watsoninstitute.org/infopeace/vy2k/marinetti.cfm (A Brown University site containing a translation of Marinetti's "Futurist Manifesto" of 1909. Alternative versions are available online.)

www.wordspy.com (More fresh and edgy than Dictionary.com; more linguistically reputable than Urban Dictionary.)

www.worldwidewords.org ("Michael Quinion writes on international English from a British viewpoint.")

http://youtube.com: "Web. 2.0 . . . The Machine is Us/ing Us" (Michael Wesch's video essay on technology and the future.)

Index